NORTHWESTERN UNIVERSITY   African Studies

Number Thirteen

The Development of
Nigerian Foreign Policy

Claude S. Phillips, Jr.

NORTHWESTERN UNIVERSITY PRESS 1964

The material in pages 89-100 of Chapter V originally appeared in *Ibadan*, a Journal published at University College, Ibadan, No. 14 (October, 1962), in somewhat different form.

To Marguerite

Preface

During the course of my research in Nigeria, I was often told, by Nigerians as well as expatriates, that Nigeria does not have a foreign policy! What can such information mean? An obvious meaning would be that Nigeria has no attitudes, no official policies, toward areas or events outside of the state. Such a meaning is patently false on its surface—every modern state has to take a minimum of stands on many international issues simply to belong to the United Nations, the International Labor Organization, the Commonwealth, the Monrovia Powers, etc. Some of my informants, however, say that what the statement means in its refined sense is that Nigeria has no consistent policy, no predictable reaction, to beliefs and events outside its borders, and that where it does, it follows the leadership of Great Britain.

The "refined" explanation tells more about the speaker's own wishes than it does about Nigeria's foreign policy. One can probably account for the assertion that Nigeria has no foreign policy from two standpoints:

a) Some people have stereotyped new African states along the Ghana-Guinea line and are constantly surprised when Nigeria deviates from the position of these "leaders." They immediately assume that Nigeria must not be "really" independent if it dares take a position less intransigent than any other African state, and that somehow Nigeria does not know where it is going, although presumably Ghana and Guinea do.

b) Some people, accustomed to seeing patterns of reaction in a state's foreign policy, developed over many years, are frustrated that Nigerian patterns, with only three years of development, are not always clear and precise, and on some issues not even expressed at all.

Nigeria's foreign policy development and formation deserve more attention than these attitudes suggest. Nigeria is after all potentially the greatest power in Africa from the standpoint of the "elements of national power" which scholars of international politics use to determine a state's position in the power struggle: a population almost twice as large as the next most populous state in Africa, and thirteenth in the world; a relatively large land mass with many natural resources; and a competition among political parties to create a modern viable state. Compared to other African states, Nigeria has a large body of able leaders who constantly offer alternative paths for public debate. It has a free press and a number of competing daily newspapers. It has already won a position of leadership both in the United Nations and in one of the two main blocs of African states. Such a state offers an excellent laboratory for the study of foreign policy formation.

This study focuses on the foreign policy developments between 1959 and 1963, and especially notes:

a) the federal election of 1959, the first national election after it was known that Nigeria would become independent on October 1, 1960;

b) the period between the federal election and the grant of independence when legislative and partisan interests in foreign policy began to be articulated; and

c) the period from October 1960 to mid-1963 when an independent and democratic government began to respond to numerous internal and international issues and to initiate positions for the new state. [Therefore, the period since the fourth state (the Mid-West Region) was created and Nigeria became a Republic have not been dealt with at all.]

Deliberate attention is paid to detail in an effort to etch a picture of the internal struggle attendant upon foreign policy formation in these seminal years. The primary sources for this work have been the Parliamentary Debates in the Federal House of Representatives; the daily newspapers covering the period in question; party manifestoes, newspapers and pamphlets; government publications; brochures of various groups; and interviews with various government and party leaders and private individuals.

I cannot, however, exaggerate the tentative nature of this study. There are many gaps which can only be filled in as studies-in-depth are made on particular issues and organizations. Needed, for example, are studies on the decision-making process in the Ministry of Foreign Affairs and Commonwealth Relations; the relative power in the decision-making process of various Cabinet members; the compromises in policy made necessary by the coalition of the NPC and the NCNC; and the influence of Sir Ahmadu Bello on Sir Abubakar Tafawa Balewa. It may be years, if ever, before scholars are permitted to see the documents and memorabilia to such significant matters. Furthermore, studies-in-depth are needed on the political parties, the youth groups, the labor unions, and other pressure groups as well as on inter-Regional relations before a definitive picture of foreign policy formation can be drawn.

Nevertheless, it is hoped that this study will serve as a base of reference for future scholars. After all, policies have been enunciated and patterns of action and reaction begun in the first three years of independence. Nigeria is a "going concern" and in spite of charges of "lack of dynamism" there appears to be little about the country that can be said to be static. Although the pages which follow deal primarily with the formation of foreign policy, they also demonstrate something about the problems of a society rather suddenly forced to create a world position for itself. Tentative though it may be, therefore, it is my hope that it contributes something to the understanding of Nigeria, a country I have come to respect and esteem.

Acknowledgments

The debts incurred in the preparation of this book are many. I am especially indebted to the Carnegie Corporation of New York for a large grant to the Institute of Regional Studies of Western Michigan University which made it possible for the University to award me a grant for study in Nigeria. I am likewise indebted to the Nigerian Institute of Social and Economic Research, University of Ibadan, Ibadan, Nigeria, for the appointment as an Associate Research Fellow for the 1961-62 school year. The Faculty Research Committee, Western Michigan University, also gave me a small grant to gather material located in the United States. Without these various forms of assistance, the study would have been impossible.

A number of individuals have given generously of their time in assisting me. James O'Connell, Lecturer in Government, and John P. Mackintosh, then Lecturer in Government, University of Ibadan, both read an early draft of the manuscript in its entirety. Their insights and criticisms have been of incalculable value. Parts of the manuscript were also read by K. W. J. Post, then Lecturer in Government, and Jerome Wells, then Visiting Lecturer in Economics, University of Ibadan; Grady Nunn, Professor of Political Science, University of Alabama; and Roy Olton, Associate Professor of Political Science, Western Michigan University. Each offered useful advice. None of the readers, of course, is responsible in any way for what appears here.

It would be impossible to list the names of all the Nigerians who supplied me with information and insights, but my debts to them are no less real because of this.

Russell Seibert, Vice President for Academic Affairs, Western Michigan University, was helpful in getting me typing assistance. Finally, my wife Marguerite assisted in many ways, from proofreading to being a highly enthusiastic companion in our Nigerian sojourn.

CLAUDE S. PHILLIPS, JR.

Western Michigan University
November 26, 1963

Contents

The Development of Nigerian Foreign Policy

I. Foreign Policy and
a New State

The foreign policy of old established states is rarely ever so clearly defined that prediction of future action can be made with certainty. It is questionable whether anyone could have predicted the United States decision to fight in Korea, the British decision to join the French and Israelis in the Suez venture of 1956, the Soviet decision to grant some autonomy to Poland, or the United States decision to blockade Cuba. While these decisions make sense in retrospect, a refusal to make them at the time would subsequently have been regarded by scholars as merely part of the maneuvering of states for survival. While each of these decisions now appears to have been a focal point in the history of international relations, a contrary decision at the time would have merely continued historical trends. Each decision of a major power, deliberately or through miscalculation, may of course lead to a world war, but a refusal to make decisions which depart from trends may also lead to such a war.

It is a truism to say that the future is unknown, but it is no truism to say that decision-makers of states must attempt to shape the future. Older states do have one advantage over the new states: they have their practice over the past decades to give some indication of both their interests and other states' reactions to them. The blockade of Cuba surely has roots dating back to the Monroe Doctrine in spite of twentieth-century changes in that concept; and Russia's refusal to side with India in its struggle with China, in spite of the precipitate action of its ally, seems to square with Russia's past concern with holding the Communist bloc together as best it can. The study of the foreign policy of older states, therefore, is concerned with the history of how they have in fact behaved. Coupled with such studies, of course, are the foreign policy pronouncements of governments, the relative military power of states, the number and power of each state's allies, the various policies of its allies vis-à-vis specific issues, and the various internal forces in a country which affect foreign policy decisions. Added to these traditional factors must be each state's commitment to the United Nations and its concern for the new states, whether aligned or neutralist. These factors intertwine in countless ways and, over a period of time, reveal state behavior which gives some indication of state interests and thereby some predictability of reaction to specific events or issues.

However, new states (those which have gained independence since 1945 or have emerged to world prominence from isolation or unequal status) provide few of the factors needed for the study of foreign policy. A history of fifteen years or less reveals little about how a state will react to future world crisis. The absence of a long pattern of behavior is merely one of the problems we face. New states, by virtue of the fact that decision-makers are for the first time "on their own," are properly characterized as unstable. The social forces which produced the independence are not necessarily the forces essential for orderly, stable growth. In fact, the forces of independence were subversive, bent on destroying a power relationship, not on building a viable political structure. Nor is there any reason why nationalists, fighting together for independence, should agree either on state forms or state goals after independence has been achieved. Independence, furthermore, has almost invariably meant (relative to older states) weak military power, an absence of highly trained administrators, an insufficient and inefficient civil service, a poorly developed economy, and a largely a-political population. It has also often revealed the absence of a nation, there being instead numerous nations, tribes, or regions to which the masses owed loyalty.

As such states gain their independence they are immediately faced with the problem of relations with other states—those close by, those with whom they believe they share values, those in the United Nations, the Big Power blocs, their former rulers. Ultimately necessary for the task of formulating a foreign policy are concepts of both international interests and national goals. While national goals (images of what the nation ought to be) and international interests (images of the state's proper concern for areas and events outside its borders) probably exist chiefly in the minds of elites,[1] the elites in the new states face problems different from the elites of the older states. Their most formidable challenge on the international scene is to establish a position in a bi-polar world. The alternatives appear limited to two: to join one of the blocs or to pursue a policy of unilateralism.[2] This is no easy choice. For a state which has just won its independence, joining a bloc can appear to be the substitution of one form of restriction on freedom for another; but playing the "lone wolf," as India has seen, may invite attack from a stronger neighbor. Furthermore, internal problems (economic de-

1 See especially Joseph J. Spengler, "Theory, Ideology, Non-Economic Values, and Politico-Economic Development," in Ralph Braibanti and Joseph J. Spengler (eds.), *Tradition, Values, and Socio-Economic Development* (Durham: Duke University Press, 1961), p. 4 ff.

2 The term "unilaterialism" is borrowed from Frederick H. Hartmann, *The Relations of Nations* (New York: Macmillan, 1957), p. 283, which he defines as a pattern in which "a state relies on its own power, makes no alliances, and has no obligations to defend others."

Collective security is sometimes suggested as an alternative but, since the breakdown of collective (that is, universal) security, whereby all states agree to resist any aggressor as envisaged in the United Nations, this is no real alternative.

velopment, education, national consciousness, widespread acceptance of drastic changes) related to all the facets of creating a viable state frequently force the decision-makers to neglect the world scene: to rely on the United Nations or to assume that if they do not align the great power conflicts will bypass them.

Alignment is but one of the numerous problems faced by the leaders of new states, each problem at the beginning devoid of a national precedent. Shall the new state recognize its foreign-drawn boundaries or make claims on territory controlled by a neighbor? Shall it create an army capable of pressing its claims against neighbors, or one merely capable of defense? Shall it maintain economic ties with its former ruler, increase them, or reduce them in favor of other states? What relations shall it seek with more powerful neighbors, and what with weaker neighbors? Are international problems to be given precedence over domestic ones? What role shall be given to the former metropole? Does a new state have an international role different from that of older states, and if so what is it? Shall the new state seek aid from any state willing to grant it or from certain states only? It is obvious that national goals and international interests soon become intertwined.

New states, of course (like older states), do not always attempt to give clear-cut answers to these questions, preferring to feel their way cautiously. Some feel compelled at the beginning to state a position on some questions and not on others. Some are faced with international pressures which preclude a definite national position on certain issues. All, however, find it necessary to state some positions, not only because leaders do have views of international import, but because they become on independence members of an international world. The decision-makers of new states (like those of other states) must concern themselves with their nation's survival. They must determine what external threats, if any, exist to their state and assess their nation's power in relation to such threats. But survival is the common interest of all state leaders and has to be given content by such ideas and practices as expansionism, status quo, compromise, trade agreements, alliances, international organizations, regional cooperation, and other matters of war and peace. Since such ideas and practices cannot be pushed with equal vigor on all issues, state leaders must soon establish a priority of preference or hierarchy of interests. It is these which, over a period of time, reveal permanent interests and provide patterns of foreign policy.

ENTER NIGERIA

Nigeria is one of the new states, having obtained independence only on October 1, 1960. Our purpose is to examine foreign policy formation in this potentially great African state. The approach here is analytical, and foreign policy is defined "as the legislative aspect . . . of managing foreign relations."[3]

3 Kenneth W. Thompson and Roy C. Macridis, "The Comparative Study of Foreign Policy," in Roy C. Macridis (ed.), *Foreign Policy in World Politics* (Englewood Cliffs: Prentice-Hall, 1962), p. 18.

The analytical approach begins with the assumption that a state's geographical postion and size, its history, its role in international decision-making, and its "elements of national power" all combine over a period of time to provide a consistent and meaningful policy, regardless of changes in national decision-makers. Setbacks and variations in application do occur, but interests, once asserted, have a way of remaining interests to states. New states, however, have only the most limited history of relations with other states and therefore no pattern of "hierarchy of interests" which have been defended with various degrees of intransigence, compromise, or indifference. This raises the question of whether there is anything one can say about a potential state *before* it becomes independent. What, for example, could one say about Nigeria's foreign policy in 1958 when it was first known that it would become independent in 1960? Were there characteristics of this state-to-be which would indicate its probable foreign policy? By attempting to avoid hindsight and dealing only with conditions known in 1958, it is submitted that the following policies might well have been anticipated:

1) Having a large area, the largest population of any African state, and the resources necessary for a potentially powerful industrial and military state, it was likely that Nigeria would attempt to assert strong leadership in areas of its interests.

2) Being potentially the most powerful state in a continent of rapid change, it would undoubtedly place African affairs high on its priority list.

3) Having won independence with a minimum of rancor, it would not likely break all or most ties with Great Britain.

4) Having argued the evils of colonialism to justify its independence, it would probably join similarly-situated states in condemning colonialism wherever it continued.

5) Like most other British colonies, it would join the Commonwealth (in fact, this had been agreed upon and was already approved by all leaders).

6) Like any new state, it would seek the advantages of membership in the United Nations.

7) Having a federal structure, with one conservative region likely to dominate the two more radical regions, its policies in all areas would likely be cautious and moderate.

8) There being no evidence of Communist leanings among the potential leadership, it would appear quite unlikely that Nigeria would seek more than friendly relations with the Soviet bloc.

9) There being strong pro-British and pro-American sentiments among the potential leadership, it would appear likely that close relations would be established with these two powers.

However, these evaluations in 1958 would only have provided guidelines. They would not tell us many things we need to know about Nigeria's foreign policy. Was its closeness with Britain to lead to military alignment, or would it join the neutralist sentiments of other new states? Would it be aggressive and expansive, or would it insist on the maintenance of current boundaries? Would it seek closer ties with English-speaking Ghana than with other African states? Would its anti-colonialism support gradualism or haste? Would its interests in Africa lead it to support early political union or some less rigid form of cooperation? Would hatred of apartheid lead it to encourage military action against South Africa or would it encourage less harsh action?

In retrospect, answers to some of these questions appear quite clear, but they were not clear in 1958. What has made them clear has been the actual practice of an independent state. It is the purpose of this monograph to examine the practice of Nigeria, not only since independence, but during the fifteen months preceding independence. Those preceding months saw a national election in which politicians began for the first time seriously to concern themselves with foreign policy; and the meetings of a parliament whose members began to assert what they regarded as the national interests of an independent Nigeria. Such a study can only be a beginning, however, a study in foreign policy *formation*. Only time will reveal the extent to which the first attempts to identify Nigeria's national interests really embraced the permanent interests of Nigeria.

The obvious weakness of this study is that many of the documents related to decision-making are not only not available but in many cases may not even exist. Where careful records of secret and executive sessions have been kept, they will not be available for scholarly perusal for years, possibly decades. Nevertheless, it is believed that some insights are available even at this early date into Nigerian foreign policy formation. Political parties have foreign policy planks in their platforms; the Government has announced, enacted, and defended certain policies; an Opposition has arisen to challenge forthrightly, and with trenchant arguments, the position of the Government; articulate groups in the society have arisen to criticize the Government's foreign policy; and the Government itself has shown change (some would say maturity) in three action-packed years.

We have had to rely mainly on open documents (such as parliamentary debates), government pronouncements, public debates, internal conflicts, actual government action, news stories and journalistic articles, and to a lesser extent on interviews and whatever insights one can gain from living in the country for almost a year in 1961-62. Not being privy to actual decision-making in secret sessions of the executive branch, we face the problem of dealing with appearances rather than realities, as Henry Bretton has asserted so forcefully.[4] However tenuous this study, the forces at play in foreign policy formation during the restless seminal years should have value for understanding whatever "reality" finally emerges from this dynamic and changing state.

THE FEDERAL SETTING

The outstanding feature of Nigeria is that it is a federation, and that fact (as in the United States) has come to color every important policy whether domestic or foreign. The very essence of federalism is the lack of

4 Henry L. Bretton, *Power and Stability in Nigeria* (New York: Praeger, 1962), *passim*.

sufficient national consensus to create a unitary state; hence, the idea in many minds that it is a "second best" form of government. However, the fact that a federation emerges at all is evidence that some common values are held by leaders from various regions, and Nigerian leaders no less than British came to accept a federal system, although with reluctance in some quarters. The result for Nigeria was a federation of three regions and a federal territory (Lagos). Such decentralization makes governing difficult enough even after decades of experience, as the history of other federal states will demonstrate. But Nigeria adds to this system another feature— that in which one region is larger than the remaining ones combined, in both geography and population. It is difficult to see how such an arrangement can survive indefinitely, particularly when the dynamic forces for rapid change exist mainly in the smaller regions. A brief description of the Nigerian setting, therefore, appears necessary before the central problem of foreign policy can be treated.

THE REGIONS

The Northern Region, which has over three-fourths of the land mass, is land-locked. It has over half of the population of the country, is ethnically made up chiefly of Fulani and Hausa, is overwhelmingly Moslem in religion, and has a long tradition of autocratic rule by Moslem emirs, a system hardly touched by the British. This region has the fewest educated people, is the least developed economically, and has little or no tradition making for democracy. Allowing such a region so effectively to dominate the new federation does indeed appear to represent "one of the greatest acts of gerrymandering in history."[5]

Both the Western and Eastern Regions, located on the coast, are much more developed than the North, have a greater number of educated people, are mainly Christian or pagan, have fought longer and more vigorously for independence, and have supplied most of the leaders of the country. Their differences, however, are also great. The East is dominated by the Ibo, and the West by the Yoruba, each with its own language and social order. They have a long tradition of animosity and distrust of each other.

Because of these tribal differences, organizations sprang up in each Region to defend the interests of the dominant group against encroachments from the other Regions. The oldest political party in contemporary Nigeria grew out of such a movement. Formerly called the National Council of Nigeria and the Cameroons (NCNC), it is now called the National Convention of Nigerian Citizens (in order to preserve its famous initials). It sprang chiefly out of the Ibo Federal Union, an Ibo cultural organization in the East headed by Dr. Nnamdi Azikiwe. It fought against federalism for a number of years before finally giving up what was obviously a losing battle. It claims to be Fabian-Socialist in outlook, appeals mainly to the Ibos in

5 *Ibid.,* p. 124.

the East and minority groups in the other Regions, and "is the principal advocate in the country of Pan-Africanism and a policy of Nigerian non-alignment with international power blocs."[6]

In 1949, a group of intellectuals in the Northern Region formed a cultural organization called the Northern People's Congress, one of whose leaders was Alhaji (later Sir) Abubakar Tafawa Balewa. In 1951, having won the support of Alhaji (later Sir) Ahmadu Bello, the Sarduana of Sokoto, the Congress formed itself into a party by the same name. With the support of the Sarduana and the emirs of the Region, the party definitely became conservative in outlook (indeed it actually delayed rather than speeded independence). Its appeal is restricted almost entirely to the North, and mainly to Moslems.

In the Western Region, in 1948, Chief Obafemi Awolowo established the *Egbe Omo Oduduwa,* a Yoruba cultural organization which he had founded earlier in London. This organization became the basis for the Action Group, the dominant political party in the West, which now provides the opposition in the Federal Parliament. Its appeal is mainly to Yorubas in the West, but it also gets support from minority groups in the other Regions. It has always favored federalism for Nigeria.[7]

One other important party, the Northern Elements Progressive Union (NEPU), should be mentioned, although it did not grow out of a cultural organization and is largely restricted to the North. It was formed in 1950 by Mallam Aminu Kano. It regards the NPC as too conservative, seeks the reform of Islam, and eschews foreign alignments. It aligned itself quite early with the NCNC, although it is regarded as slightly more radical than the latter. After the elections of December 1959, it was faced with a real challenge when its partner formed a coalition with its main enemy, the NPC.[8]

The above-described factors provide the setting for Nigeria's entry onto the world stage as a sovereign state. No one party had anywhere like a national following. Parties were identified by the regions of their origins. In each region there was a tendency for the dominant party to thwart and frustrate the activities of the minority parties, occasionally to the point of murder, and frequently to the point of violation of civil rights. Opposition parties were often treated as enemies, or even traitors, of Nigeria. Yet out of this melee Nigerians were to elect politicians who were to form a government which was to steer the country, among other things, into a meaningful foreign policy, one which would not only secure the survival

6 Ronald Segal, *Political Africa* (London: Stevens and Sons, Ltd., 1961), p. 376. Cf., however, *infra,* Chapter II. Cf., also *Zik, A Selection of the Speeches of Nnamdi Azikiwe* (Cambridge: The University Press, 1961), pp. 163-208.

7 See *Awo: The Autobiography of Chief Obafemi Awolowo* (Cambridge: The University Press, 1960), pp. 160 ff., 213, ff., and *passim.*

8 For fuller discussions of Nigerian politicians and political parties see Segal, *op. cit., passim; Zik,* pp. 301-34; and Kenneth W. J. Post, *The Nigerian Federal Election of 1959* (London: Published for The Nigerian Institute of Social and Economic Research by Oxford University Press, 1963), *passim.*

of the state, but would assist it to rapid economic and industrial growth, the goal of all underdeveloped countries.

NIGERIA: A TRULY NEW STATE

Most of the new states of the world (those which have emerged since World War II) have gained their independence from a European power. Nigeria is no exception to this generalization. What this meant in the case of Nigeria was, not the resurgence of a former state which had lost its independence for a while, but the emergence of a state which had never existed before. The extent to which Nigeria is a state depends entirely on the fact that Great Britain assumed control over a large part of Africa which lay in the watershed of the Niger and Benue Rivers. The geographical area covered 373,250 square miles (larger than Texas and Oklahoma), and at the present time the population is thought to be near 40,000,000. In this area there exist at least 300 tribes, most of whom have their own language. However, 58 per cent of the people belong either to the Fulani-Hausas of the North, the Ibos of the East, or the Yorubas of the West.[9] This vast area of many diverse cultures saw little in common among the people. Much of the territory was occupied by warring tribes, although much of the North had been united in the Moslem *jihad* (holy war) of the early nineteenth century. Before the British came, the area as a whole had never known a common ruler.[10] Nigeria, therefore, is to a large extent the history of the last 60 years of British rule.

As far as international politics is concerned, perhaps Nigeria's lack of a national history is its greatest virtue.[11] Like the United States in the nineteenth century, Nigeria in the twentieth century is free to find its position in the world largely unrestrained by repressive traditions. It has no national past, real or fancied, to recover; it has no traditional enemies; it has no common mythology with holy scriptures to which national policy must be made to appear to conform; it has no competition among religious leaders, each claiming to know the true way as laid down in ancient revelations; it does not have to appeal to past national principles to compel present national acceptance of new objectives; it has no common economic history to which national policy must conform, or which must be repudiated

---

9 See George P. Murdock, "The Traditional Socio-political Systems of Nigeria: An Introductory Survey," in Robert O. Tilman and Taylor Cole (eds.), *The Nigerian Political Scene* (Durham: Duke University Press, 1962), pp. 3-16.

10 Cf., *The Economist*, June 17, 1961, p. 1240, for a report which ascribes to Prime Minister Balewa the assertion that Britain united squabbling villages and made a nation of them; and *Awo*, p. 252, where the leader of the Action Group said of his party: "We acknowledged the fact that Nigeria was a British creation. . . ."

11 This is not to say that Nigerians have no cultural history. Every Nigerian belongs to some social group with a long cultural history, and anthropologists are constantly pushing the time limits of that history further and further into the past. For a brief account see the excellent volume by M. C. English, *An Outline of Nigerian History* (London: Longmans, 1960).

in order to have a viable contemporary policy; it has no common traditional political structure to restrict the direction it may take; it does not even have a common religious hero to whose teachings policy must conform in order to get universal acceptance; in short, Nigeria *as a nation* is more fully free than India, Burma, or even China. Being freer, however, means that Nigerians have a greater responsibility to compromise differences in order to produce some national consensus. For whereas Nigeria has no national history, the various peoples who make up the federation *do* have a history. The struggle at the center, therefore, involves the element of compromise on issues. But compromise does not necessarily mean that the traditions of one group or the other will prevail; for inside each tribal or traditional group is a new, educated elite whose objectives are to change the traditional ways. The social structure of the Federal Parliament demonstrates the level at which that body operates in shaping the new policies: 67 per cent of its members in 1960 were forty years old or younger; almost all of them were literate (as opposed to more than 80 per cent illiteracy in the country); and most of them were either teachers, professional men, or businessmen.[12]

This is not to say, of course, that Nigeria started in 1960 with no governmental patterns, no common language, and no common values. The governmental structure, though imposed by the British, was an evolutionary creation, involving in recent years active participation by the leading Nigerians from all the regions; the common language is English; and the common values are those of the European democracies, however weakly instilled. Nigeria did not start its national history from a void. On independence it had already had six years experience as a federal state; the regions had had some experience in self-government; political parties had been in existence for more than a decade; and the articulate leaders had been putting forth various and numerous proposals for national policy. The political struggle was already occurring within the British parliamentary framework, which agreed that the majority should govern but the minority should be protected with rights.[13]

FOREIGN POLICY BEFORE INDEPENDENCE

It would also be wrong to assume that no thought had been given to foreign policy before independence. For decades Nigerian leaders had felt a kinship with other Africans, particularly Negro Africans. One of Nigeria's own great nationalists, Dr. Azikiwe, had for twenty-five years been in the

---

12 For statistics for the period 1951-57 see James S. Coleman, *Nigeria: Background to Nationalism* (Berkeley: University of California Press, 1958), pp. 380-83. See also Royal Institute of International Affairs, *Nigeria: Political and Economic Background* (London: Oxford University Press, 1960), p. 3. Cf., *Awo*, p. 252, where the writer referred to his party members as "a number of detribalised politicians and journalists living in the urban areas of the South."

13 Bretton, *op. cit.*, pp. 22-23, argues that the "Westminster model" is so alien to traditional Nigerian thinking that it will surely be replaced by a system "more closely corresponding to local tastes and requirements."

forefront in preaching Pan-Africanism.[14] Jomo Kenyatta and Kwame Nkrumah were heroes to Nigerians as to other Africans. Colonialism, being the enemy to Nigerians, became the enemy (in the minds of Nigerians) to other colonial peoples, and produced identification of Nigerians and other colonials, particularly African ones. Nigerian leaders were trained mainly in Britain (and a few in the United States) and had as a result interests which led them to maintain a closer identification with Western democracies than with totalitarian systems.

As early as 1949, Dr. Azikiwe was questioning whether Nigeria (or any African state for that matter) should align with the West. In a speech in London, he pointed out that Africans had been called on in two world wars to fight Kaiserism and Hitlerism to make the world safe for democracy —"a political theory which seems to be an exclusive property of the good peoples of Europe and America." He did not say that he would not align with the West in the "cold war," but his words had an ominous ring:

Now the peoples of Africa are being told that it is necessary, in the interest of peace and the preservation of Christianity, that they should be ready to fight the Soviet Union, which the war buglers allege is aiming at world domination. Since the end of World War II, Field Marshal Lord Montgomery has been visiting several countries in Africa, including my country, Nigeria, which harbours uranium-233. Military roads are being constructed under the guise of economic development. American technicians are flooding Africa, and feverish preparations are being made for World War III. Certain factors have necessitated the stand which my organisation, the National Council of Nigeria and the Cameroons, have taken in respect of the next war. In Nigeria and the Cameroons we face the inescapable reality that the blood of our sons has been shed in two world wars in vain.[15]

In 1955 Dr. Azikiwe delivered a blistering attack on the Afro-Asian states which convened the Bandung Conference for having invited the Gold Coast (Ghana) but not Nigeria. In his address, he said:

I may say without fear of contradiction that any decision made at Bandung on the future of this continent that does not take into account the fact that every sixth person in Africa is a Nigerian, is bound to be like a flower that "is born to blush unseen and to waste its sweetness in the desert air." . . . But it is obvious that they blundered when they decided to invite one West African State-to-be and chose to ignore the other West African State-to-be. . . . The Asian Powers will do well to appreciate the historic mission and manifest destiny of Nigeria on the African continent. . . . Moreover, there is nothing to prevent us from convening a Pan-African Conference or a Pan-Afro-Asian Conference when the time comes. Nevertheless the Asian Powers must be warned that Asians in Africa should live up to expectations in their relations with Africans, and that they should not exploit Africans; I have in mind Afro-Asian relations in East Africa and the Union of South Africa.[16]

14 The NCNC had even had a foreign policy plank in its platform of 1945, to wit: "To secure for the people of Nigeria and the Cameroons an effective voice in international affairs which directly or indirectly affect them." *Zik*, p. 314.

15 *Ibid.*, p. 62.

16 *Ibid.*, pp. 63-65.

In February 1959, Azikiwe said that the Pan-African Conference held in 1958 in Accra had opened a new chapter in the history of Africa. "We are on the eve of great events," he said. "A future Federation of independent West African States has made a beginning. It is my earnest hope that the Federation of Nigeria, soon to be independent, will play a worthy part in that larger Federation."[17]

As early as 1938 the Charter of the Nigerian Youth Movement, the precursor of contemporary political parties, had listed as one of the goals for a united Nigeria its "complete autonomy within the British Empire. We are striving towards a position of equal partnership with the other member States of the British Commonwealth of Nations."[18] While this may not have been a profound foreign policy, it was nevertheless significant in view of the fact that not even Asian states had been admitted to the Commonwealth —at that time it was entirely white. Furthermore, this objective has hardly been challenged by Nigerians since it was first enunciated.

However, we must not leave a false impression. As one writer said, when Pan-Africanism was getting considerable attention in the late 1950's, "in Nigeria . . . the several provinces were far too busy negotiating their own differences to worry about the gigantic problem of West African unification."[19] Indeed, Nigerian politics, until 1959, was concerned almost entirely with internal struggles over constitutional arrangements, the beginnings of self-government in the regions, and the effort to get from the British a specific date for independence. Only with the assurance of a fixed date for independence did the Nigerian leaders concern themselves with Nigeria's place in international politics.

17 *Ibid.,* p. 68. In a reminiscence he pointed out that as a journalist in Accra in the 1930's his newspaper, the *African Morning Post,* had for its motto: "Independent in all things and neutral in nothing affecting the destiny of Africa." *Ibid.*
18 *Awo,* p. 121.
19 Paul-Marc Henry, "Pan-Africanism: A Dream Come True," *Foreign Affairs,* April 1959, p. 446.

II. Foreign Policy in the Federal Election of 1959

At the end of the Resumed Constitutional Conference in 1958, Nigerian leaders in London knew that the country could have its independence by October 1, 1960, merely for the asking. The report of the Conference described this momentous concession of the British Government as follows:

... The Secretary of State said that ... he was authorised by Her Majesty's Government to say that if a resolution was passed by the new Federal Parliament early in 1960 asking for independence, Her Majesty's Government would agree to that request and would introduce a Bill in Parliament to enable Nigeria to become a fully independent country on the 1st October, 1960.

The Conference warmly welcomed the Secretary of State's statement. The Prime Minister [of Nigeria] and the Premiers [of the three Regions] made statements accepting the Secretary of State's statement, and expressing their desire that on independence Nigeria should become a full member of the Commonwealth and that there should continue to be close co-operation between Britain and Nigeria.[1]

The "new Federal Parliament" referred to was to be the result of the federal election to be held sometime in 1959. That election, therefore, was to be the first one held in Nigeria in which the policies of the various parties could advocate a course of action for an independent Nigeria (no one doubting that the new Parliament would request and get the promised independence). This meant, also for the first time, the right of, and necessity for, politicians to concern themselves with foreign policy, for before independence that had been the prerogative of Great Britain. Two moves were already a foregone conclusion: Nigeria would seek admission both to the Commonwealth and the United Nations—no one ever seriously challenged these assumptions. Much talk had already occurred in Nigeria, as throughout all Africa, on Pan-Africanism, neo-colonialism, white settler

1 *Report by the Resumed Nigeria Constitutional Conference* (Lagos: Federal Government Printer, 1958), p. 33.

rule in east and south Africa, racism, French atomic bomb tests in the Sahara, and other issues that affected Africans, emotionally or otherwise. But it would be wrong to assume that Nigerian political parties, at the beginning of the election campaign, had definitely formulated policies for the nation to follow in world affairs.

THE BEGINNING OF PARTY INTEREST IN FOREIGN POLICY

The importance of the election, in the minds of Southerners at least, is revealed by the fact that both Dr. Azikiwe (leader of NCNC and Premier of the Eastern Region) and Chief Awolowo (leader of the Action Group and Premier of the Western Region) relinquished their premierships to seek the Prime Ministership at the center by running for Parliament. On the other hand, Sir Ahmadu Bello (leader of the NPC and Premier of the Northern Region) decided to hold his regional office, thus allowing the deputy leader (Sir Abubakar Tafawa Balewa) to become the Parliamentary leader of the Party.[2] Balewa had already been playing this role for some time and for two years had been Prime Minister. Thus, the 1959 election saw three of the top four men in Nigeria vying for national leadership after independence.

The campaign began, haltingly, in the summer of 1959, although the election itself did not occur until December 12. The first policy paper to be published, the "14-point programme" of Chief Awolowo, leader of the AG, on June 4, ignored foreign policy altogether. In fact, it was not until August 20, in a statement by Dr. Azikiwe, leader of the NCNC, that foreign policy got any attention. At that time "Zik" announced his policy for encouraging foreign investment: no enterprise in existence before October 1, 1960, would be nationalized, but the right would be reserved to regulate commerce and industry "in accordance with International Law and the usages and practices of the civilised nations of the world."[3] Continuing, he promised an efficient armed force and intelligence service; adherence to the United Nations; continuing Commonwealth membership; a "neutralist" foreign policy, with adherence to "no axis of geopolitics"; and the policy of a "good neighbour" toward African states, with the attempt to establish closer economic and political relations with them.[4]

These statements were indeed quite general and hardly revealed anything positive about Azikiwe's plans. Nevertheless, Awolowo chose the occasion of the Sixth Annual Conference of the Action Group, on September 11, not

---

2 Sir Ahmadu's move would correspond in the United States to a politician's rejection of the presidency in order to continue as governor of a state. This writer has learned of no satisfactory explanation for such a move, except for one observer who believed that Sir Ahmadu has religious aspirations to become the Sultan of Sokoto, and thus religious leader of all Moslems in West Africa. Also, it was always possible that the Southern parties would coalesce, thus leaving the NPC to serve as the Opposition, a role which Bello apparently did not want.

3 *Daily Times,* August 22, 1959.

4 *Ibid.*

only to answer the Eastern Premier but to give a rather comprehensive statement of foreign policy. He began by asserting that it was "unrealistic to labour for the emergence of United States of Africa, or even of economic co-operation such as exists in Western Europe." Such activity, he added, is not only "visionary," but was "the pursuit of what is quite frankly an *ignis fatuus*." Besides an unwillingness of new states to give up their independence, he said, two other difficulties stood in the way of a political union of African states. One stemmed from the position of Egypt in the Arab world, which "regards it infra dig to be regarded as having any social and cultural affinity with the black races of Africa." Under the "undisguised totalitarianism" of Nasser, political cooperation "would be possible only if the black races of Africa are prepared to remain as satellites in Egypt's orbit as Syria is now." The second difficulty stemmed from the dominant position of white settlers in east and south Africa with whom he saw no chance of cooperation.

Chief Awolowo went on to point out that no nation is absolutely good or absolutely evil, that color bars still exist in the United States and Great Britain, but that in the Western democracies the people are fighting this evil

without risk to their lives or personal freedom. If you did likewise behind the iron curtain you would not live to fight another day.

These then are my promise and my test as to which of the two opposing Blocs of the world is to be preferred, whilst we maintain friendly relations with all. The world in which we live is still far from perfection. We have got to take it as we find it and, like conscientious and honest people, strive to contribute towards its peace, progress and happiness. . . .

The question is, as between the Western Bloc and Eastern Bloc, where can a man freely exercise his natural right to hold and express any opinion subject to such restrictions as may be laid down by Laws enacted by the freely elected parliament of the land? The answer is obvious: it is in the Western Bloc. . . .

In the present world contest, when atheistic materialism is threatening to destroy or stifle all that is best and noblest in man, neutrality in international affairs, whether passive, positive or independent, is an unmitigated disservice to humanity. My own analysis has led me to the conclusion that neutrality, as the basis of the foreign policy of certain nations, is no more and no less than the projection, conscious or unconscious, of the deepseated prejudices which those nations have had towards the countries of the Western Democracies. . . .

There is a policy which appears to be in vogue amongst some of the developing countries of the world. In their quest for financial and technical assistance, they adopt the tactics of wooing the nations of the two Blocs at the same time, in the hope that in the latter's anxious bid for new supporters or converts, they (the developing countries) would get the best of two worlds. I consider these tactics to be both disreputable and dangerous.

. . . If we want help from more than one nation, by all means let us seek it. But it is immoral to play two opposing forces against each other in the process. . . .

The tactics are dangerous because acts of double-dealing, whether diplomatic or otherwise, never pay in the end.

To sum up, Nigeria should do everything in her power to foster co-operation among all the countries of West Africa in economic and cultural matters. She should fearlessly champion the cause of the oppressed peoples in Africa and other parts of the world. She should take her place in the British Commonwealth of Nations, and should not hesitate to make her attitude, towards the ideals for which the Western Democracies stand clear beyond any shadow of doubt.

In so far as is compatible with her honest convictions, national interests, and her legitimate obligations as a loyal member of the British Commonwealth, she should maintain cordial relations with all the other nations of the world, and do her best to promote peaceful co-existence between the Western and Eastern Blocs.[5]

It is difficult to escape the conclusion drawn by Kenneth Post: "Though Chief Awolowo never in so many words called for an alignment with the West, the inference to be drawn from his analysis and conclusions was obvious."[6] In fact, Dr. Azikiwe drew the same conclusion. He charged Awolowo with advocating an alignment with the Western democracies, and added that such an alignment would "entangle Nigeria in military alliances which are not in our national interest and which could endanger our corporate existence." He said the term "Western democracies" included many states which, "with the exception of Britain have ruled Africa with force and with inhumanity. Belgium, France, Italy and Portugal are among the world's worst colonial powers." Finally, he said: "We will bind ourselves closer to the United Kingdom and the United States of America but it would be foolhardy to align ourselves with the Western democracies as a whole in the way the Action Group suggests."[7]

The Action Group's own newspaper apparently believed also that Awolowo had advocated some form of alignment, but denied that any military alliance was envisaged. Said the editorial: "Those who argue that alignment with Western Democracies commits Nigeria to war and to military alliances against her will have only distorted the facts." The proof that such alignment does not automatically create such commitments, the paper said, was found in the ability of the United States and Canada to oppose their allies, Britain and France, in the Suez crisis of 1956.[8] At this stage of the campaign, therefore, it might appear that the Action Group advocated closer ties with the West than the NCNC, although Dr. Azikiwe's reference to ties with Great Britain and the United States cast some doubt on the extent of the differences.

A new development, in the form of a manifesto of the NPC, occurred the

---

5 *Daily Service,* September 12, 1959. Cf., a similar statement in his autobiography, *Awo* (London: Cambridge University Press, 1960) , pp. 309-313.

6 Kenneth W. J. Post, *The Nigerian Federal Election of 1959* (London: published for the Nigerian Institute of Social and Economic Research by Oxford University Press, 1963) , p. 311.

7 *Daily Times,* September 12, 1959. Earlier Dr. Azikiwe had charged the Action Group with seeking to align Nigeria "with the Western democracies which, with the exception of the United States are the self-same colonial powers, who held Africa and Asia in political bondage for centuries." *Ibid.,* Sept. 9, 1959.

8 *Daily Service,* September 15, 1959.

day following the *Daily Service* editorial. "Above all our Government will be based on the fear of God," the manifesto began, and asserted that on foreign policy the NPC will "rule out completely any idea of adopting a policy of neutrality in international affairs." Continuing, Nigeria must join with countries whose policies are animated by the same beliefs as hers, and, therefore, Nigeria "must maintain the closest relationship with the United Kingdom," it must join and support the United Nations, and it "should aim at retaining and expanding her existing ties of friendship with the United States of America." The NPC regarded a West African federation or union "as at present premature"; while it did not rule out such a union in the future, "for the present we feel that it will be better for us to direct our energies to developing the potentialities latent in each country." Finally, the manifesto summed up the foreign policy of the NPC as follows:

(1) A dynamic policy adaptable to circumstances but founded on our fundamental beliefs.

(2) Membership of the Commonwealth.

(3) Closer ties with the United Kingdom.

(4) Increasing friendship with the United States of America.

(5) Friendly relations and closer co-operation with all countries in the African Continent, particularly those in West Africa.

(6) Friendly relations with all countries sharing common interests with Nigeria and respecting Nigeria's sovereignty.

(7) Acceptance of the principles and obligations of the United Nations' Charter.[9]

Post says the policy of the NPC "differed considerably from that of the NCNC, and was much closer to Action Group's, a fact which that party was not slow to point out in its newspaper."[10] Indeed, it would appear that at this particular point in the campaign the NCNC was offering an alternative to the foreign policies of both the NPC and the AG; its leaders had advocated neutralism, adherence to "no axis of geopolitics," and closer economic and political ties with other African states. These apparent differences, however, faded away when the NCNC-NEPU Alliance issued its manifesto on October 9, and when the NCNC alone (the NEPU apparently not agreeing) issued its policy paper on foreign affairs on October 22. The Alliance manifesto read as follows:

We shall not commit Nigeria to joining any military pacts. But we shall develop our armed forces on the basis of neutrality, as has been the case with Switzerland. But whether a position of neutrality in military matters will be in the national interest of Nigeria or not will be decided after relevant factors have been taken into consideration on the attainment of independence.

In any case, we shall frame our foreign policy to enable us to maintain friendly relations with any sovereign State which either declares as a matter of policy its adherence to the Universal Declaration of Human Rights or guarantees to enforce Human Rights and Fundamental Freedom. Clearly, this will

9 *Daily Times,* September 18, 1959.
10 Post, *op. cit.,* p. 314.

make the respect for human dignity an important element in our foreign relations. We will maintain a policy of non-alignment with any particular axis of
geopolitics, Eastern or Western—a policy which will definitely place us at a
maneuverable advantage to be independent in our approach to problems of
international relations.

. . . we shall neither be partisan nor be neutral but we shall be independent
in our attitude.

. . . we shall remain as a full-fledged member of the British Commonwealth
of Nations and exchange diplomatic representatives with the other members
wherever possible. We shall apply to join the United Nations. . . .

. . . in Africa, we shall develop a policy of 'good neighbour'. . . . We shall
not deliberately give cause to our African neighbours to be apprehensive that
the Nigerian Colossus has any designs either to interfere in their domestic affairs
or to seek to draw them into its political orbit.

. . . We will spike neutrality because it is defeatist and lacks moral conviction. We shall be opposed to partisanship because it is an exhibition of
prejudice.[11]

This statement would be instructive if for no other reason than its
attempt to advocate neutrality only in relation to military pacts, but to
renounce it in all other contexts. Yet, after saying its neutrality in military
matters would be like that of Switzerland, the statement qualified this
position by saying that whether a position of neutrality in military matters
"is in the national interest or not would be decided after independence."

It is equally instructive in that it totally ignores Pan-Africanism, and
gives both sides in the cold war equal treatment. Part of the vagueness of
this manifesto is due, no doubt, to the difference between the two parties
making up the Alliance. However, the NCNC is very much larger and far
more significant in Nigerian politics than the NEPU. This fact was demonstrated when, on October 23, the NCNC issued its own policy paper on international affairs.

The NCNC policy paper was the only one which attempted to place a
Nigerian political party's policy within a theoretical framework. The paper
began with the assertion that foreign policy is a struggle for power, but
pointed out that there are two schools of thought on politics: the "idealistic,
moralistic conception which considers politics in terms of abstract moral
principles"; and the "realistic one to which the political scene presents itself
as an unending struggle for interest and power." Without saying categorically
which position the NCNC accepted, the paper said: "our national interest
would be defined not in terms of ambiguous and universal moral platitudes
but in terms of the power we have available and can make necessary for the
attainment of our objectives."

Following this brief excursion into theory, the policy paper then launched
into the party position:

There can be no doubt about the fact that Nigeria would continue to be
friendly with the West. It has always been emphasized that the NCNC strongly
believes that an independent Nigeria should remain within the Commonwealth.

11 *Daily Times,* October 9, 1959.

. . . The NCNC equally believes that Nigeria's relations with the United States should be one of very intimate and cordial relationship. Needless to emphasize our deep admiration of and affection for the United States, its ways of life, its championship of the freedom and equality of man everywhere and, no less important its greatness.

One cannot help but admire a country born in revolution from the depths of colonial status to the majestic height of world leadership. We believe that membership in the Commonwealth invariably, though not automatically, means a relationship of one sort or the other with the United States. If this be correct, then the saying that 'All roads in the Commonwealth lead to Washington' may also be true.

[Reserving the right to win friends anywhere, the paper continued:]

Although the NCNC prides itself as a Fabian Socialist party, which is stoutly opposed to Communism as a way of life, yet we do not believe that anti-Communism in and of itself, is a sufficient basis for a foreign policy. Our relations with the Eastern bloc should generally be based on a policy of peaceful co-existence while specifically it should be dictated only by Nigeria's national interest. . . .

The NCNC views with favour the idea of the Federation of the West African States. But we realise that in view of the onerous difficulties involved in the implementation of such a federation, the issue should remain a long term one, pending the attainment of independence by all, or at least, a majority of the countries that comprise the geographical stretch of West Africa and the successful social and economic integration of its peoples. There is another major obstacle to the scheme, namely, the integration policy of Metropolitan France with her overseas territories—a good portion of which lies in West Africa.

The policy paper then went on to advocate a West African Consultative Organization made up of the governments of West Africa to "keep alive the cultural links of the territories concerned and for exploring the avenues of implementing the federation question as early as possible." It referred to Pan-Africanism as

a desirable philosophy and a long term objective. . . . As a philosophy, it is anti-communist or ought to be so; but as an objective of policy, it is a clarion call made by Africans themselves for the liberation of all African peoples, racial equality and racial tolerance—the most passionate and yet the most constitutional appeal made in the history of modern nationalism.

As a last point, which it did not elaborate, the policy paper suggested a "Monroe Doctrine" for Africa but "advises caution in its methods of approach."[12]

ESSENTIAL AGREEMENT AMONG PARTIES

It is impossible to escape the conclusion that the three most important parties had now come remarkably close in their foreign policy principles,

12 *Daily Times*, October 23, 1959. In view of the policy statement's reference to anti-communism, it is interesting to note that on the day after its release Dr. Azikiwe charged that the Northern Region's law requiring a permit for political rallies was a situation conducive to the growth of communism. *Ibid.*, October 24, 1959.

albeit those principles were for the most part quite general and gave only vague indications of each party's reaction to specific situations. Furthermore, it must be conceded that the NCNC official policy coupled with Dr. Azikiwe's explanations of it often appeared unclear and occasionally contradictory. This was due, presumably, to day-to-day maneuvering to score points against the opposition. Nevertheless, the main parties were in agreement on a number of important points: they all favored membership in the United Nations and the Commonwealth; a rather definite identification with the Western democracies (particularly Great Britain and the United States) as opposed to the Communist states; and they were unanimous that Pan-Africanism was at best an ideal, certainly not something to be achieved immediately, although it is not so certain that they were in agreement on some form of union of West African states. On the last point, it appears that the NCNC and the AG each held on to some hope that states in West Africa might somehow work more closely together than states normally do, although the NPC apparently considered this as much of a dream as Pan-Africanism. Except for the fact that the politicians continued to denigrate the foreign policy statements of the other parties as being insincere, one could assume that there were no basic differences among the major parties.[13]

It is obvious that such agreement was highly fortunate for a young state, and doubly so for a federal state already threatened with numerous centrifugal strains, not merely from traditional regional interests, but from strong political parties which represented tribal and religious groups in each region (with principles therefore which are difficult to compromise) rather than something so vague as the national interest. Certainly, the history of Nigeria would have been different if one of the political parties (particularly the NCNC or the NPC) had advocated principles diametrically opposed to those enunciated; e.g., if one of them had rejected the United Nations or the Commonwealth, or had advocated an alliance with the Soviet bloc or with the Arab bloc, or had demanded an immediate union of African states. In fact, it is somewhat surprising that no such divergent group or position appeared at all; surprising, that is, until one notes that even on domestic issues the parties tended to disagree more on methods than objectives. And where they disagreed most on objectives was in areas involving the exercise of political power; e.g., the power of the Federal Government as opposed to that of the Regions, the creation of new states, the use of national police instead of regional police in the Regions, and the reduction of the power of native courts, particularly in the North.[14]

13 Three minor parties also published manifestoes but, except for the Dynamic Party, led by Dr. Chike Obi, were almost exclusively concerned with domestic affairs. Even Dr. Obi's foreign policy statements were quite general with no ramifications of importance. He called for a strong Ministry of Defense, specializing in guerilla warfare; a West African Monroe Doctrine; the formation of a West African Republic to consist of Nigeria, Ghana, Liberia, Guinea, and the colonies of France, Portugal, and Spain in West Africa; and a strong defensive alliance with India directed against the Union of South Africa. *Daily Times,* November 6, 1959.

14 Cf., Post, *op. cit.,* Chap. VIII, pp. 284-328.

It is probably not difficult to account for the unanimity of agreement among the political leaders. Obviously the method of British rule, and especially the way Britain had relinquished colonial control, had created good feelings toward the metropolitan power. Nigerians had not been split over the emotion-charged question of whether or not to wage war on the British in order to gain independence. The issue never really arose. In fact, all factions had been represented in the pre-independence government so none felt left out in the decision-making processes leading to independence.[15] Furthermore, all the leaders had been trained in the United Kingdom (or the United States) and had absorbed the values of Western democracy which they all defended from time to time in some form or other. Also, like most of the other leaders of the world, and especially those of new states, Nigerian leaders saw survival most clearly in a strong United Nations; certainly they were convinced that they had no chance of survival in a power struggle with the big powers apart from the ameliorating influence of the United Nations. Pan-Africanism was indeed an ideal—it had been discussed for years, and offered wonderful visions of a colossal state, powerful and viable, peopled and run by black men. But none of the leaders could see even that dream come true if it meant giving up a more certain dream, the existence of a free and sovereign Nigeria.

We must now ask the question: what permanent interests appeared as soon as leaders began to think in terms of an independent state? First and foremost was the idea that Nigeria intended to remain sovereign in Africa, in spite of the deeply imbedded ideal of Pan-Africanism. Second, Nigeria would not break its numerous ties with Britain and other "Western" states. Even if its leaders had been inclined to break such ties immediately, the experience of Guinea must surely have informed them. Certainly trade channels already established were not to be cut until others had been created. Third, the importance of the continent of Africa became apparent, although in retrospect it does appear that there was a remarkable neglect of many African trouble spots, due perhaps to what the Prime Minister later called the African's general ignorance of continental affairs. A lack of experience in international politics may also explain why no politician capitalized on Nigeria's size and potential power to assert a policy of dominance for that country in African affairs. Such an assertion (though veiled) was to come shortly, however, and from the Prime Minister. The fourth and fifth permanent interests were memberships in the United Nations and the Commonwealth. How "permanent" these permanent interests were to be would depend on history, but they appeared to be the only logical ones in 1959, given the geographical setting of Nigeria, its history of British rule, its world position as a new and weak state, and certainly not least the attitudes of the powerful leaders of the three dominant parties. Time and political stability would fill in the details, but the main interests in the international field seemed set.

15 Cf., Coleman, *op. cit.,* p. 371.

THE RESULTS OF THE 1959 FEDERAL ELECTION

For clarity, a few words must be said about the election results. Contests were held for 312 seats in the enlarged House of Representatives: 174 from the North; 73 from the East; 62 from the West; and 3 from the Federal Territory of Lagos. From the Northern Region, the Northern Peoples Congress (NPC) elected 134 members, the Action Group (AG) elected 25, the National Council of Nigeria and the Cameroons/Northern Elements Progressive Union (NCNC/NEPU) elected 8, and minority parties and independents elected 7. From the Eastern Region, the NCNC/NEPU elected 53, the AG elected 14, and small parties and independents elected 1. From the Western Region, the AG elected 33, the NCNC/NEPU elected 21, and small parties and independents elected 8. From the Federal Territory of Lagos, the NCNC/NEPU elected 2 and the AG elected 1.[16]

It will be noted that the NPC elected all of its members from the Northern Region; it did not elect a single person from the other regions, although some Southern independents later aligned with the Northern party. On the other hand, the NCNC/NEPU and the Action Group, while electing their largest bloc from their Regions of origin, also elected some members from each of the other Regions and the Federal Territory. Comparisons by party and Region were as follows:

Region	Northern Peoples Congress	NCNC/ NEPU	Action Group	Others	Total
Northern	134	8	25	7	174
Eastern		58	14	1	73
Western		21	33	8	62
Lagos		2	1		3
Total	134	89	73	16	312

The largest single bloc, the NPC with 134 members, was still short of an absolute majority (which was 167), thus making a coalition imperative. Rumors existed to the effect that leaders of the Action Group offered to form a coalition with either of the other two major parties, but Chief Awolowo denied this.[17] In any case, the two largest parties did agree to form a coalition. Thus the NPC and the NCNC/NEPU (with 223 members out of 312) formed the Government, while the Action Group (with 73 members) formed the Opposition. Sir Abubakar, leader of the largest bloc in the coalition, demanded and got the Prime Ministership, and Awolowo became the official Leader of the Opposition. Dr. Azikiwe then resigned as leader of the NCNC and member of the House of Representatives to become President of the Senate. The actual bargaining which had gone on,

16 *Report on the Nigeria Federal Elections, December 1959* (Lagos: Federal Government Printer, 1960), p. 24.
17 *Daily Times,* December 23, 1959; K.W.J. Post, "Forming a Government in Nigeria," *The Nigerian Journal of Economics and Social Studies,* June 1960, p. 3.

however, was revealed after independence when Dr. Azikiwe was appointed the Governor-General of Nigeria, the first native of the country to be so honored.

Sir Abubakar immediately appointed a cabinet of fifteen members, nine from the NPC and six from the NCNC. He retained the portfolio of foreign affairs for himself, however, until the summer of 1961, that is, until eight months after independence. The Government was, until October 1, 1960, still theoretically subject to the control of the British Governor-General, Sir James Robertson, on behalf of Her Majesty's Government. For all practical purposes, however, most of the British Government's powers had disappeared as the Regions became self-governing. The same results occurred at the federal level; thus, in effect, giving the Central Government complete freedom in legislation and policy formation in the period immediately preceding independence.[18]

18 On April 1, 1960, in Parliament, Sir Abubakar said: "Now the Leader of the Opposition knows very well that though in name and legally we are not independent, the Prime Minister is really responsible for the defence of the country, and also our foreign relations. No Consulate could be opened in this country without my consent, and foreign delegations visiting this country must have my blessing." *House of Representatives Debates,* April-May session, 1960, p. 33.

III. *The Gathering Storm: Foreign Policy in Parliament, 1960*

In Chapter I foreign policy was defined as "the legislative aspect of managing foreign relations." This concept, of course, involves much more than the formal discourse of legislative bodies, colored as all such discourses are by executive initiative and judicial decisions. Until records of actual decision-making struggles in the executive are available, however, we must rely to a large extent on the Parliamentary record for our account of the struggle. Formal executive proposals, coupled by defenses from Government spokesmen, should reveal much about the bases for Government policy. General debate should reveal the nature of the interests of other segments of the society.

The year 1960 is significant for this study, not only as the year of Nigerian independence, but because of the gradual unfolding of foreign policy views which were clearer and fuller than those of the election period and were often contradictory of campaign statements. Such contradictions, of course, are to be expected in a dynamic setting where decision-makers are suddenly confronted with a "real situation" as opposed to the more theoretical one of election campaigns.

The Government faced the need (for its own direction as well as public information) to fill in the generalizations of 1959 by applying them to particular issues. Even more important was the need for the two main parties making up the coalition to explore the extent to which each could accommodate the foreign policy views of the other. There is no doubt that the important discussions in this relationship occurred in secret executive sessions. Nevertheless, it is obvious that the NCNC developed a split between one faction identified with its Parliamentary leadership under Chief Festus Okotie-Eboh, and another faction representative of militant youth, whose spokesman in the Parliament appeared to be Dr. Kalu Ezera.[1] As a result

1 In Nigeria these factions were generally referred to as conservatives and radicals. The conservatives rarely identified themselves by that term, but those who were called radicals by others also called themselves radicals frequently. Because of the rather

of this cleavage in the NCNC it is possible to witness some of the decision-making struggles, for the radicals in the party were constantly making their position known in the Parliament and elsewhere.

The year 1960 also saw the incubation of the "about face" of the Parliamentary leadership of the Action Group on foreign policy affairs. Such a radical shift in such a short time without a change in leadership will undoubtedly be analyzed for years to come. Some tentative evaluations will be offered later in this work.

One writer has said that "Nigeria's introduction to the battles of world politics has been sudden and rude,"[2] and events in Parliament in 1960 would support the observation. Attention here will be mainly on the House of Representatives, which met four times during the year. The highlights of each session on questions of foreign policy are indicative of the unfolding interests and positions.

FAIR WEATHER

The new Parliament met for the first time in January and for one purpose only—to pass a resolution asking for independence from Great Britain. The occasion is important in that the Prime Minister made a number of statements which would indicate his Government's attitude toward Great Britain, the Commonwealth, Nigeria's neighbors, and the general tone of his foreign

---

common usage of these terms in Nigeria, and because they appear to be quite inoffensive to the individuals and groups to whom they are applied, they also have been used in this work frequently.

Occasionally, however, those who were called radical by other Nigerians called themselves liberal. All of these terms are obviously relative. This writer has attempted to use them, therefore, with the following meanings (realizing of course that they may bear no relation to the meanings intended by Nigerians who use them, particularly when used opprobriously) :

Conservative: cautious, slow to make change, hesitant to break existing power relations, nostalgic, reliance on existing social patterns, general focus on the social elite and current leadership.

Liberal: belief in need for constant change ("growth"), willingness to innovate and to disrupt social patterns which slow down moves toward established goals but preferring legal or constitutional means, focus on the masses ("the people"), mistrust of social and political elites, hopeful.

Radical: extremes of the above. The radicals referred to in this study appear to be extreme liberals, demanding change rapidly, resentful of both legal and traditional restraints, filled with a conviction that they "know" what is the right way, and a tendency to see events in the sharp dichotomy of right and wrong, with little middle ground. Radical conservatives, restricted it would seem to Moslem traditionalists, are quiescent at this writing. However, Bretton, *op. cit.*, pp. 85, 109, divides the society into only two groups: the elite (ruling groups and their supporters) and counter-elite (composed of three distinct sub-groups: "the conservative and reactionary, the moderate-liberal, and the social revolutionary . . .").

2 L. Gray Cowan, "Nigerian Foreign Policy," in Robert O. Tilman and Taylor Cole (eds.), *The Nigerian Political Scene* (Durham: Duke University Press, 1962), p. 116.

policy which, he made clear, would not be announced until much later.

Balewa himself moved the momentous resolution to the effect:

That this House authorises the Government of the Federation of Nigeria to request Her Majesty's Government in the United Kingdom as soon as practicable to introduce a legislation in the Parliament of the United Kingdom providing for the establishment of the Federation of Nigeria on October first, 1960 as an independent sovereign state, and to request Her Majesty's Government in the United Kingdom at the appropriate time to support with the other Member Governments, of the Commonwealth Nigeria's desire to become a member of the Commonwealth.[3]

The Prime Minister defended his motion by pointing out the difficulties and obligations which approval would involve. He said that whereas on two previous occasions when Nigeria had asked for independence it had been a challenge to Great Britain, now it was Great Britain who was challenging Nigeria, for the former had already promised that if the Nigerian House approved the motion, Great Britain would grant independence on October 1, 1960. He said that some people had said that it was better "to govern ourselves badly than to be governed well." He added that: "Perhaps it is better, for those who do the governing, but we must think of those who are going to be governed by us." He assured the House that he did not anticipate a bad government, but added:

Nevertheless that question of good or bad government is really the substance of the challenge now made to us. The United Kingdom Government do not grudge us our independence: they do not attach conditions. No, they merely ask us to affirm that we fully understand the course of action which we are about to pursue.

Moving on, he asserted that: "Independence is very different from self-government—it is far, far wider in scope." Independence, he said, is like "a son who has left his father's compound and has now to make his own way in the world." The two greatest responsibilities of independence, he pointed out, are "defence and external affairs. Both of these subjects are vitally important and our assumption of responsibility for them is the full measure of our independence." As to defense, he said that "Nigeria is a peaceful country which has no territorial ambitions and no intention of attacking her neighbours. . . ." He expressed fear, however, that Nigeria's neighbors might attack her. "Over the past year or so there has been a good deal of trouble going on in some of the countries which border on Nigeria and as I see it, the danger is that disaffected elements in those countries will come over the Nigerian border to hide and will then carry on sporadic raids in their own country." Consequently, he called for "adequate military forces to safeguard our long land frontier," and added that it is "my earnest hope

3 *House of Representatives Debates,* January session, 1960, p. 27. (Hereinafter referred to as *H. R. Debates.*)

that the visible strength of Nigeria will have a stabilising effect in this part of the world."[4]

Turning to external affairs, the Prime Minister set the tone for his Government's foreign policy. Obviously recognizing Nigeria's great size in relation to other states in Africa, he said that in the United Nations "Nigeria will have a wonderful opportunity to speak for the continent of Africa." He went on to say that:

we must not deceive ourselves into thinking that provided we ourselves are honest and well-intentioned it will be easy to follow a successful foreign policy. First of all I want to make it clear that no country can afford to have an inflexible foreign policy, and whatever foreign policy Nigeria may adopt after Independence it will have to be capable of being adapted to the changing circumstances in the world. (Hear, hear). To carry on a foreign policy in the best interests of Nigeria, and of the many hundreds of thousands of Nigerians who are living temporarily in foreign lands, is not going to be easy at all, but we shall do it. I do not for one moment under-estimate the difficulties which lie ahead, and I have felt compelled to underline them to-day, but nevertheless given sincerity of purpose and goodwill we shall not fail and on this score too I am prepared to say on behalf of my fellow countrymen that we are ready for independence.[5]

Sir Abubakar then turned to the question of the Commonwealth, reminding the House that all the Nigerian delegates to the Resumed Constitutional Conference in 1958 had expressed the desire for Commonwealth membership. Almost as an aside, he said: "I am grateful to those officers who have helped us to catch up with the twentieth century. Many of those officers devoted the whole of their working lives to the service of Nigeria and dedicated themselves to our welfare." On the whole, he added, "we and the British have got on very well together and the road to Independence has not seen any bloodshed or ill-feeling between us and the British." Getting to the main point, he said:

The reason why I personally want to see Nigeria taken into the Commonwealth is this. I know very well the immense opportunities and the great need for development in our country and I want to ensure so far as is possible that the development is on sound lines. At present we are [an] under-developed country. In order to expand our economy we must seek investments from the richer and more developed countries, investments both of money and technical skill. It is going to be very difficult sometimes to sift the genuine from the self-interested and that is one reason why I should warn that Nigeria must be careful in recognising her real genuine friends.

Another important reason is that for some time to come we cannot possibly be represented in every country in which Nigeria has interests or in which

4 *Ibid.*, p. 29. Presumably the Prime Minister was referring to a series of border incidents between the Southern Cameroons and the Cameroun Republic. There seemed to be some fear that when these two areas were united guerilla forces might move over into the Eastern Region of Nigeria and use that area as a staging ground for subsequent attacks on the new Cameroun Federation.

5 *Ibid.*

Nigerians are living. Not only is the foreign service very costly, but it also requires our very best men and at present we cannot spare enough from Nigeria. But in those countries where Nigeria cannot be directly represented we shall have the other members of the Commonwealth to look after our interests.[6]

The Prime Minister closed his moderate speech with a plea for national unity. After the motion was seconded, the first supporter was the Opposition leader, Chief Awolowo, who said that the Government and the Opposition "are in perfect accord" on the motion. In his brief speech, he dwelt almost entirely on the momentous nature of the occasion.[7] Not so with most of the members who spoke on the motion. Member after member (in all, fifty-nine spoke) rose to support the motion only to move quickly from the subject of independence to the question of Nigerian unity. Numerous members launched into attacks on Regional Governments with which they disagreed. Opposition political parties were accused of violations of civil rights, hooliganism, and duplicity, as opposed to the defense of the national interest which characterized the speaker's party. No party and no Regional Government escaped abuse of this kind in the three days of debate which occurred on the motion for independence. In the mélange of recriminations, the future foreign policy of the nation, soon to be independent, was almost totally ignored. The Prime Minister had said almost all that was to be said at this time on the subject.[8] The motion for independence, however, was

6 *Ibid.*, p. 30.

7 *Ibid.*, pp. 31-33.

8 Some exceptions, brief as they were, are worth noting. Mallam Aminu Kano (leader of NEPU, in alliance with NCNC) doubted that Nigeria faced any threats from the Cameroons, and called for a vigorous policy for Nigeria in the United Nations on all African matters, in acquiring foreign aid without strings, and in working for "a great African Union." *Ibid.*, pp. 77-78.

Jaja Wachuku (NCNC, who eighteen months later was to become Foreign Minister) gave a discourse on the greatness of Africa, on the fortuitous size of Nigeria which would not "abdicate the position in which God Almighty has placed us," and on Nigeria's "mission to rescue the Black Africans from destruction, oppression and repression." He congratulated the Prime Minister for having said that if South Africa did not change its way there would not be room for it and Nigeria both in the Commonwealth, and then launched a vigorous attack on the Central African Federation, winding up on a plea for unity: "we are not here to attack ourselves." *Ibid.*, pp. 89-91.

J. S. Tarka (leader of the United Middle Belt Congress, allied with the Action Group) suggested that Nigerians must be either Western democrats or Eastern democrats—"and since we are not disciples of the Marxist theory, we are Western Democrats." *Ibid.*, p. 102.

M. T. Mbu (Minister of State for Naval Affairs) suggested that "no nation to-day can fully say she is neutral; whether she likes it or not her interest is still protected by other blocs, and Nigeria can well be accommodated and be protected within the Western bloc." This would be possible because, among other things, "on the 21st of October, 1959, the Committee on Foreign Relations of the United States Senate in their report on the study of the United States foreign policy in Africa published that the United States should recognise that it is for the interest of the West that the African States should pursue a policy of non-alignment." *Ibid.*, p. 103.

passed unanimously. It was clear that at this time, apart from the Prime Minister's embellishments, little attention in advance of the party positions during the election campaign (which had only ended the month before) had been given to a more definitive foreign policy.

CLOUDS FORM

Parliament re-assembled on March 30. Apart from the question of alignment (to be discussed in the following section), the session is important for the first glimpse of the radical wing of the NCNC on foreign policy matters. The Government itself attempted to stave off debate in this area by having the Governor-General devote merely one paragraph to foreign policy in his Speech from the Throne. He said the Ministers were giving "anxious consideration" to the question and would "have a well thought out policy" by independence. While the policy would be based on a "free, equal and friendly association" in the Commonwealth, he felt it necessary to add that the Government "deplores the recent tragic bloodshed in South Africa."[9]

In the debate on the Speech from the Throne certain NCNC members joined the Action Group in condemning its weakness, particularly for ignoring South Africa's racial policies, French atomic bomb tests in the Sahara, and the question of Pan-Africanism.[10] That certain NCNC members wished to force the Government to take a more positive stand in these and other areas was revealed by motions which they offered and managed to get debated. A few examples will suffice.

Mr. Lamuye (NCNC), as a result of the Sharpeville killings in South Africa, moved: "that, in resentment of the apartheid policy of South Africa, this House urges the Government to take appropriate steps to ban the importation of South African goods into this country."[11] The tone of the discussion, agreed to by thirteen other speakers, was set by the mover of the motion, as follows:

In moving this seemingly hostile Motion against the Union of South Africa, I am motivated by a patriotic desire to see my fellow Africans down in the Union of South Africa as free, if not freer, socially and politically, than those of us in this part of the country [sic]. I hardly need to go over the spate of intolerance, hate, oppression and unbelievably violent subjection to which millions of our brethren are faced by a Godless, heartless, despotic government headed by a merciless, bloodthirsty Dutchman in the person of Dr. Verwoerd.

Mr. Odigbo (NCNC) resented the fact that embassies were planned only

---

Other references to foreign policy, though few in number, tended only to agree with Sir Abubakar that it should be flexible.

9 H. R. Debates, March-May session 1960, pp. 20-21.

10 See ibid., for statements by Chief Mariere (NCNC), p. 28; Dr. Okeke (NCNC), p. 38; Mr. Akpan (AG), p. 41; Mr. Muhtari (NPC), p. 65; and Dr. Chike Obi (NCNC), pp. 106-07.

11 Ibid., p. 134.

for Britain, the United States, and "a few other places in the Western bloc."[12] In a similar vein, Dr. Nzeribe (NCNC) criticized the fact that "our foreign affairs personnel are being trained in London, some in Washington and some in Khartoum." He questioned whether any should be trained "by colonial powers," but suggested it was all right to train them in India, Israel, or America.[13] The strongest comment on this subject came from the leader of NEPU, the Northern Region minority party aligned with NCNC. Mallam Aminu Kano, who later became a Government Whip, made the following "neutralist" statement:

There are many nations now waiting at the door to come in, but when the time comes these people will be quite ready to come into Nigeria. Even now there are certain great powers, for example, the United States of America is not only interested in Nigerian affairs but is interested in training Nigerian diplomats for Nigeria. I have reason to believe that we in Nigeria should not allow certain nations to train our diplomats. The training of diplomats is entirely our own concern. There is the Carnegie Foundation Fund to be used in Nigeria and all the African countries for the training of diplomats which I think we must be very careful about because if we allow American foundations or Government or Institutions to give scholarships specifically to Nigerians to be trained as diplomats in America then naturally the door is open for the Soviet Union to train Nigerians in Moscow as diplomats in their own way. Then we open our own way to the danger of being wooed by these big powers whose policy is economic superiority or ideological superiority.[14]

Although himself a Moslem, he was equally distrustful that Moslem nations might pressure Nigeria to align with them because of its large Moslem population. Referring especially to Egypt, Iraq, Morocco, and Tunisia, he said "some people think . . . we should fall in line with Moslem countries against Israel."[15]

A third illustration of NCNC fears came from a motion by Mr. Akwiwu and Dr. Ezera calling for the creation of a ministry or at least a department charged with the responsibility for Pan-African affairs.[16] Dr. Ezera gave the fuller defense of the motion, basing the need on a channel for Nigeria to "project her personality adequately," and to dispel the ugly impression

12 *Ibid.,* p. 405.
13 *Ibid.,* p. 409.
14 *Ibid.,* p. 411.
15 *Ibid.* He also warned that Nigeria must not make its visa requirements as difficult as some countries. "My experience," he said, "of going to America, for example, was that I was questioned whether I had ever read a communist book. I told them that I had never read any communist book or even met a communist. I told them that I had never committed an offence for which I was imprisoned other than traffic offence. All these—more questions—would not necessarily matter. I think we must make Nigeria a place where people willing to come in can come in." *Ibid.,* pp. 411-12.
16 *Ibid.,* p. 516. Mr. Akwiwu was concerned with the ignorance in Nigeria of things African. For example he said he had been informed that the Bank of West Africa, which operates in Nigeria, was controlled by the Standard Bank of West Africa, which is controlled by South Africans. A department of Pan-African affairs would be able to look into this matter. *Ibid.,* p. 517.

that Nigeria has been "aiding and abetting imperialist designs on the continent of Africa." He said that Pan-Africanism "is a powerful force sweep-
ing through Africa," that the "historical future . . . of black Africa and
indeed of the peace of the world depend on the success or failure of this
movement," and he "could see no reason why Nigeria cannot lead" this
force. He defined Pan-Africanism as a "force that seeks the general liberation of all African peoples." Like all revolutionary ideas, he added, "this
noble concept has earned the opposition of imperialist powers and their
agents because it seeks not only to liberate African peoples but also to unite
all African peoples under a single state." He admitted that "as a philosophy
it is regarded as a long-term objective. But to-day it is becoming a meta-
physical fact. . . ." He went on to commend the Prime Minister, who, he
said, "is fastly [sic] becoming not only a strong advocate of Nigerian unity
but also becoming a Pan-Africanist." He said he remembered very well,
"around 1948, it was the same Prime Minister who stated that he would
lead a *jihad* against the South and push us to the sea if we drove away the
British imperialists." He concluded by noting that the South African Government was Nigeria's greatest threat, for South Africa feared Nigeria and:

This fear is definitely going to drive the South African Government to invade
Nigeria if our policy supports Pan-Africanism, and I have it on good authority
that the timing of the South African attack on us is tentatively scheduled
for early 1961 when we shall still be finding our feet immediately after
independence.[17]

The Government appeared to recognize the fears and frustrations expressed by the radical members of the coalition, but in doing so made its
own moderate position known also. For example, on the question of banning
the importation of South African goods, the Minister of Commerce and
Industry, Mr. Dipcharima (NPC), accepted the motion in the name of the
Government, but cautioned that "We shall be, I hope a member of the
G.A.T.T., and according to this international Club, you cannot take unilateral economic action, even when we do not want it, we have to confine
ourselves to collective action." Nevertheless, he said, "the Government
accepts the Motion in principle and will try to co-operate in every way
possible to make it effective."[18] The Prime Minister also spoke, but charged
that some speakers had been unfair in condemning Britain for abstaining
in the United Nations vote which condemned the Union for its racial policy.
He said that Mr. Macmillan had condemned apartheid "in very clear
terms" and that Britain had abstained only on "a technical matter."[19]

17 *Ibid.,* pp. 519-20.
18 *Ibid.,* p. 139.
19 *Ibid.,* pp. 148-149. Supporters of the motion, representing all parties, advocated the
    expulsion of South Africa from the Commonwealth; proposed that on independence
    day all white South Africans in Nigeria be arrested; proposed that white South
    Africans in Nigeria be placed in concentration camps and made to work in
    Nigerian coal mines and on their farms; and suggested that the Dutch Reformed
    Church should be banished from Nigeria and its property turned over to "the

On the question of training personnel for the foreign office, the Government spokesman, Mr. Mbu (NCNC), Minister of State for Naval Affairs, merely pointed out the importance of such training. But Sir Abubakar himself dealt with the questions raised by Dr. Ezera. He questioned whether the terms "African personality" or "Nigerian personality" had any meaning and whether they were nearly as useful as the term "human personality." He promised, however, that there would be a section in his Government to deal with the affairs of African countries.[20]

The Government's efforts to conciliate the developing radical position, without committing itself to specific action, even extended to a motion by an Action Group member, Mr. Omisade, calling on the Government to condemn French atomic bomb testing in the Sahara and, should France continue, to suspend trade between the two countries and freeze French assets in Nigeria. After the motion was seconded, but before it could be debated, the Prime Minister said he wanted to speak. He pointed out that he had already led a delegation to London to protest. There, he said, he had been assured by scientists that there would be no harmful effects from the tests on Nigeria, but in spite of the assurance "I and all my colleagues in England insisted that the best thing would be that France should not explode the bomb." He added that:

> . . . I found in the United Kingdom that neither they, nor the United States, nor any country in the world could stop France from exploding the bomb, as they did. I found also that the United Nations had not power to force France to stop it. . . . I understand the United Kingdom protested on our behalf when they heard about it [i.e., the test of April 1], but that protest had very little effect.[21]

He concluded by saying that the Government would like to accept the motion. Speakers from each of the parties then rose to support the motion in the terms already used, and it passed unanimously.

The Action Group itself was also conciliatory during the 1960 spring session. Apart from Chief Awolowo, its main spokesman on foreign affairs was Chief Anthony Enahoro, "Shadow Minister of Foreign Affairs." Enahoro said it was "a matter for regret that four months before the attainment of Independence . . . the Government has not yet made up its mind on the foreign policy which it will pursue after 1st October." Consequently, he said, there was no alternative but to demand, "before Independence, a comprehensive White Paper on the foreign policy which can be debated and adopted by this House."

The Action Group spokesman offered "to take foreign policy out of the

---

Methodist Church or other voluntary agencies that have a background of the love of mankind at heart." The Minister of Commerce himself promised that: "From to-day onwards, no white South African will be employed by this Government. . . ." See *ibid., passim*, pp. 134-52.

20 *Ibid.*, p. 520.
21 *Ibid.*, p. 131.

field of sharp controversy," and asked the Prime Minister to attempt "a common understanding" among the parties. In a statement which appears to be a ramification of the Action Group's policy in the campaign of 1959, he reminded the Prime Minister that some people thought, erroneously, that there were only two sides to the question of alignment, i.e., total alignment or non-alignment. There was, he explained, a third position of selective alignment, and he illustrated by asserting that since Nigeria wished to remain in the sterling area this meant she was economically aligned with certain powers. Continuing, he said:

We are aligned with the State in this particular regard which believes in the same things which we believe. We do not want to make enemies of others. We agree with the Western concepts of liberty and the dignity of the individual. And so in this field we have our commitments. Even in the military question, the Prime Minister suggested that he hoped that we would continue to take advantage of the training facilities offered by the United Kingdom.

But having allowed for all these commitments, there is one important reservation which Nigerians wish to make and it is this one reservation which is now advanced as the broad definition of non-alignment. Members wish to be free to do business with the whole world; we want to make friends; we do not want to be dragged into NATO or into a watertight bloc. But this is not non-alignment. I suggest, Sir, that the appropriate package label for all these beliefs, our commitments, our desires and our reservations, is independent alignment, and we commend it to the Prime Minister and to the House.[22]

The Prime Minister refused Enahoro's plea to attempt a common understanding and answered him simply:

The Federal Government cannot have a foreign policy now. My friend knows very well. We can only have a foreign policy after [the] attainment [of] independence. At present all the political parties in the country have got their foreign policies—what they think should be their foreign policies—and it is not for the Government now to give a foreign policy for Nigeria.[23]

In conclusion, a few words can be said about foreign policy in Nigerian Parliamentary thinking in the spring before independence. The Government was clearly unprepared yet to assert a policy. Nevertheless, the primacy of Africa in Nigerian thinking seemed to be firmly accepted on all sides. Even Balewa's rejection of African personality in favor of human personality was not thought of as minimizing the importance of Africa. There was, on the other hand, a general restlessness throughout the Parliament on various questions of foreign policy. The radical wing of the NCNC began to reveal its frustrations with a moderate Government (of which it was a part) which might not be as vigorous in condemning imperialism as they defined it, and in promoting Pan-Africanism. The Action Group, however, appeared to be opposing because it was expected to. Its acceptance of some

22 *Ibid.*, p. 403. In the light of Enahoro's implied willingness to accept the training facilities for the Nigerian army offered by the United Kingdom, cf. *infra*, pp. 35-36, 44-45 for Action Group opposition to the Defense Pact.

23 *H. R. Debates*, March-May session 1960, p. 407.

form of alignment, reaffirmed even later, merely reveals that party leaders had not yet decided on a new policy. All in all, the session demonstrated how "sudden and rude" the grant of independence had been for foreign policy making. A potentially mighty nation of Africa was moving onto the world stage with only vague ideas of its position. Still, until a free government was itself fully responsible for specific reactions to real problems, generalizations may have been the only policy. Even well-defined permanent interests do not lend themselves to rigidly fixed responses to hypothetical situations. Even so, a clear conception of national purposes was not yet apparent.

THE STORM THREATENS

The most serious issue of foreign policy discussed in the spring session of Parliament involved alignment. This issue has been given a special section because: (1) it came to public attention through a non-Parliamentary group; (2) it affected the London Conference in May which drew up the Independence Constitution; (3) it put serious strains on the Government coalition; (4) it was the chief vehicle by which the Action Group made its now-historic reversal in foreign policy (although this was clear only in retrospect); and (5) it was the issue, more than any other, which divided the articulate Nigerian society in the first year after independence. The interplay of forces in such a momentous question deserves careful attention.

The question of alignment came to the forefront (probably in March) when leaders of the Zikist National Vanguard, militant youth wing of the NCNC, exposed the fact that the Government intended to sign a Defense Pact with Great Britain. Chief Awolowo, however, was the first to raise the question in Parliament, on April 1. He said there was "widespread speculation" that one of the issues to be discussed at the Constitutional Conference was such a pact and asked the Prime Minister to take the House into his full confidence on the matter. The speculation, he added, had been "given credence" by the fact that the Prime Minister had just been handed the portfolio for Defense by the Governor-General, presumably so he would have the legal competence to "commit this country to military agreements and pacts abroad." Furthermore, he said, it was of "the utmost public interest" for the Prime Minister to announce whether "any secret condition" in the form of a defense pact had been attached to Nigeria's independence.[24]

Chief Awolowo's charge apparently took the Prime Minister by surprise. In his rebuttal he said the "Federal Government is not going to commit Nigeria to anything which we know will not be in the best interests of the country." He denied that he had taken over the portfolio of Defense in order to "commit Nigeria to something." Rather, he said, he took the portfolio because Nigeria had been responsible for its military forces since April 1958.

24 *Ibid.,* p. 30.

He then attacked Awolowo's economic policies, and sat down without ever mentioning the question of military pacts.[25]

That even members of the Government coalition were not happy with the Prime Minister's response was revealed on April 12, when Mr. R.B.K. Okafor (NCNC, and later Parliamentary Secretary to the federal Minister of Justice) introduced the following motion:

That the Government of the Federation should not enter into any Military Alliance, or sign any Mutual Defence Pact, or grant any part of Nigerian land to any foreign Government for the purpose of building a Military Base without the prior approval of the Legislature.[26]

In defense of his motion, Okafor said that his purpose was not to prohibit the Government from entering such agreements, but only to assure that any such move first had the approval of the Parliament. He pointed out that during the previous election the political parties had not included the question of military alliance in their campaign tactics, and to enter such now without reference to the people would violate representative principles of government. Furthermore, he said (without supporting his opinion), such a move would require consultation with the Regional Governments. He added that Britain always attempted to get bases from her former colonies "to protect her economic interests in that country and also to serve as a launching pad for her imperialistic design." He cited a number of instances to support his position: India's refusal to enter such a pact; the postponement of independence for Cyprus for refusing to sign a pact; the fact that "Sudan, in view of constant aggression and fear of Egypt, signed a Military Pact with Great Britain"; the fact that "the former Prime Minister of Ceylon was defeated and his party thrown out on this question of military pacts"; the "Suez Canal dispute"; the "Persian Oil Dispute in which the United States of America is involved"; and the recent "troubles in Okinawa." "I mention these interests," he said, "because they have always been the chief reasons of wanting Military Alliances and naval bases by world powers."[27]

Okafor suggested that military bases in Nigeria "can only be useful as theatre for underground atomic tests," and would "undoubtedly make us hewers of wood and drawers of water to that nation in all aspects of life." Besides, he added, Britain had abstained from voting in the United Nations against South Africa's apartheid policy, and Britain and South Africa had abstained from voting against the French atomic bomb tests in the Sahara.

This is food for thought for every true son of Africa. We must remember that all African eyes are on Nigeria. Every African race is waiting for Nigeria's independence for her emancipation. Shall we fail our race? It will mean cutting our nose to spite our face. What will generations yet unborn call us?[28]

25 *Ibid.*, p. 33.
26 *Ibid.*, p. 332.
27 *Ibid.*, pp. 333-34.
28 *Ibid.*, p. 335.

The motion was supported by two other NCNC members before the Prime Minister announced that the Government would accept the motion. He was obviously prepared to discuss the matter this time, albeit in vague terms. He said the extent of cooperation in defense matters between Nigeria and Great Britain had already been agreed upon between the Prime Minister and the Regional Premiers of Nigeria on the one hand and Great Britain on the other. What was agreed, he said, was

that there would be mutual advantage to Britain and Nigeria in co-operating in the field of defence and that they had exchanged views and reached unanimous agreement on the facilities and help which each country would render to the other after independence.

The Prime Minister added that:

the House will be well aware that our military forces are being trained in some of the military establishments in the United Kingdom. We have not got a full military Academy in Nigeria and we have to send some of our potential officers to be trained in Sandhurst and other places. We hope these facilities which are at present offered will continue to be offered to us even after independence. . . .

. . . I repeat again what I said the other time, we shall not commit Nigeria to anything which we know is not to the interest of the country.

I give the House the assurance that we shall not enter into any agreement without their approval.[29]

The issue continued to crop up in Parliament and the press for the next month. A new element, with the impact of an explosion, intervened just before the Constitutional Conference convened in London, when Chief Awolowo exposed the fact that he and the three other leaders (Sir Abubakar, Dr. Azikiwe, and Sir Ahmadu) had initialed a Draft Agreement in 1958 granting military bases in Nigeria to Britain and that the agreement was a pre-condition to independence.[30] He said that he *personally favored some form of cooperation* but some parts of the agreement may be unsuitable to Nigeria, so he felt the whole issue should be publicized.[31]

Immediately, Dr. Azikiwe and Sir Ahmadu denied that the initialing of the agreement was a pre-condition to independence. At the beginning of the Conference, Mr. Macleod, Colonial Secretary, also denied that there were any conditions attached to Nigeria's independence.[32]

On May 11, Awolowo wired Macleod chiding him for not admitting that there were strings tied to independence before he (Awolowo) had exposed the deal. He told Macleod that he had initialed the agreement because he felt that when discussion of it occurred in Nigeria it "was bound to break down somewhere."[33]

29 *Ibid.*, p. 339.
30 *Nigerian Tribune* (Ibadan) , May 4, 1960.
31 *Daily Times,* May 5 and 7, 1960.
32 *Ibid.*, May 11, 1960.
33 *Ibid.*, May 12, 1960.

Whether due to Awolowo's criticism or not, at the end of the Conference, Mr. Macleod told the British House of Commons that:

It was thought originally, a year or two ago, that it would be appropriate for Nigeria to lease some land to this country on which, if we wanted, we could construct additional facilities. We have decided not to ask for that and that was very welcome by the Nigerian authorities.[34]

Also at the end of the Conference, Dr. Azikiwe said that Britain had decided "not to press" some points in the original agreement, and Chief Akintola (Deputy Leader of the Action Group and Premier of the Western Region, a delegate) said that conditions had been withdrawn due to public pressure in Nigeria.[35] The latter also said that independence "will be absolute."[36]

When Sir Abubakar returned, the press met him at the airport and asked about the pact. He assured the reporters that "there will be no military bases in Nigeria." He was asked whether he did not think that the Nigerian public ought to be informed if any agreement on military matters was reached and said, "That's not the way Governments are run." He added that he thought it was wrong for leaders to disclose private discussion: "I say it is wrong—very wrong. It is not how international issues are discussed and debated." When asked to illustrate what he meant when he said that the military arrangements made in London were of a technical nature, he replied: "For instance there might be an agreement on aircraft passing over Nigeria or using our aerodromes." He added that there was no question of spy planes taking off from Nigeria for spy planes "will take off from military bases, and we are not having bases in Nigeria."[37]

When Dr. Azikiwe returned to Nigeria in July he said the delegates, on arriving in London, had told the British that it would be unwise to "press for the privilege of establishing military bases in our country." He stressed a number of times the point that Parliament would have to approve any agreement and added the following significant observation:

Personally, I have always felt that the establishment of land bases for military purposes by stronger nations in the territories of weaker nations is anachronistic in the realm of international politics. In this age of sputniks and luniks, we cannot agree to any portion of our territory being transformed into a military base since in times of war it becomes a military objective. If our foreign policy is one of neutralism, then it is wise that our people made their views heard against the establishment of military land bases in Nigeria. As I have said earlier on, the credit should also go to Britain for having the good sense to appreciate and respect our feelings on this delicate matter.[38]

It was now clear that intransigence in the NCNC, abetted by the Action Group, had forced the Government to give up any idea of British bases

34 *Ibid.*, May 21, 1960.
35 *Nigerian Tribune*, May 21, 1960.
36 *West African Pilot*, May 20, 1960.
37 *Sunday Times*, May 22, 1960.
38 *Daily Times*, July 7, 1960.

in Nigeria. It was equally clear that the question of alignment had become the sharpest issue dividing the Nigerians as they attempted to ascertain the "permanent interests" of their new state. It was also clear, however, that some form of defense agreement with Britain had been entered. It was not clear what the agreement entailed. Nor was it clear whether Awolowo was merely opposing for the sake of carrying out the role of an official Opposition or because of a radical shift of viewpoint. Parts were not to fall into place until after independence.

THE LULL OF INDEPENDENCE

Parliament re-assembled from August 3 to 20, the last session before independence. The high light of the session was the Prime Minister's formal announcement of a foreign policy. The continued interest of legislators in matters of external affairs was shown, although for the most part there was restraint in obvious anticipation of the official announcement. The chief concern of the session was a military appropriation bill, and statements on foreign policy were generally gratuitous, tending to reflect uneasiness in NCNC/NEPU circles about the Government's intentions.[39] There was an

39 For example, Mr. Okafor (NCNC) suggested that only capable men be appointed to serve Nigeria overseas. *H. R. Debates,* August session 1960, p. 66. Dr. Ezera (NCNC) noted that embassies had been planned only for London, Washington, Khartoum, Accra, and Jeddah and suggested that one also be established in New Delhi. He also warned against allowing foreign policy to be made in the Regional capitals (a not-so-sly reference to the Premier of the Northern Region, and leader of the Prime Minister's party, the NPC). *Ibid.,* p. 69. Mr. Chiedezie (NCNC) suggested that government ministers travel widely in order "to project the personality of Nigeria in international affairs." *Ibid.,* p. 72. Mallam Monguno (NPC) cautioned that Nigeria would be only one member among many in international organizations and "we must never resort to segregating ourselves with a view to taking unilateral action on any international matter." *Ibid.,* p. 73. Dr. Okeke (NCNC) encouraged ministers to travel abroad "to acquaint themselves with what is happening abroad." *Ibid.,* p. 75. Mallam Aminu Kano (NEPU) urged that embassies be established in Asia and Latin America. *Ibid.,* p. 84. Several others spoke in a similar vein. See *ibid.,* pp. 116-21.
   On August 12 Dr. Ezera (NCNC) noted that the Minister of State, Dr. Esin, had denied newspaper accounts which said the Minister had warned that it would be foolish for the Nyasaland Malawi Congress Party to attempt secession from the Central African Federation. Dr. Ezera charged that the denial was "not only feeble but vague," and that the alleged statement had "not only shocked world liberal opinion but also greatly embarrassed all Nigerian nationalist elements." Furthermore, he added, it was an "unnecessary and dangerous interference in the internal affairs of a sister African country." Sir Abubakar defended Dr. Esin by saying that he did not know "whether the statement . . . shocked the world. It might have shocked a few individuals in Nigeria." He said that he accepted the Minister's explanation that the newspaper reports were "twisted" and added that Nigeria was "out to assist any African race." He also made a further plea against "these catch-phrases and words, 'African personality,' 'Nigerian personality.' We Nigerians are human beings. I want us to project the human personality in this country. . . ." *Ibid.,* p. 78.
   On August 15, Mr. Akwiwu (NCNC) complained that the residence of the United Kingdom High Commissioner was located within yards of the Prime Minister's and

attempt to get a motion before the House to withdraw the invitation to the Government of South Africa to attend the independence ceremonies, but the Prime Minister refused to permit it to be debated. He said a withdrawal might offend other Commonwealth members, and besides he doubted if South Africa would send a delegation "knowing fully well our views and how we feel about their policy." He admitted that "every day my views are becoming stronger and stronger against the policies of South Africa," but he did not think a debate was necessary to demonstrate the House's "abhorrence" to that country's policies.[40]

The long-awaited statement on foreign policy was made on August 20, 1960 in the House of Representatives.[41] It must surely have disappointed Chief Enahoro (foreign policy spokesman for the AG), who had called for a "comprehensive White Paper," for the statement had only 864 words. The Prime Minister himself said it was only in "general terms," and merely attempted to show "how the mind of the Government is working." Because it was the first official pronouncement of Government policy on foreign affairs, the statement follows in full:

In formulating its policy for the conduct of foreign affairs the Federal Government recognises that its primary duty is to safeguard and promote the interest of the Federation and its citizens. We have already declared our intention of a plan to join both the Commonwealth and the United Nations. In regard to the former, it is important to understand that all members of the Commonwealth are autonomous communities equal in status and in no way subordinate one to another in any aspect of their domestic or external affairs. While therefore benefiting greatly from the free interchange of ideas and consultation between the members of the Commonwealth and from their experience within the framework of the United Nations, we shall, nevertheless, have a free hand to select those policies which we consider to be most advantageous for Nigeria, subject always to our belief in the principles of the United Nations.

We shall, of course, endeavour to remain on friendly terms with every nation which recognises and respects our sovereignty (Hear, hear) and we shall not blindly follow the lead of anyone; so far as it is possible the policy on each occasion will be selected with proper independent objectivity in Nigeria's national interest. (Hear, hear). We consider it wrong for the Federal Government to associate itself as a matter of routine with any of the power blocs. (Applause). This freedom of action will be an essential feature of our policy and will ensure that full attention is paid the opinions expressed by our representatives. Our policies, as I have said before, will be founded on Nigeria's interest and will be consistent with the moral and democratic principles on which our constitution is based.

---

the Governor-General's homes, and the Parliament and Secretariat buildings. "What security have we there?" he asked. He suggested that Nigeria's diplomatic offices in Washington not be "carried into the bedroom of the F.B.I. . . ." *Ibid.*, p. 116.

40 *Ibid.*, p. 190.

41 By holding the statement until the last day of this particular session, the Prime Minister was able to bypass a debate on it at this time.

Very particular attention will be devoted to adopting clear and practical policies with regard to Africa. It will be our aim to assist any African country to find a solution to its problems and to foster the growth of a common understanding among all nations and especially among the new nations of this continent. We are determined to encourage the development of common ties between all the states. The difficulties which will confront us in promoting the friendly association of independent countries in Africa are fully appreciated, but we believe they can be overcome if a start is made by emphasising and building upon the cultural and economic links which already exist. This will be followed up by a policy of securing an agreed plan for the improvement of inter-territorial communications and transport facilities and by the pooling of resources for higher education and scientific research. Although it will be premature at this state to think in terms of a Common Market for Africa, we are intending to work towards the expansion of trade and travel and to secure an agreed plan for the improvement of inter-territorial communications and the like.

On the problem of boundaries our view is that although in the past some of these were created artificially by the European powers which even went so far as to split some communities into three parts, each administered by a different colonial power [sic]. Nevertheless those boundaries should be respected and in the interest of peace must remain the recognised boundaries until such time as the peoples concerned decide of their own free will to change or to merge into one unit. We shall discourage any attempt to influence such communities by force or through undue pressure to change since such interference could only result in unrest and in harm to the over-all plan for the future of this great continent.

It is true that Africa is changing everyday. We rejoice to see so many countries becoming independent but with the good developments there are bound to be some bad ones and we are troubled by the signs which we see of the ideological war between the Great Powers of the world creeping into Africa. We shall therefore take steps to persuade the African leaders to take serious note of this distressing trend. We shall make every effort to bring them together so that having been made aware of the danger we may all find a way to unite our efforts and prevent Africa from becoming an area of crisis and world tension. (Hear, hear).

We shall not, however, allow our direct and primary interest in African affairs to blind us to the grave and vital issues which dominate the wider international scene. In the United Nations and in any other way possible we shall direct our energies and influence to helping to reach solutions which will contribute to the peace of the nations and well-being of mankind.

To sum up, we shall do everything in our power to foster co-operation among the countries of Africa and particularly of this part of Africa and in-so-far as is compatible with national interest and with our membership of the Commonwealth and of the United Nations we shall maintain cordial relations with all the other nations of the world, firmly opposing all forms of aggression and striving always to maintain the observance everywhere of those human rights which all parties in Nigeria have agreed upon as fundamental; in particular freedom from racial discrimination.

Sir, this is a statement which, I hope, the House will debate after Nigeria has attained Independence. (Loud applause).[42]

42 *Ibid.*, pp. 289-90.

The statement reveals much for what it does not say. Gone, for example, is any reference to the position of all the three major political party manifestoes in the campaign of December 1959, to the effect that closer ties must be sought with Great Britain and the United States. Absent also is any reference to neutrality or non-alignment. Pan-Africanism is totally ignored, except for the vague reference that a common market for Africa is regarded as premature. No reference to great international issues is made, except for the statement that Nigeria would not join either power bloc "as a matter of routine." Except for a vague concern over ideological conflicts of the Great Powers in Africa, and the general admission that Nigeria's primary interests were in African affairs, no policy looking to solutions of African problems (nor even stating what those problems were) is enunciated. This was indeed a "general statement," obviously intended to placate all parties at this auspicious interim immediately preceding independence. Certainly everyone could read his own views into the statement, except, perhaps, for those who wanted more direct ties with the West, and even that was not ruled out by anything stated in the paper. No one could quarrel with a policy which advocated independence for maneuvering, membership in the United Nations and the Commonwealth, and the importance of Africa to Nigeria. As a harmony statement, it was excellent; as a statement indicating Nigeria's position to world and African problems it revealed little. The statements of frustration made by many NCNC members in the preceding months had revealed to the NPC the need to reconsider its no-neutrality position of the election campaign, if the coalition was to work. Holding the coalition together seems to have become one of the hallmarks of Sir Abubakar's administration, of which more will be said later. Independence celebrations, however, had merely been a lull in the gathering storm.

THE STORM BREAKS

The first Parliament after independence met from November 14 to 29, 1960. The first full debate on foreign policy had been promised for this session. When the debate on general foreign policy occurred, however, it was anticlimactic, for the storm had already broken over one aspect of that policy: the question of alignment. In what may have been profound foresight, the Government, before permitting debate on the Prime Minister's statement of August 20, first proposed that Parliament approve the Defense Pact with Great Britain. It will be recalled that on the previous April 12, the Prime Minister had promised that no agreement would be entered without the approval of the House. It had already been made clear also, after the Constitutional Conference the previous May, that some sort of agreement affecting Nigerian defenses had been made, although the Prime Minister had asserted categorically that "there will be no military bases in Nigeria." The nature of the agreement was now to be brought fully to light.

On November 19, Alhaji Ribadu, Minister of Defense, moved the following resolution:

Be it resolved that this House notes with approval the steps taken by the Government to arrange for the proper training of the armed forces and for the acquisition of the weapons necessary for the defence of Nigeria, and authorises the Government to conclude the Defence Agreement with the Government of the United Kingdom of Great Britain and Northern Ireland in the terms presented to this House in Sessional Paper No. 4 of 1960.[43]

Alhaji Ribadu pointed out that it had been obvious for some time that after independence Nigeria would require outside assistance for officer training, for staffing and administration during the period of Nigerianization, and for supplies of military equipment including warships. As a consequence, he said, discussions were begun at the Resumed Constitutional Conference in 1958 for the Defense Agreement[44] which the Government was now supporting. He said Article I was a "reaffirmation of the friendly and cordial ties which already exist" between the two countries.[45] Nothing in Article I, he added, commits either party to come to the defense of the other, and "in no way derogates from the full sovereignty and independence of action of Nigeria." Article II, he said, provides that Britain will supply Nigeria the personnel and training which are needed. The remaining articles stipulate that Nigeria shall provide the United Kingdom "with facilities for tropicalisation trials of aircraft both above land and sea and over-flying and air-staging facilities." He concluded that "there is no provision in it for giving up any piece of Nigerian land or airfield to the United Kingdom. There is no question of the United Kingdom having a base in Nigeria." The whole agreement is justified, he said, "to arrange for the needs, at least over the next years, of the Armed Forces. . . ."[46]

Chief Festus Okotie-Eboh (NCNC), Minister of Finance, seconded the resolution and reminded the House that the leaders who went to the Constitutional Conference had agreed to a defense treaty. He said:

43 *H. R. Debates,* November session 1960, p. 56. The Defense Agreement is a document of eight articles and an annex on Status of Forces. Sessional Paper No. 4 of 1960, mentioned in the Minister's resolution, is a copy of the Defense Agreement with a brief introduction of its relationship to discussion and agreements reached at the Resumed Constitutional Conference in 1958, a copy of which appears in the Appendix.

44 In the *Report by the Resumed Nigeria Constitutional Conference* (Lagos: Federal Government Printer, 1958), p. 32, appears the following statement: ". . . the Federal Prime Minister and the Premiers [of the Regions] were at one with Her Majesty's Government in believing that there would be mutual advantage to Britain and Nigeria in co-operating in the field of defence and that they had exchanged views and reached unanimous agreement on the facilities and help which each country will render to the other after independence."

45 This is not an accurate statement of Article I which does not mention friendship at all, but provides for each Government to "undertake to afford to the other such assistance as may be necessary for mutual defence," and to consult on what measures shall be taken. See Appendix.

46 *H. R. Debates,* November session 1960, pp. 56-58.

We are not the type of people who say one thing to-day and change to-morrow, like a chameleon. Sir, having initialled—and Sir, this is important—having initialled those Heads of Agreement on something that we need now even more than in 1958, and considering that the United Kingdom met our requirements for the deletion of certain of the Heads, we were happy to conclude the negotiations for the draft Agreement.[47]

He justified the treaty on the grounds that Nigeria's responsibilities to the United Nations required it to have "forces trained and equipped in the modern way." "Surely," he added, "no Nigerian would like to hear in the case that is going on in the Congo today that Ghanaian soldiers are better than Nigerian soldiers!" He asserted that there was nothing to be ashamed about in relying on others for weapons. "Ghana and Morocco have recently concluded negotiations for the supply of Russian planes for their respective Forces and Ghana is following that with negotiations to try and attract Royal Air Force officers to Ghana to help and train her own airmen."[48]

The Minister of Finance denied that either party was obligated to help the other if it committed aggression, but added that: "If we were attacked only would we be entitled to ask the United Kingdom to come to our aid." He did not claim that this aid would come automatically as a right, nor did he even hint as to whether this entitlement was reciprocal, that is, whether Britain, if attacked, could ask Nigeria to come to its aid.[49]

The Leader of the Opposition, Chief Awolowo, led the attack against the resolution. He was in a most awkward position, for he had to admit straight away that he had initialed (along with the current Prime Minister, Sir Abubakar; the current Governor-General, Dr. Azikiwe; and the current Premier of the Northern Region, Sir Ahmadu Bello) the document agreeing to a defense pact. He followed this admission with a most remarkable statement:

May I say, Mr. Speaker, that the circumstances under which Britain obtained our initials to that document, in my view, amount to a bare-faced, unabashed and undue influence. The four of us were bundled to No. 10 Downing Street and were asked to initial this document on the understanding that unless this document was initialled, it would not be possible for Her Majesty's Government to make a declaration fixing the date for our Independence.[50]

He was asked, of course, why he had initialed the document and replied: "Because we would not have been able to bring back the declaration of independence—and this would be so simply because we failed to initial a cer-

47 *Ibid.*, pp. 58-59.
48 *Ibid.*, p. 59.
49 *Ibid.*, p. 60.
50 *Ibid.*, p. 61. Each of the four had been asked to initial the agreement on the assumption that one of them would be the Prime Minister after the 1959 elections, and thus obligated to it. As it turned out, only two of the four were at this time in the Parliament: Sir Abubakar and Chief Awolowo.

tain document and the whole country would have been up in arms against all of us."[51]

Awolowo's opposition was based on the allegation that the treaty itself did not tell all. There was also, he added, the "unknown and hidden document" which had been initialed and which was an attempt "to swindle this country out of its sovereignty." This "secret" document, he said, provided that:

> it is of great importance that Nigeria should lease to the United Kingdom on terms to be agreed upon a piece of land in Kano of up to 150 acres on which the United Kingdom may construct facilities and station personnel for staging purposes.

Furthermore, he said, Britain was to get another piece of land of about 1000 acres, to build an airport, if for any reason the airport at Kano became unavailable. Finally, in "time of emergency" Nigeria was to afford the United Kingdom "such port facilities at Lagos and Port Harcourt as Her Majesty's Government may request."[52] He then followed with the admission that "as a result of public outcry, this Agreement has been shelved."[53]

In the course of his argument against the treaty as proposed, Chief Awolowo admitted that there was "no express mention of the leasing of a base in this agreement but it is necessarily implied—you will find it in the annex." It is implied, he explained, because the annex provides for soldiers to come to Nigeria and obviously they must have a place to stay.

Chief Awolowo concluded by saying that "the country is already irrevocably committed to military alignment and involvement with Britain." Even if the treaty is rejected, he added, Nigeria has already been committed

> by the Prime Minister in the exchange of correspondence between him and Viscount Head. In the exchange of correspondence, it is clearly stated that Nigeria will assume all obligations and responsibilities of the Government of the United Kingdom which arise from any valid international agreement entered into by the United Kingdom Government.[54]

The Prime Minister himself challenged the truth of what Chief Awolowo had said. He said he was

> most disappointed with the speech and the untruth in the speech of the Leader of the Opposition. I always regard the Leader of the Opposition as a good Christian and I think, Sir, either in Christianity or in Islam, that it is a sin for one to tell a lie.[55]

---

51 *Ibid.*, p. 63. He had even gone so far, when he saw the Prime Minister shaking his head, as to say: "I was saying that Dr. Nnamdi Azikiwe made a statement some time ago which corroborated what I now say, namely, that it was a condition precedent to the making of a declaration for independence that we should initial this Outline Defence Agreement, and he said at that time that he knew what he would do if he were to win the election, and I knew what I would do if I won the election." *Ibid.*, p. 62.

52 *Ibid.*, p. 61.

53 *Ibid.*, p. 62.

54 *Ibid.*, p. 64.

55 *Ibid.*

He added that it was "completely untrue" that the four leaders were "bundled into No. 10 Downing Street." Furthermore, he said, the Prime Minister of the United Kingdom was not present at any of the discussions on the Agreement.[56] He said that it was true that the "original Agreement" contained a proposal for a military base but it was then referred to the Nigerian Council of Ministers and "it was as a result of the discussions in the Ministerial Committee that we have exactly the form of the Agreement in which it is now before us."[57]

That there was uneasiness in quarters other than the Action Group can be seen in the remarks of Mallam Muhtari, NPC Chief Whip, and Mr. Abii (NCNC), both of whom supported the resolution. Mallam Muhtari said: "I must, in the first place, however, admit that for the first three or four months public opinion in this country was very much against this Pact. . . ." He later said that he had gone through the agreement very carefully and that "it is wholly acceptable to me."[58]

Mr. Abii was even less positive. "There is no need saying that we are not going to accept it," he said. "We are bound to do so." He went on, however, to plead as follows:

I am suggesting very humbly to the Government that a little examination be given to certain words in the draft Agreement in order to make things plain to our people. For example, I feel that if you take Article II, it will be absolutely necessary to get the lay people of the country to understand what it means. By adding after the words 'Closest co-operation' add 'whenever such is to be in the best interests of both countries.' I suggest this because the closest co-operation must be accepted by our own country before we are bound by it.[59]

56 *Ibid.*, p. 65. On November 23, in a press conference, Awolowo asserted that the British Prime Minister, Mr. Macmillan, *was* present at one of the meetings. See *Anglo-Nigeria Military Pact Agreement* (n.d.) issued by the Action Group Bureau of Information.

57 *H. R. Debates*, November session 1960, p. 66. During the course of his defense, the Prime Minister made one other charge which was quite damning of Chief Awolowo: "I said [at the 1958 London Conference] that Kano Aerodrome was a civil aerodrome but I would have no objection to the United Kingdom having another aerodrome somewhere else. (Interruptions). And, Sir, the Leader of the Opposition, at our meeting, said, 'If you cannot have it in Kano, come to the Western Region.' (Prolonged interruptions). Honestly, Mr. Speaker, Sir, I am telling the House the truth." *Ibid.*, p. 65.
Chief Awolowo, off the floor of the House, charged that the Prime Minister's statement was a "bare-faced falsehood." *Nigerian Tribune*, November 24, 1960.

58 *H. R. Debates*, November session 1960, pp. 70-71.

59 *Ibid.*, pp. 71-72. He suggested further changes to the same effect throughout the Agreement, but then before anyone could discuss his proposed changes, he moved that the question be put, and it was.
One other speaker of note on the resolution was Dr. T. O. Elias, Attorney-General and Minister of Justice, who spoke on the position of the Agreement in international law. He said that an international agreement signed by accredited representatives of a country "must be binding on them whether it was signed under duress or not," and that the signing of any agreement necessarily meant a surrender of "part of its sovereignty." However, he added: "If we are bound by the initialling which was made

Needless to say, the resolution passed the House, in this case by a vote of 166 to 38, the only negative votes being supplied by the Action Group and its allies with the exception of Dr. Chike Obi, leader of the Dynamic Party but holding an NCNC seat.[60] It is probably impossible, however, to reveal fully the antagonism which this resolution engendered. The Nigerian House of Representatives is not known for its decorum during debates, but in this case the Official Record is filled with admonitions of the Speaker calling for order, and the record is interspersed with (Interruption), (Prolonged interruption), and (Loud interruption). There were no less than fifteen of these interruptions while the resolution was being moved and seconded, nine while Chief Awolowo spoke, twenty-two while the Prime Minister spoke, and ten thereafter. There is no doubt that the Defense Agreement has been the most unpopular act of the Government to date among Nigeria's articulate groups.

Further proof of the resentment occurred on November 25 when a group of students from the University College, Ibadan, marched on the house of Dr. Kalu Ezera, then Lecturer in Government and NCNC member of the House of Representatives, to ask him why he had supported the resolution. Dr. Ezera is quoted as saying that the NCNC had already prepared an amendment which it would propose to the already approved Defense Agreement.[61] This apparently did not satisfy the students, for on Monday, November 28, they were joined by students from two other colleges in Ibadan, and over 1000 strong,[62] they boarded "23 buses and mamy wagons" bound for Lagos. There the irate students gate-crashed into the House of Representatives, broke through a police cordon to get into the Senate chambers, and manhandled at least two federal ministers.[63] They carried placards which read: "No Bases in Nigeria"; "Balewa betrays us"; "Defence Pact Betrays our Foreign Policy"; and "Britain, Leave Nigeria Alone." Police used tear gas to disperse the students and arrested six of them, but Dr. Tunji Otegbeye "a bearded private medical practitioner [and President of the Nigerian Youth Congress] stood surety for them."[64] The students were later bound over to keep the peace. The judge said they had acted out of "youthful

---

between an independent country and a dependent country then we would not be here asking you to ratify this agreement." *Ibid.*, p. 70.

60 *Ibid.*, pp. 75-76.

61 *Nigerian Tribune*, November 28, 1960.

62 The *Nigerian Tribune*, November 29, 1960, said there were over two thousand students.

63 *Nigerian Tribune*, November 29, 1960; *West African Pilot*, November 29, 1960; and *The Service*, December 3, 1960.

64 *The Service*, December 3, 1960, p. 2. Mr. Dapo Falase, President of the Students' Union, University College, Ibadan (who was in the crowd but was not one of those arrested), had written a letter to the Regional Premiers saying the Pact "weakens Nigeria's claims to the respect of the African nations." *Ibid.*

A correspondent for *The Service* said it seemed suspicious that Britain which had never before had tropicalization trials should suddenly need them now. *Ibid.*

exuberance" and if given a chance "may reform and turn out to be useful to the country in dire need of trained personnel."[65]

The reasons for the objections to the Defense Pact are at once simple and complex. Chief Awolowo charged that it was an attempt to "swindle this country out of its sovereignty." Since Chief Awolowo had openly advocated alignment with the West only eleven months earlier, and had openly admitted that he was not above using deceit to win what he wanted, many people have discounted his position as mere opposition for the sake of opposing. But there was something more than objection for the sake of objection in the remarks of the NPC Chief Whip and NCNC member Mr. Abii quoted above. Chief Olugbade of the Action Group certainly expressed one of the fears of many Nigerians when he protested against the Pact as follows: "Now we are inviting a situation whereby Nigeria's voice will be looked upon with suspicion in the comity of African nations because we have all been suffering, we know that, for years."[66] This fear had not been helped any by the criticism of all defense pacts by Dr. Kwame Nkrumah of Ghana the previous summer, and his assertion that Commonwealth obligations already entailed helping members in an emergency situation, for this is "part of the general understanding of the Commonwealth."[67]

The Pact itself seems mild indeed. In return for some very basic needs for Nigeria's military forces, Britain merely has over-flying and air-staging facilities, and the right to consult for mutual defense purposes. In monetary value Nigeria appears to get far more than it gives. There certainly appears to be no foreign base on Nigerian soil. But the opposition points out, rightly, that other states in the Commonwealth get what Nigeria gets without a defense agreement.[68] Furthermore, a materialistic approach ignores the psychological meaning of "independence," which seemed to trouble the members of Parliament as much as it did the irate students.[69] Coupled with this is the further problem of what it means to be neutral or non-aligned. Although these two terms were used often, and approvingly, by many Nigerian spokesmen on foreign affairs, it is still questionable whether the

65 *Daily Times,* December 23, 1960.

66 *H. R. Debates,* November session 1960, p. 68.

67 *West African Review,* Vol. XXI, No. 392, July 1960, p. 6. See also *Daily Times,* May 14, 1960.

The Action Group weekly newspaper, *The Service,* on December 17, 1960 said:

"Ghana's Minister of Foreign Affairs, Mr. Ako Adjei, has said in effect that Dr. Nkrumah excluded Nigeria from the list of African States to whom he sent proposals for an African Military command because 'Ghana holds the view that it is improper for an African State to enter into a defence agreement with any other state outside the African Continent.'"

The Service, while opposing the Defense Pact, also said it felt it was not Ghana's place to determine Nigeria's foreign policy.

68 See *West Africa,* August 26, 1961.

69 John West, writing for *The Service,* December 10, 1960, said: "I know for certain that the majority of those who voted for the Pact did so in the knowledge that they were doing the wrong thing."

Government wanted or cared to use them.[70] Evidence for this came six days after the debate on the Defense Pact when the House was permitted to debate the foreign policy statement made by the Prime Minister on the previous August 20.

The Prime Minister himself led off the debate on November 24, 1960. His address on this day was to be an elucidation of his earlier statement, but after a brief statement on power blocs, was devoted chiefly to African affairs. On the question of blocs, he reiterated his earlier position that Nigeria would not join any power bloc "as a matter of routine," which latter phrase he now interpreted to mean that "Nigeria as a country will not join either the Western or the Eastern, or any other bloc, but Nigeria will follow an independent line no matter from where the truth comes, whether it be from the East or the West, Nigeria will go to the path of truth."[71]

The Prime Minister had much more to say on Africa, however. Here, he first reiterated his intention to regard every other state on that continent as an equal, disclaiming the need for big states to dominate smaller ones near it. But that he did not expect Nigeria itself to be treated as an equal by the other African states was revealed in the following aside:

Well, possibly, Sir, if we conduct ourselves well and if we appear well-meaning to the countries of Africa, there is no reason why they should not give us our recognised position by virtue of our size and population, but it is not for us to go out to show to those smaller countries that we are big in size and population and therefore they have to come trailing behind us.[72]

He emphasized, however, that his prime concern at the moment was for "peace and stability."

He again asserted that there was no need to station troops on Nigeria's borders with Dahomey, Niger, and Chad, pointedly leaving out the Cameroun Republic.

He agreed that Nigeria must work to "bring about closer understanding, to bring about more exchange of visits and ideas between all the countries of Africa," and asserted that contacts for such purposes had already begun. He made it clear, however, that one of the drawbacks to any sort of union was the fact that Africans really were quite ignorant of each other. The first course for Africa, then, is for states to come to some understanding of each other, to discover both what is common and what is different. It is true, he added, that the greatest problem was to keep Africa out of the ideological war.

When I say ideological war, Sir, I do not particularly refer to either belief or any kind of association which might exist in other parts of the world. I mean we should try to keep out from Africa the evils which we believe are menacing

70 The Prime Minister had said earlier that he regarded his foreign policy as neither one of neutralism nor non-alignment. *Daily Times,* October 5, 1960.

71 *H. R. Debates,* November session 1960, p. 196.

72 *Ibid.*

not only Europe, not only Asia, not only South America but the world as a whole.

To achieve this aim, he was prepared to "work closely to follow up this idea that we have, to draw up a list of matters in which we think we have common interests." There was not, however, to be any talk of political union "before knowing exactly what our problems are." While such a union might come "sometime in the future—only God knows the future—" he could see no "easy and stable" union at that time.

Pressing his point, he said that he had warned "a very important politician" from one of the West African countries in 1957 that the proposed merger of his state with another would fail, and it did. Presumably he was speaking of the Mali Federation, but he did not make that clear. The reason such federations are immature, he said, in a rather sharp criticism, was because "of the personal ambitions of individuals in two or three states," which therefore is why "we think it is unnecessary and unwise for separate countries to federate." Furthermore, he saw no chance that newly independent states would give up their sovereignty in the near future.

That he expected Nigeria to be a leader was again demonstrated in his concluding remarks to the effect that Nigeria would not impose itself on others, but would be willing to assist others if called upon.

But, Sir [he added], we are not going to ask to give advice, we are not going to ask to give assistance. People must make requests to us. We have to be approached. That, Sir, is our policy, and I call it "live and let live in Africa."[73]

The inoffensive nature of the Prime Minister's statement was revealed by the mildness of criticism which it invoked. The Opposition Leader said the policy was "not bad as far as it goes." He criticized the Government Leader for not stressing the fact that Nigeria was a liberal democracy and must therefore attempt to "translate" the ideals of such a system "into realities both at home and abroad." Also, he felt that it was wrong not to have stated definite positions on Kenya, South Africa, Congo, Algeria, and the Central African Federation, and he again criticized the Defense Pact as having jettisoned the principle of non-involvement.[74]

In all, twenty-seven members of Parliament spoke on the resolution to approve the Government's foreign policy. There was little opposition, except that some believed, with Chief Awolowo, that it did not "go far enough." The resolution was carried by a voice vote.[75]

---

73 *Ibid.,* pp. 197-98.

74 *Ibid.,* pp. 199-202. The previous month Awolowo had said: ". . . we do not support his [Balewa's] foreign policy which we consider to be vague and hypocritical in the extreme." *Daily Times,* October 6, 1960.

75 *H. R. Debates,* November session 1960, p. 252. The Opposition even suggested that a committee be set up in the House representing all parties to "work out the details" of a bi-partisan policy. *Ibid.,* p. 233. Balewa rejected the suggestion on the grounds that foreign policy was a Government prerogative. *Ibid.,* p. 250.

CONCLUSIONS

The year 1960 was a formative one for Nigerian foreign policy. Certain attitudes and fears were revealed which the campaign of 1959 had hidden. One would have assumed, reviewing the election platforms of that year, that Nigeria would identify itself clearly with the West. The NPC and the Action Group had openly advocated it, and the NCNC had spoken with two voices —one which advocated "neutralism," and one which renounced neutralism in favor of an independent course of non-alignment with military blocs but positive friendship with the West. It became readily apparent, however, that such an identification with the West was far from universally desired. While Nigeria's dominant values appeared to be those of the West, independence of action seemed to be stronger than such identification.

The NPC/NCNC coalition had joined an essentially conservative party with an essentially liberal party, the latter with a strong radical wing. The leadership was in the hands of conservatives, but part of its support depended on placating radicals of the NCNC. The radicals, even when supporting the coalition with their votes, made their voices heard. The fears of the radicals were too strongly pressed to be ignored. They revealed concern over the fact that Nigeria might not follow a "neutral" or "non-aligned" course, and insisted on using these terms rather than Balewa's. They feared that Nigeria might align with the West, that is, with some of the NATO powers; that Moslem states might pressure Nigeria to oppose Israel; that diplomacy might be left in the hands of non-Nigerians; that African affairs might be neglected in an undue consideration of world issues. This wing was wont to talk about African personality, and to insist that some form of Pan-Africanism was not only possible, but was to be actively sought. They believed that colonialism and "neo-colonialism" were Africa's greatest dangers.

The Opposition Party shared many of the above views, but revealed an inconsistency that made its policy appear to be one of opposing merely for the sake of opposing. While Awolowo at first was still interested in some form of identification with the West, by the end of the year he and his party had dropped most references to such ties. From mild approval of the Defense Pact in May, the Action Group had come to rabid rejection of it in November. It seemed to be searching for expressions of popular will, with a view to espousing whatever would get the party elected in the future. Its attempt to have the foreign policy labeled as "independent alignment" seems only a slight modification of the other terms commonly used, that is neutralism and non-alignment. Nevertheless, it frequently added its voice to the NCNC radicals, thus strengthening opposition to NPC conservatism.

For the most part, one gets the impression that 1960 saw the NPC literally lifted by the articulate radicals of the NCNC, abetted by the Action Group and the press, and re-directed toward goals which that party had not even dreamed of before. A mixture of all these forces impinged on the Government and undoubtedly colored its decisions. By the end of the year, and somewhat hesitantly, the coalition Government had come to have a foreign policy. While it was admittedly quite general, certain standards stand out which can be described as follows:

1) Nigeria would continue its Commonwealth membership. The Prime Minister himself, however, had revealed a hardening of his distaste for South Africa, and he had indicated that he was considering strong opposition to continued Commonwealth membership for that country.

2) Nigeria intended to work with the United Nations. The Prime Minister had gone personally to New York and addressed the international organization on Nigeria's becoming the ninety-ninth member of that body. In that address he reviewed Nigeria's foreign policy, made some suggestions on the Congo situation (which will be discussed later), and added that he believed that it was "the intention of the original promoters [of the United Nations] to see that countries which are now backward should be assisted in every possible way to develop so that they become world assets and not liabilities."[76]

3) Nigeria would not align with any power bloc. It is clear that the Prime Minister did not regard the Defense Pact as a violation of his policy, that is, it was not "a matter of routine," but merely one of those ties which would benefit Nigeria. It would be left to the course of history to determine what Nigeria would take from the other Big Power bloc. Furthermore, Sir Abubakar seemed to be saying that he was not in favor of any kind of bloc, not even an African one, which implied that Nigeria would not seek an alliance even of African states whereby that continent would attempt to speak with one voice on world issues.[77] Nevertheless, the Defense Pact had not gone down easily with many articulate people and opened the Government to charges of gross inconsistency in relation to non-alignment. Apart from the Defense Pact, however, the Government's policy, while not openly pro-West, was certainly not anti-West. Even among the opponents of any identification with the West, there appeared to be no support for a positive pro-Soviet position. By and large, the Soviet bloc was ignored.

4) Nigeria would make no attempt at a political union of African states in the forseeable future. There was to be a host of independent African states for an indefinite period of time. While expecting other African states to recognize its great size, Nigeria would not attempt to bring about a hegemony of such states under its control. Each state, including Nigeria, had its own internal problems to deal with first. Concentration had to be placed on these problems and solutions found which would produce internal viability, before union with other states could be attempted.

The main difficulty with talk of political union at this time was due to the fact that African states knew very little about each other. Knowledge about the world had, for the most part, been acquired through contacts with the European metropole, and colonies which had existed side by side frequently spoke a different European language, and were devoid of even rudimentary communications such as roads, railroads, or telephones. Cer-

76 *Federal Nigeria*, September/October, 1960, p. 14.
77 In his address to the United Nations he had said: "I hate the very idea of blocs in the United Nations: it seems to me to be a contradiction in terms." *Ibid*.

tainly, the Nigerian Government maintained, something more than a belief in Pan-Africanism was necessary to bring about a political union of such states. Furthermore, the Prime Minister made it clear that he distrusted the personal ambitions of some of the African leaders, and had no intention of aligning Nigeria to some union which would be dominated by any of these individuals. Presumably, his fears were directed chiefly at Mr. Nkrumah of Ghana.

5) Nevertheless, some form of African cooperation was required and would be attempted. Consequently, Pan-African conferences would be held to map out the common problems, the common agreements, and the strong differences. When these were known, then machinery could be created to encourage inter-African cooperation. Especially fruitful at this time appeared to be the fields of communications and trade.

6) Nigeria would press for the elimination of all colonialism on the African continent. At this time, however, no date or timetable was suggested.

Thus, while Nigeria was clearly feeling its way on a foreign policy, it was also clearly beginning to shape a position. It was setting forth a statement of values within which to judge day-to-day events. However, it must be admitted that it would be difficult to predict Nigerian reaction to a particular situation from the policies so far stated, apart from the probability of cooperation with the United Nations, and caution on any proposal for African political union. The phrase "live and let live" is even less clear than "neutralism" or "non-alignment." In fact, the Government's position was sufficiently vague and the values expressed sufficiently universal, that, apart from the Defense Pact, there was no serious opposition to it in either the Parliament, the press, or the political parties. Nigeria, however, at the end of 1960, was barely beginning its existence as an independent state. There is no doubt that a considerable accommodation of values had developed in the coalition parties in a short period of one year, that fluidity characterized the views of many parliamentarians, and that an Opposition was beginning to develop in the Action Group.

IV. Internal Pressures Affecting Foreign Policy Formation

The parliamentary attitudes discussed in the previous chapter did not occur in a vacuum. They reflected values, fears, and interests which exist in Nigerian society. The fact that such divergent positions could be so freely expressed in the Parliament revealed something of the nature of the democratic setting in which they occurred. A democratic setting, however, which is characterized by large blocs of extreme viewpoints, often accompanied by intolerance, frustrates government action. The test of democratic government, therefore, is whether, in the face of a society sharply divided as to values and goals, it attempts to silence the voice of opposition or accommodate it. This was the challenge faced by the Nigerian Government in its formative periods immediately before and after independence.

Internal, that is, non-official, pressures on the Government existed from the beginning. While that is not unusual for any government in a pluralistic society, it is quite clear that extreme divisions in a new state not only weaken the chances of governmental survival but of the survival of the state itself. The nature of the internal pressures on foreign policy formation must therefore be examined in some detail. Of particular concern will be the various groups which served to articulate opinion in Nigeria, as well as the strains resulting from the federal structure of the state.

THE ALL-NIGERIA PEOPLES' CONFERENCE

In the April 1960 session of the Parliament, some NCNC members had supported a motion calling for the creation of a ministry or at least a department of government to deal with Pan-African affairs. The Prime Minister rejected the suggestion, but did agree that there would be a section in his Government to deal with the affairs of African countries.[1] After independence, the Ministry of Foreign Affairs and Commonwealth Relations was organized into eight divisions, among which is the Africa Division.

1 See *supra*, pp. 31, 33.

Perhaps even more important in the eyes of many people was the Prime Minister's appointment in May 1961 of a Personal Adviser on African Affairs. For this position he appointed Dr. K.O. Mbadiwe, an American-educated NCNC leader from the Eastern Region. "Dr. Mbadiwe has, in his time, been a firebrand in Nigerian politics and in 1958 he caused a national sensation by breaking with Dr. Azikiwe on grounds that Zik's nationalism was too moderate."[2] The breach was healed in 1960 when he rejoined the NCNC. The subsequent appointment of Mbadiwe as Personal Adviser was regarded by *The Economist* as Sir Abubakar's "shrewdest domestic political move" for he can "now appear to be listening to the extreme nationalists without needing to take their advice."[3]

One of Dr. Mbadiwe's first moves was to call the All-Nigeria Peoples' Conference in August 1961. This was, he said (in a personal interview with the author), a result of his own personal initiative and not that of any pressure groups. It was the fulfilment of a pledge, he said at another time, "that I will seek the views of all shades of opinion in this country on Nigeria's role on African Affairs."[4] To get "all shades of opinion" he resorted to the device of a conference of selected individuals representing political parties, trade unions, students, Parliament, women's organizations, war veterans, intellectuals, and clergymen.[5]

The theme of the Conference was "Nigeria's Role in African Affairs." The Prime Minister identified himself with the Conference to the extent of making a short address at the opening session, the gist of which was as follows:

I should therefore like you to ask yourselves the following questions, the answers to which I think might produce some solutions to the many problems in Africa: How can we bring the peoples of Africa closer together so that all of us could have the feeling of oneness? Should we tackle our problems in Africa regionally—West, East, North, South, Central Africa—or should we do it by taking the Continent as a whole? How are we to assist the remaining dependent territories in Africa to attain full independence within the shortest time possible? How do we tackle the problems of territories where there are European minority settlers? Do we aim at achieving an immediate political union of all-African States or do we at the beginning start by co-ordinating economic and cultural relations? At present we lack the necessary capital and the technical skill to develop our resources by ourselves alone, and so how are we to obtain help from outside and still keep free from being under the influence of one power

---

2 *The Economist,* June 17, 1961, p. 1240.

3 *Ibid.* For a fuller account of Mbadiwe, see Ronald Segal, *Political Africa* (London: Stevens and Sons, 1961), pp. 177-8. In the fall of 1961, the NCNC called upon one of its members to resign his seat in Parliament so that Dr. Mbadiwe might run for it. In the January by-election resulting therefrom, he was returned to the Parliament. See *Nigerian Morning Post,* February 1, 1961.

4 Unpublished Records of the All-Nigeria Peoples' Conference held in Lagos, August 19-21, 1961. The Records are in mimeographed form only, and pagination is impossible to follow. No page references, therefore, can be given.

5 *Sunday Times,* August 20, 1961.

bloc or the other? How can we in Africa help to preserve world peace and promote the happiness of mankind in general?[6]

"The Federal Government," he concluded, "is very anxious to know your thoughts on all these matters."

The first day of the Conference was devoted to the making of speeches from the delegates, who were encouraged to state their views "without qualifications." Over two dozen people accepted the challenge. At the risk of distortion through summarization, the concerns of the delegates can be reduced to a few points. The most consistent theme was the need for Pan-African union. Speakers deplored the fact that blocs exist, although there was an attempt to deny the reality of such blocs in Africa. Casablanca Powers and Monrovia Powers "are names quoted by Fleet Street Journalists, the 'New York Times' etc., who hope to divide us sufficiently in order to rule us," said Mr. Abuka, a university student; while Mr. Ijoma, President of the Students' Union, Nsukka, said "the existing differences between the two powers is brought about by the imperialists"; and still a third delegate, a Chief Durosaro, wanted African union in order to stop the "bad propaganda . . . that Africa is divided into two blocs. . . ." There appeared to be a general belief among the participants that African unity awaited only the approval of the Nigerian Government. Consequently, there was practically no concern with machinery for implementation of such unity.

The second theme, equally unchallenged, was that Nigeria was "under the influence of imperialists," and "pro-West" in its views.[7] Consequently, the Defense Pact was repeatedly denounced, and the Government was called upon to become truly neutral or non-aligned, even to the point of restricting the quantity of news about Britain and the United States over Nigerian radio.

The third theme was that Nigeria would have to attain internal unity before it could expect to join in an African union of any kind. Internal unity, however, meant abrogation of the federal structure and revealed a desire to re-open the whole struggle over state form (unitary vs. federal) that had occupied most of the early 1950's. Delegates here were of the school which believes that federalism would never allow national identification to develop. One delegate (Mr. Imoudu, leader of one of the trade unions) opposed a coalition Government, but did not suggest how the country could be run otherwise.

The fourth theme expressed by the delegates was that Ghana somehow represents African aspirations better than Nigeria does. Said one delegate, a student from the new University of Nigeria, Nsukka: "I would prefer to be a prisoner in Ghana than to be a free citizen in this country because everywhere you go, they ask you 'Are you from Ghana?'" Mallam Aminu Kano, leader of NEPU and a government whip, said Nkrumah "enjoys total confidence of the people of Ghana." Another delegate, unnamed but

6 Unpublished Records of the Conference.
7 The term "pro-West," when used by Nigerians, does not seem to mean "to favor Western Civilization." Rather, it means "to favor, or sympathize with, the Anglo-American bloc," as opposed to the Soviet bloc.

representing the Supreme Council of Ex-Service Men, deplored the fact that Ghana's leaders regarded Nigeria as having only "partial independence." Another delegate, a Mr. Femi, said: "Everyone is impressed by Mr. Nkrumah in Ghana because he shows he is militant. So, Sir, we want our Federal Government to show they are militant." It was in this same vein that Michael Ogon (militant member of NCNC, Provincial Commissioner, Port Harcourt) resented having Nigeria identified with the "moderate French West African" states rather than with the "militant" states of Guinea, Mali, and Ghana.

The viewpoints represented in the general meeting help explain the reports of the various committees into which the Conference was divided. Two committees were especially concerned with questions of foreign policy: the International Relations Committee and the African Affairs Committee.

The International Relations Committee was chaired by Mallam Aminu Kano, and had for its *rapporteur* Chief O. I. Dafe, Administrative Secretary of the NCNC. In the introduction of its report, the committee listed certain weaknesses in the Federal Government which included: discrimination against the Soviet Union; allowing the British High Commissioner's residence to remain too close to that of the Prime Minister and the State House;[8] entry into the Defense Pact ("unnecessary . . . in view of the existing mutual defence arrangements among commonwealth countries"); failure to support activities of African bodies abroad; allowing the Head of Security in the British High Commission to advise the Federal Government on security; passport restrictions on Nigerians wishing to travel to countries of Eastern Europe; allowing expatriates to serve as secretary-typists in the Government; banning of Communist literature; fear of Russia; allowing Nigerian diplomats to be trained abroad; allowing foreign governments, particularly the United States, to hold conferences in Nigeria; and the use of "Lisbon Airport by our Government."

On the basis of these "weaknesses," the committee made a number of recommendations "with a view to resuscitating the lost grounds and prestige of Nigeria in International Affairs." The gist of the recommendations, largely paraphrased here, were as follows:

1) The Government, to counter the dangers of neo-colonialism, should "control the influx of several agencies of neo-colonialism which come to our country in the guise of friends, such as the Moral Rearmament, International Co-operation Administration, Kennedy Peace Corps, Experiment in International Living, Operation Crossroads, and others."

2) No foreign nation should be allowed to hold a conference in Nigeria, "e.g. the Conference of the American Diplomats recently held in Lagos."

3) The Soviet Union should be given accommodations equal to that of any other nation.

8 Said the Report: "For instance, the possiblity of monitoring and other espionage activities cannot be overlooked. And besides, the Committee disapproves of special protection and privilege accorded to the British High Commission, which privileges are not accorded to other Embassies."

4) The Soviet Union should have equal facilities to those granted to other diplomatic missions, "particularly the U.S.A. and U.K. This recommendation is borne out by the following discriminatory practices: (a) the restriction on the U.S.S.R. to limit the number of their Diplomats to 10, whilst other Embassies experience no restriction; (b) discriminatory allocations of diplomatic car plate numbers as follows:—5 allocated to U.S.S.R. as against 100 to each of U.K. and U.S.A."

5) Mr. Krushchev and Mr. Nkrumah should be invited to visit Nigeria, and Nigeria should attend the Belgrade Conference of Neutral States.[9]

6) Students and other bodies should be encouraged to hold international conferences in Nigeria to promote international understanding.

7) The Governor-General and the Prime Minister should visit all independent African states so that the Prime Minister will lose his reluctance to speak about the African continent as a whole.[10]

8) The Government should support all African nationalists fighting for the independence of their countries, and should grant asylum to such nationalists "forced by imperialists" to leave their countries.

9) The Government should either recognize both North and South Korea, or neither of them until the country is unified "in view of the fact that the Korean issue is still on the agenda of the United Nations."[11]

10) The Government should condemn French action in Bizerta.

11) Full recognition should be given to the Algerian provisional government.

12) The Government should support two important African organizations in the United Kingdom, namely, the Committee of African Organizations and the West African Students' Union.

13) The Government should desist from "communist witch-hunting" whereby:

(a) Passports are denied to Nigerian Nationals wishing to travel to East European countries and China;
(b) Intelligence Reports are . . . written by British Intelligence Officers in the Nigerian Civil Service and elsewhere;
(c) Intelligence Reports about Nigerian Nationals by British Diplomats in places where we do not have Embassies are accepted unchecked by the Nigerian Government;
(d) Importation of literature from East European countries and China is banned;
(e) Expatriate Professors, Lecturers, Academicians and Graduates from the East European countries are not allowed to teach in Nigerian institutions.

14) The Government should recall about £300,000,000 sterling reserves

---

9 The disparate topics are treated in the Report as recommendation Number 5.
10 Reference here is to Sir Abubakar's oft-repeated statement that Africans really know very little about each other.
11 The committee made no mention of the fact that the United Nations supported South Korea, nor did it mention the Central Congo-Katanga dispute, also on the agenda of the United Nations.

from the United Kingdom and other countries for the development of Nigeria.

15) Government insurance companies should be promoted, and other insurance companies should be made to re-invest their premiums in Nigeria.

16) The Government should encourage loans and discourage investments.

17) A republican form of government should be established "to enhance the prestige of Nigeria in Africa and in international affairs."

18) "Nigeria should have nothing to do with the European Common Market but instead should actively contribute towards the formation of an African Common Market and Monetary System."

19) Nigeria should "sever relations immediately" with the "so-called Central African Federation which is not even a sovereign state," and is furthermore rejected by Africans there.

20) Nigeria should establish diplomatic relations with East Germany.

There were only two criticisms of the report. One delegate suggested that an amendment should be added encouraging Jomo Kenyatta to visit Nigeria. Another amendment was suggested by Dr. Mbadiwe himself, calling on the Government to "control foreign investments," not "discourage" them as Point 16 had recommended. Both amendments were accepted and before discussion could occur the chairman, Dr. Mbadiwe, said "everybody is in favour of the report. There is, therefore, no need to call for more debates." The report was accepted by the Conference as amended.

The African Affairs Committee was chaired by Chief H. O. Davies, prominent lawyer, "nationalist," and leader in the NCNC; its vice-chairman was Chief Kolawole Balogun, former High Commissioner to Ghana, colleague with Dr. Mbadiwe in his break with Azikiwe in 1958, and now an active member of the NCNC again; and its *rapporteur* was Dr. Eze Ogueri II, Editor-in-Chief of the Nigerian magazine, *Africa,* and a member of the NCNC. The committee decided to approach its problems by first identifying "sovereign African States." It found fifty-eight of them including Ifni, Canary Islands, Fernando Po, and other islands and enclaves. It also, for reasons which never appeared in the report of the committee, did not consider Somalia independent but did so consider Algeria.

This committee, like the International Relations Committee, also listed a number of weaknesses in the Government. It agreed that there was much ignorance about other parts of Africa; that Nigeria lacked "internal unity"; that Nigeria still relied heavily on foreigners as revealed in its economic planning, its internal security, its "obvious bias towards the Western Block [sic]," in permitting cable and wireless services to remain in the hands of Britons, and in the Defense Pact; that Nigeria was inconsistent in its claim to non-alignment as is revealed by its recognition of West Germany but not of East Germany; that Nigeria has not "pronounced unequivocally for political union of African states"; that Nigeria does not enjoy the confidence of African nationalists abroad because it recognizes the Central African Federation, has not encouraged nationalist refugees to seek asylum in Nigeria, and has permitted Nigerians to accept foreign titles; that "Macarthyism, that is, exaggerated ideas of Communist influence, seems to obtain in Nigeria"; and that the Nigerian Constitution itself is favorable to "sectional loyalty," and is therefore a "handicap to Nigeria's full participation in African Affairs."

In the light of these weaknesses, the committee proceeded to recommend that:

"Nigeria should establish with all deliberate speed an Institute or Council on African Affairs ... as a centre for channeling information and dealing with all phases of African Affairs";

Nigeria should accept Pan-Africanism positively and "accept in principle the idea of a Political union of African States on [a] continental basis";

Nigeria should initiate economic, scientific, and cultural cooperation with neighboring states, "but the realisation of both political union and economic and cultural co-operation should be persued [pursued] simultaneously";

Nigeria should attempt to bring the Casablanca and Monrovia Powers together;

Special contacts should be made with the Casablanca Powers;

Nigeria should support the principle "one man one vote" in countries dominated by white minorities;

Nigeria should seek aid from "both the East and the West" but in doing so should guard its sovereignty jealously;

Nigeria should establish at least one embassy in each of the five regions of Africa; that is, north, west, east, central, and south;

Nigeria should extend educational facilities to students from other African states by offering scholarships "tenable in our universities"; and

A Ministry of African Affairs should be created immediately for "the effective projection of Nigerian personality in Africa."

The Records of the Conference do not indicate whether the recommendations were debated or not, but the magazine *Africa,* edited by the committee *rapporteur,* asserts that the report was accepted by the Conference.[12]

---

12 *Africa,* October 1961, p. 15. However, it must be pointed out that a conflict was later revealed which exposed Dr. Mbadiwe to the charge of "rigging" the Conference. Mr. Mbazulike Amechi, Parliamentary Secretary to the federal Minister of Information, said that the African Affairs Committee had originally proposed "that the Government should accept positively and make an unequivocal statement on the Principle of Pan-Africanism, and that also Nigeria should support the creation of an African Military High Command for mutual defence of any African State that may be attacked by a foreign imperialist power."

Mr. Amechi said the Conference accepted the committee's wording, but that after many delegates had left, Dr. Mbadiwe had proposed to modify the recommendation so as to accept "'in principle' the desirability of possible political union of African states and should recommend also the desirability of a Joint Military action whenever the occasion arises." He charged further that Mbadiwe refused to allow anyone to speak on the amendment except two supporters.

On the other hand, the Secretariat of the Conference issued a statement denying that the amendment had been proposed to a decimated conference, although it admitted that "Dr. Otegbeye and a few of his friends" walked out during the voting. It further explained that the purpose of the amendment was to refuse "in clear terms

The All-Nigeria Peoples' Conference has been treated here at length because of the attention which it has since received from both the national and international press, and because its subject matter is appropriate to this study. In assessing the importance of the Conference on Nigerian foreign policy formation, however, a number of questions have to be raised. How were the delegates picked? Since Dr. Mbadiwe himself said the Conference was to reflect all shades of opinion, is one to assume that there are no Government supporters in the country? After all, almost no opinion favorable to the Government's policy was voiced.[13] Did restrictions on debate indicate that the Conference was intended to reveal only one body of opinion? Why were the questions raised by the Prime Minister ignored, or dealt with, if at all, in a most perfunctory manner? Considering its assigned tasks, how could the Conference fail to come to grips with some very great problems in Nigerian foreign policy? As examples: Is the policy one of neutrality or non-alignment, or does it matter? Should Nigeria concern itself with the important non-African problems of the world such as Berlin, Laos, West New Guinea, disarmament or Arab-Israeli relations, and if so, on what basis? Does a constant attack on the Anglo-American bloc, while practically ignoring the Soviet bloc, really constitute an independent policy? What are the dangers to Nigeria from the two Big Power blocs? Should Nigeria admit that there are two very real blocs in Africa and plan its policy accordingly? What role can small, weak states play in solving world problems? Are there really two sides to almost every international issue?

In view of the fact that the Conference failed to deal with any of the questions posed, was critical of almost every Government action, and proposed easy solutions to complex problems by assuming that the "bad" in Nigeria came from the Anglo-American bloc while the "good" came from those who advocated Pan-Africanism and the loosening of ties with Europe, what conclusions can one draw from the Conference? One well-known Nigerian, who refuses to be identified, told the writer that the Conference was "merely a means of allowing the radicals to let off steam and it served its purpose well." This viewpoint seems to be well supported by the records

---

to ape any other country in Africa or to borrow the language of any other people besides that of Nigerians." *Daily Mail*, August 25, 1961.

The *Daily Mail*, the Government newspaper of the Northern Region, had an informative reaction to the above dispute. In a front page editorial it referred to Amechi as "a young man who likes to open his mouth very often and too wide. His youthful impetuosity may prove dangerous to the coalition government formed between his party, the NCNC, and the Northern People's Congress." Having charged him with attempting to precipitate a crisis at the Conference "unbecoming of a Parliamentarian who holds a ministerial position," the vitriolic editorial closed with the admonition: "He should be WARNED by his leaders." *Daily Mail*, September 5, 1961.

13 The only positive pro-Government statement was made by Mr. M.T. Mbu, federal Minister of State for the Navy, who gave a feeble defense of the Defense Pact. He said it had not yet been ratified and "if it is your wish that it should not be signed [ratified?], it will not be signed." He did insist, however, "that most of you here are not as nationalistic as those in the Government."

of the Conference. However, it must also be concluded that a strong, articulate segment of the Nigerian intelligentsia is displeased and frustrated with Nigeria's international position. This segment, largely identified with the radicals of the NCNC and the AG, resents any ties with the Anglo-American bloc; regards true independence as requiring some positive attempts at rapproachment with the Soviet bloc, free of any alliance; and believes that every possible effort to bring about African political union must be made immediately, that the only alternative is the "balkanization" of Africa along South American lines and with the concomitant weakness of that continent in economic and political viability. This segment sees the Government as slow, ponderous, conservative, much too sensitive to Anglo-American views, and unwilling to use its powerful position in Africa to lead, or even coerce, African unity. The Conference, with the implied blessing of Sir Abubakar, gave the radicals a form of legitimacy, and assured them of a ready platform—which the Government had promised to consider—to which they could appeal in future debates. Their position was now clear. No longer were they many disparate voices crying in the wilderness of the multi-party system—now, at least, they were recognized as an identifiable body holding positive positions about the role of Nigeria in world affairs.

The All-Nigerian Peoples' Conference, therefore, gave the radicals a channel of communication with the Prime Minister through his Personal Adviser on African Affairs; provided a platform not identified with any particular political party; indicated the strong emotional commitment to the radical view which many Nigerian leaders held; and, since it claimed to represent many classes of Nigerian society, provided a pressure on the coalition Government which probably could not be safely ignored. That such a conference could be called to condemn the Government's policy, while none exists to praise it, indicates the serious cleavage which divides the country. On the one hand are the politically dominant Northern conservatives (maintaining power through a traditional structure to which parliamentary democracy has been grafted) and on the other hand are the more modern, liberal- and radical-minded, but less numerous Southerners (squeezed out of political control by a process which they probably believe in more than the Northerners).

THE CHANGING PLATFORM OF THE OPPOSITION

It will be recalled that Chief Obafemi Awolowo is not only Leader of the Opposition in the Federal House of Representatives but is, and has been from its founding, the President of the Action Group. He is, in fact, the only leader of a major party in the Parliament; the Leader of the NPC (Sir Ahmadu Bello) being Premier of the Northern Region, and the Leader of the NCNC (Dr. Michael Okpara) being Premier of the Eastern Region. When Chief Awolowo speaks, therefore, it is with the voice of his party.

It will also be recalled that in the federal elections of 1959, Awolowo had indicated an open preference for the "Western Bloc," by which he meant the Anglo-American bloc, and had asserted that "it is immoral to play two opposing forces [that is, the Big Power blocs] against each other." He had also stated that "Neutrality in international affairs, whether passive, positive or independent, is an unmitigated disservice to humanity." Furthermore, he had labeled as "unrealistic" any attempt to form a United States of Africa or even to try to establish close economic cooperation among African states.

After his defeat in the federal elections, Awolowo began to make radical changes in his position. Many attribute this to his bitterness over losing the election. Others say that he had to change in order to fulfil the proper function of a loyal opposition. If such change were called for, however, it is obvious that he had two alternatives: to defend even more sharply his previously stated positions, or to adopt new positions entirely. Had he chosen the first alternative, he could have charged that the Government's policies revealed a constant shift to the center and thus indicated the undue influence of the NCNC. By choosing the second alternative, he has appeared to be trying to outflank the NCNC, has opened his party to charges of hypocrisy, and produced what appears to be a bewildering array of contradictions.

From the beginning of his role as Opposition Leader, Awolowo has engaged in bitter attacks on the Government. His role in the Defense Pact debate in 1960 has been discussed in Chapter III, and he has repeatedly denounced that pact again and again. In the November 1960 debate on foreign policy, he condemned the Government's moderate stand on the Congo. If "we have correct orientation," he said, there was no alternative to all-out support of Lumumba.[14] At the same time he asserted that Nigerian ideals "are contrary to the ideals for which the Eastern bloc stands." However, he added, "we have no right . . . to discriminate against the countries of the Eastern bloc," particularly in the field of technological education. The two leading countries in this field are, "in order of merit, Russia and America," and Nigerians must be encouraged to study in both.[15]

In June 1961, after a visit through West Africa, he startled many people by asserting that Nigerians should join the Ghana-Guinea-Mali union. At this time, he also first charged that the Monrovia Conference was financed by "certain Western powers."[16]

In July 1961, in *The Service,* the weekly paper of the Action Group, Awolowo published an article entitled "My Plan for Africa." Here he charged that many of the "ostensibly independent" states of Africa are not free, and this included all of the Monrovia Powers, since they had had military and economic ties forced on them by the European metropole. He also charged that "Belgium and her allies in NATO" had contrived to

14 *H. R. Debates,* November session 1960, p. 200.
15 *Ibid.,* p. 202.
16 *Africa Report,* July 1961, p. 11.

subvert Congo independence, and that "Western Imperialists" had revealed their true intentions in Africa by the Angola brutalities. To counter these influences, he said three alternatives were open: (1) to allow "Western imperialists to continue to hold us in thrall"; (2) to fall "prey to the sweet advances of Western imperialists" and in doing so to enhance the "forces of extremism" which will "gather strength and subsequently erupt, with disastrous consequences for all of us"; or (3) to "see wisdom in purposeful unity." He chose the third alternative, of course, and proposed the formation of an Organization for African Community, to be open to African political parties and nationalistic movements, but not to governments. "Governments," he explained, "are bound by international law and usage which nationalistic movements are not obliged to observe."

The purpose of the Organization would be to seek the fulfilment of ten "aims and objectives" as follows: (1) "complete freedom and sovereignty for all those African States which are at present only nominally independent"; (2) setting of target dates "in the very near future" for the independence of all African colonies; (3) "immediate termination of the existence of any military base in any part of Africa"; (4) extermination of apartheid in South Africa; (5) outlawing of all discrimination against "black people in particular and Africans in general" in Africa and other parts of the world; (6) defense of the "dignity of the African"; (7) establishment of "a community of interests among all the people of Africa"; (8) division of the continent "into zones" as a first "practical step towards the emergence of an All-African political union"; (9) introduction into each zone of a customs and monetary union and other forms of cooperation; and (10) non-involvement "of all African countries in the present East-West power politics and struggles as well as non-partisanship in the Arab-Israeli dispute and conflict."

In September 1961, Awolowo continued his attacks on the Government by delivering a speech, highly resented in Government circles, in London to Nigerian students. He charged, among other things, that Viscount Head "is generally regarded as the de facto ruler of Nigeria"; the Defense Pact is "notorious"; NATO "still operates an exclusive secret wireless frequency in most parts of Nigeria"; "Nigeria is a submissive British subaltern or satellite"; Sir Abubakar never takes a stand "until after he has had a chance of personal contact with Mr. Macmillan or one of his lieutenants"; the Prime Minister agreed to "team up with the radicals from Malaya, Ghana, Canada and India" over the Commonwealth membership of South Africa only at the last moment, and on returning to Nigeria "was given a hero's welcome for the exploits of other people"; the Monrovia Conference was "inspired and completely financed by the more important countries of the Western Bloc"; while other leaders of Africa attacked the European Common Market, Balewa has been "noncommittal"; in seeking "foreign aid for our development, our Government has allowed itself to be led into a blind alley by its Western masters and mentors"; Balewa has allowed Britain and America to see Nigeria's economic plans for the next five years but has not allowed the nation to see them; "every obstacle is ... being placed in the way of the [Russian] Embassy being opened" in Nigeria; among "true African nationalists, Nigeria ... is thoroughly suspect"; and in "our 'neutrality' we are already militarily aligned to Britain, and hence indirectly to N.A.T.O."[17]

It was also at this time that Awolowo and his party colleagues in Parliament began to charge the Government with lack of "dynamism" in its foreign policy, and with allowing the fear of driving away foreign investments to detour it from the path of true socialism.[18]

In the light of its mounting criticism, it was only natural that the Action Group should point out that the All-Nigeria Peoples' Conference had even come to agree with it, that the Conference had the "paternal blessing" of the Government, and that the Government should, therefore, "change the foreign policy that has earned it this odium or ... resign and seek a fresh mandate from the people."[19]

A full explanation of Chief Awolowo's change may never be known fully. That he did not carry all of his party with him, however, was revealed in the extremely serious rupture which occurred at the Eighth Annual Congress of the Action Group at Jos in February 1962. In his presidential address, Awolowo spoke of the "dangerous contradictions" which divided the party "into 'inside left' and 'inside rights,' with intermediate stages in between." He refused to say which side he favored.[20] After his speech, the Congress "exploded" as Chief S. L. Akintola (Deputy Leader of the party and Premier of the Western Region), Chief Ayo Rosiji (General Secretary of the party), and their supporters walked out of the meeting and returned home. While part of the cause of the rift was due to internal policies (Akintola's resentment of party dictation to his Government; Rosiji's desire to see the party concentrate its forces in the Western Region and seek rapproachment with the parties which dominated the other two Regions), there was also resentment by many to what they regarded as Awolowo's move to the "left." One newspaper said the dissidents, among other things, felt that Awolowo's insistence on his type of democractic socialism "would drag the party to the extreme left bordering on communism."[21] Certainly,

---

17 The full address was printed in the *Daily Express,* in the editions of September 12, 13, and 14, 1961.

18 Discussed more fully *infra,* pp. 107-13.

19 O. Agunbiade-Bamishe, "Time the Federal Government Changed Its Foreign Policy," *The Service,* October 21, 1961, p. 11.

20 For the serialization of the address, see the *Daily Express* for February 3, 5, 6, and 7, 1962.

21 *Daily Times,* February 3, 1962. As early as November 1960, a political correspondent of the Action Group weekly, *The Service,* had said that Awolowo "has now shifted to the left." November 19, 1960, p. 3; and "Aiyekoto," editorial writer for the pro-AG *Daily Express,* had asserted seven months later that "Chief Obafemi Awolowo, seeing that the dictatorship of the Right is creeping in slowly but steadily now flirts with the dictatorship of the Left." June 20, 1961.

Chief Awolowo, himself, in his autobiography had said: "The pendulum of my attitude to British administration in Nigeria has always oscillated between the middle-of-the-road and the left wing. From the time I returned to Nigeria in 1946 up

from the newspaper accounts, one would have to conclude that much of the opposition to Awolowo and support for Akintola came from the wealthy business and financial interests and many chiefs in the Western Region which support the party. There seems to be little support for any form of socialism among this group.[22]

The rupture in the party was quite serious, with most of the eminent party leaders taking one side or the other. Chief Awolowo seemed to have the majority support of the Congress, however, for he succeeded in getting his supporters elected to the general secretaryship (Mr. Samuel G. Ikoku, a militant leader of the party from the Eastern Region) and the two vice-presidencies (Chief Anthony Enahoro, militant "Shadow Minister of Foreign Affairs" in the Federal Parliament, and Alhaji Ibrahim Imam, Bornu Youth Movement-Action Group leader in the Northern House of Assembly). An uneasy reconciliation with Akintola occurred later, but lasted only until May, at which time the Premier removed some officials previously appointed by Awolowo. The latter called an executive meeting of the party and ordered Akintola to resign his premiership on grounds of party indiscipline. Akintola refused and instead called on the Speaker of the Western Region Assembly to convene the Assembly. When the Speaker refused, Akintola called on the Governor of the Region (Sir Adesoji Aderemi) to dissolve the Assembly and call for new elections. The Governor refused to do this and instead appointed a new premier. The Speaker then called the Assembly into session to approve one or the other of the two premiers. The Assembly was interrupted twice by violence among its members and the federal Prime Minister refused to allow it to attempt a third meeting. Rather, he called a special session of the Federal Parliament which passed an emergency power act declaring that "a state of public emergency exists."[23] Under the emergency powers granted by Parliament, the Prime Minister restricted the movement of Chief Awolowo, Chief Akintola, and a number of other officials of the Action Group as well as of the Western Region (such as the Leader of the Opposition, an NCNC member), and appointed an administrator to run the region (Dr. M. A. Majekodunmi, federal Minister of Health, a Yoruba member of the NCNC).

The emergency was lifted in January 1963, and Akintola and his followers,

---

to 1951 when the Action Group was inaugurated, I stayed permanently on the left." *Awo* (Cambridge: the University Press, 1960), p. 249. However, in his presidential address to the Eighth Congress of his party, he denied that he was a Communist—in fact, he strongly condemned Communist planning as totalitarian and therefore contrary to democratic socialism. *Daily Express*, February 3, 1962.

It was also necessary, it would appear, for Mr. S.G. Ikoku, who was subsequently elected as General Secretary of the party, to deny that he had ever been a Communist or had ever been "associated with any communist organisation." *Daily Express*, February 6, 1962. Another newspaper had been careful to point out, however, that Ikoku had "recently visited countries behind the Iron Curtain." *Daily Times*, February 3, 1962.

22 See, for example, Increase Coker, "Explosion of a Myth," *Sunday Post*, February 11, 1962.

23 *Supplement to Official Gazette Extraordinary*, No. 38, Vol. 49, May 29, 1962, Part B.

in a newly organized United People's Party, were allowed to resume power in coalition with NCNC. In the interim, Chief Awolowo and some of his followers were indicted for treasonable conspiracy. Awolowo was found guilty and sentenced to ten years in prison.

The swift action of the Federal Government in the Action Group rupture appears precipitate. There certainly was no breakdown of law and order in the region and it seems likely that with a little time the Assembly would finally have voted and resolved the legal issue of who was premier. The Prime Minister's action can only be explained by the deep hatred for the Action Group in both the NPC and the NCNC; and the party rift, coupled with regional government confusion, provided the coalition at the federal level with the opportunity to punish the Action Group. Furthermore, it is obvious that the Federal Government leaders, as well as the leaders of the NPC and the NCNC, preferred the Akintola faction and feared that Awolowo was going to win. There is no doubt that the Federal Government hopes that the events in May, 1962, have so discredited the Action Group that the electorate will prefer anti-Action Group candidates, thus putting the NPC and the NCNC in control or near-control of all the Regions as well as the Federal Government.

One conclusion seems warranted: Chief Awolowo has been determined, since the federal elections of 1959, to sway his party to the side of the "radicals" (of whatever party or organization) who have been putting relentless pressure on the Government for more dynamism in pursuing its policies; for more positive support for African unity; and for a more neutral position between the Big Power blocs. By attempting (from his position as leader of the Action Group) to lead the Opposition to the Federal Government and at the same time to dictate the running of the Western Region, he has probably weakened both the effectiveness of the Opposition and the stability of the Western Region, and possibly set in motion forces which will destroy the Action Group. There is no doubt that he has seriously antagonized the Federal Government (and both of the coalition parties which make it up).[24] His immoderate attacks were perhaps bound to produce immoderate reactions and only history will reveal the damage, if any, done to democratic government in Nigeria.

PRESSURE WITHIN THE GOVERNMENT COALITION

It will be recalled that before independence, criticism of the Government in the halls of Parliament frequently came from the NCNC and occasionally from NPC members. This is perhaps understandable for the NCNC, for that party has been regarded as standing "for a socialist Nigeria within a united West Africa, [and] it is the principal advocate in the country of Pan-Africanism and a policy of Nigerian non-alignment with the international

24 Note, for example, that Chief Awolowo was censured by the Parliament for the foreign policy speech he made in London in September 1961. The censure was voted in the following November. See *H. R. Debates*, daily parts for November 30, 1961, p. 30.

power blocs."[25] Furthermore, it has always had "a strong radical wing opposed to economic and traditional privilege."

From the beginning of the coalition, the NCNC "radicals," as they often call themselves, have remained restless. These radicals tend to be the young, educated people who have not yet risen to important decision-making positions in the party. They tend to be somewhat bitter and resentful because the party leaders, and therefore the coalition Government, "ignore the dynamic youth and appoint middle-aged men who are uninformed. The youth are simply ignored in policy making decisions."[26]

What the NCNC, if it were ruling alone or were the senior partner in the coalition, would have done differently from what has been done, is a matter for conjecture. Nor do we wish to imply that the NCNC is a monolithic party with no differences of opinion among its members. It is evident, however, that elements in the NCNC have put pressures on the Government for changes in policy. We noted earlier that some NCNC members apparently accepted the Defense Pact with great reluctance.[27] In fact, the Foreign Affairs Officer of the NCNC aserts that it was pressure from the "more dynamic" wing of the NCNC which caused the Government finally to cancel the Defense Pact.[28] It has also been this wing of the party which has been most vocal in favor of some form of African unity; which has formed a Nigeria-Soviet Friendship Society under Dr. O. E. Ememe, Representative in the Federal Parliament from Aba;[29] which seeks closer ties with Ghana and with the Casablanca bloc;[30] and which continually warns the Government against being "pro-West."[31] Furthermore, it is common practice for all

25 Ronald Segal, *Political Africa*, pp. 374-6.
26 Ororo Okarevu, in an interview with the author on January 30, 1962. Mr. Okarevu is one of the dynamic youths of his party who has risen to the important post of African and Foreign Affairs Officer of the NCNC.
27 See *supra*, pp. 46-48. The *West African Pilot*, the most militant spokesman for the NCNC radicals, preferred to charge its hero, Dr. Azikiwe, with deceit in initialing the Defense Pact rather than credit Awolowo with true nationalistic motives. May 12, 1960.
28 See *supra*, p. 25n. Mr. Okarevu preferred the term "more dynamic" to "radicals" in referring to the militant wing of the NCNC.
29 *Morning Post*, January 5, 1962; *Daily Times*, January 3, 1962. Recently this society accused the Government of discriminating against the Russian embassy in Lagos, and also called for the establishment of a Nigerian embassy in Moscow. *Daily Express*, March 12, 1962.

   In an instructive article, Mr. Ememe has said that in the "fight to gain economic independence from an organised and armed international monopoly interests, we cannot use the example of American States since we have no radical affinity with the West Europeans from whom we must win this freedom; but from the Soviets whose experiences are similar to our own we must draw our precepts." *West African Pilot*, March 19, 1962.
30 As led by Mokogwu Okoye, referred to as the "stormy petrel of the NCNC," *Daily Express*, February 23, 1962. See also *Sunday Times*, Febuary 25, 1962. The party spokesmen do not all agree on cooperation with Ghana. Dr. Okpara, President of the NCNC, has charged "dark forces of subversion and insults directed from Ghana" with intervention in Nigerian politics. *Sunday Post*, February 18, 1962.
31 See *Daily Express*, October 9, 1961.

members of the party to insist that Nigeria's foreign policy is one of "non-alignment," not "neutrality."[32]

In the Parliament, one of the most vocal critics of the Government has been Dr. Kalu Ezera, NCNC member from Bende East. He was one of the first to charge the Government with lack of dynamism in its foreign policy.[33] It was he who asserted publicly that the NCNC coalesced with the NPC, rather than the Action Group, to keep the North from seceding from the federation.[34] It was he who was embarrassed because Sir Roy Welensky (Central African Federation) and Dr. Verwoerd (South Africa) had spoken of Sir Abubakar as a sane and moderate man.[35] It was he who called, unsuccessfully, on the Government to take foreign policy out of partisan politics by creating an All-Party Parliamentary Committee on Foreign Affairs. And it was he who led the attack on the Government for not accepting the belated invitation to attend the Belgrade Conference of Neutral States.[36] It is not charged here that Dr. Ezera is *the* leader of the NCNC radicals. He is simply the most vocal critic of the Government from the NCNC in Parliament.

Other pressures, with roots in the NCNC, have also prodded the Government. Dr. Azikiwe's newspaper continues to proclaim that the NCNC is the "only true socialistic . . . party in the Federation,"[37] at a time when the Government, including especially the Finance Minister, Chief Festus Okotie-Eboh, has been decrying talk of nationalization.[38] Dr. Azikiwe himself, as Governor-General, embarrassed the Government in the fall of 1961 by suddenly advocating a republican constitution for Nigeria, with a president of considerable powers and with a corresponding reduction of powers of the Prime Minister.[39]

Dr. Azikiwe's speech was made, apparently, without any consultation with the Government, and touched off a great debate, which still rages, on the question of the powers of a president. The Prime Minister remained silent on the issue for a number of days before finally saying that he agreed

32 See the Election Manifesto of the NCNC prepared for the Eastern Region elections in November 1961, *Daily Times,* November 7, 1961. Cf., also, *Morning Post,* September 10, 1961; and *Daily Express,* September 5, 1961.

33 *Daily Express,* September 5, 1961.

34 *Daily Times,* July 29, 1960.

35 *H. R. Debates,* daily parts for November 23, 1961, p. 12.

36 *Daily Express,* September 5, 1961.

37 *West African Pilot,* February 2, 1962. This paper has been the most militant of the national dailies in criticism of the Anglo-American bloc. An example of its editorial policy is revealed in the following paragraph:

"Gradually, the Continent of Africa is being drawn into the conflict of the whiteman's power politics. To us, they are all imperialists without qualification. America, with her own record of atrocities against the Negroes second only to the barbarism of South African fascist gangsters, is a silent supporter of British and French imperialism in Africa." June 9, 1960.

38 See *infra,* pp. 108-12.

39 *West African Pilot,* November 17, 1961. For full text of the address, delivered at the University of Nigeria, Nsukka, see the *Daily Times,* November 18, 20, and 21, 1961.

that Nigeria should become a republic. He revealed his own ability at political in-fighting by also saying that if the president in the republic were given powers greater than those now held by the Governor-General, then he would insist that the president be elected by popular vote, rather than by Parliament or some other indirect method.[40] The effect of this statement was to inform Azikiwe that the NPC would still decide who was to be the Head of State—in this case, by an NPC dominated electorate.[41]

In the same address mentioning a republican government, the Governor-General further revealed his criticism of the Government in what many regard as an unusual act for the "Queen's Representative." Under the guise of merely pointing out some of the "political tensions in Nigeria," he left many people convinced that the tensions he recognized were in reality his own and those of other people who wanted the Government to be more dynamic. He said that there had been strong criticism of the "infrequent and spasmodic meetings of Parliament"; that "Government tactics in connection with official business in Parliament embarrass both the government supporters and the official opposition at the expense of the electorate"; and that there has been a "spate of criticism" alleging "ineptitude and inefficiency" in the Executive.

On foreign policy, he said that the Defense Pact had been criticized as a derogation of Nigerian sovereignty and as implying sympathy for NATO, but added:

I think that some of the criticisms levelled against it are untrue, but after the all-Nigeria Peoples' conference, a Nigerian Minister gave indication that the pact may be reconsidered in the light of the objections made by Nigerians to its existence.[42]

40 *Daily Express,* December 1, 1961.
41 Sir Ahmadu Bello, President of the NPC and Premier of the Northern Region, emphasized Sir Abubakar's threat by saying that if a president were to be elected "I will call on all Northerners, men and women, to cast their votes, and I am confident that all Northerners will be united in support of my appeal." *Daily Times,* December 2, 1961. Note: women have never had the franchise in the North.
   Chief Adewale Fashanu, President-General of the Zikist Movement, militant youth organization of the NCNC, responded to Sir Ahmadu with an angry statement revealing the frustration which political facts produce in that wing of the NCNC. He said:
   "There is nothing preventing Sir Ahmadu from becoming first President of Nigeria, but it is a dangerous thing for political parties to gamble with such a very sacred institution.
   "I must warn, right from now, that the office of the President of a Republican Nigeria is one on which the progressive elements of this country will not compromise.
   "Enough has been compromised for the unity of Nigeria.
   "A Republican Nigeria is certainly not going to be a place where those who really suffered to win freedom for Nigeria are cast aside. It is not going to be a place for people who want to boost their ego and exploit the masses in their own selfish interest. . . ."
   "Therefore those who are now toying and gambling with this office for political favours must be warned that they are threatening the unity and solidarity of Nigeria." *West African Pilot,* February 10, 1962.
42 *Daily Times,* November 18, 1961.

Continuing, he said that there is the allegation that "Nigeria is tied to the apron strings of Britain." He added that this had caused a "lot of stories" to be woven around Anglo-Nigeria diplomacy, "some of which must be regarded as figments of the imagination." Furthermore, he said that there had been criticism to the effect that "certain nations are given preferential treatment by Nigeria whilst others are not," and refused to add his own comments as to the justification of the charge.

Finally, in a thinly-veiled reference to persons who have traveled in Communist countries and to the ban on Communist literature, he said:

It is felt that to deny Nigerians employment because they lived or studied in countries whose ideology is capitalist or socialist or to prohibit Nigerians from importing literature in the absence of any positive act which can conceivably violate our laws, is not conducive to the practice of democracy.

Another evidence of the frustration in the ranks of the NCNC came when rumors spread to the effect that Balewa might invite the Action Group to join the NPC/NCNC coalition in order to form a National Government, representing all parties. Dr. M. I. Okpara, President of the NCNC, must have believed the rumor, for he was incensed that the NCNC had not been consulted about the move. He announced that as long as he was leader of the NCNC he would not allow a National Government in which the Action Group would participate.[43] The Prime Minister allayed his fears, however, by publicly announcing that the rumor was just that—a rumor.[44]

Although the pressures on the government from inside the coalition have been overwhelmingly from the radical wing of the NCNC, it must be noted that the sharpest criticism to date of Nigeria's foreign policy came from an NPC member, and the Government Chief Whip at that. Mallam Mohammed Muhtari, Sarkin Bai, from Dambatta, refused to support an appropriation bill for the Ministry of Foreign Affairs and Commonwealth Relations on November 20, 1961. While accusing the Foreign Minister, Jaja Wachuku (NCNC), of "nepotism and partiality" at home, his most serious charge was that "Nigeria at the United Nations is rapidly losing her prestige." The greatest loss of prestige came, he charged, when Mr. Wachuku supported a move that all African colonies attain independence by 1970. This move, he added, shocked other African states who wanted an end to African colonialism at least by 1965. As a result of the Foreign Minister's motion:

Nigeria in the eyes of all African independent States is regarded to-day as a stooge of Britain. There is a strong allegation that Britain and the United States have maneuvered and succeeded in getting the Minister to stick to this date of December 1970.[45]

Mallam Muhtari's virulent and caustic attack on Mr. Wachuku has some aspects about it which are difficult to explain. The chief cannon in his arsenal of attack was, apparently, the 1970 date for African independence. Yet he

43 *Ibid.*, February 12, 1962.
44 *West African Pilot*, February 22, 1962.
45 *H. R. Debates*, daily parts for November 20, 1961, p. 32.

admitted that Mr. Wachuku was right in his claim that he first proposed the 1970 date to the Parliament in the foreign policy debate in August 1961, and that the Parliament had approved the Government's foreign policy at that time without one single objection to the proposed date.[46] Mr. Muhtari merely asserted that "it is the view of the Parliament and of all the people of this country that this date is too far and that every dependent country of Africa should be liberated not later than December 1965. . . ."[47] There are, perhaps, some explanations for this odd behavior from a leader of the Government. In the debate on the appropriation for the Foreign Affairs Ministry, other members of Parliament indicated their belief that other African states regarded Nigeria as subservient to Anglo-American desires. Resentment of what many believed was a rebuff by the Belgrade Conference of Neutrals, and sensitivity to the thrusts of Ghana which questioned Nigeria's independence, were beginning to rankle many Government supporters.[48] Furthermore, there is evidence that some people, while respecting the great ability of the Foreign Minister, resent what they regard as his arrogance.[49] Finally, there is a belief in Nigeria that the attack on Mr. Wachuku by the Government Chief Whip was "part of an NPC move to get him fired and replaced by an NPC man. The NPC wants this ministry very badly."[50]

It would be wrong to imply that pressures from inside the coalition indicate the early collapse of the Government fusion. On the contrary, with each passing crisis, coupled with the fact that the NPC has now a small but absolute majority of members of Parliament, the coalition seems to be growing stronger. However, NCNC pressures, abetted by the other pressures discussed in this chapter, have revealed to the NPC the intensity of belief held by many articulate Nigerians, mostly from the South.

PRESSURE FROM "YOUTH" GROUPS[51]

Nigeria, like other developing countries, has a growing cadre of articulate young people, made up of secondary "school leavers," university students, professional people (lecturers and professors, lawyers, physicians, teachers), businessmen, and labor leaders. Although the word "youth" is attached to many of the organizations which appeal to these people, age is not an important factor in determining membership. Many of the Nigerian "youth" leaders are in their forties or fifties.

The concept of a youth movement has emotional roots dating back to the

---

46 *Ibid.*, p. 36.

47 *Ibid.*, p. 32.

48 *Ibid.*, pp. 27-45.

49 *Ibid.*, p. 31. See also the editorial "Jaja in the Box," *West African Pilot*, November 25, 1961.

50 Statement made to the author by a prominent Nigerian politician (NCNC) who refused to be identified here.

51 Unfortunately, no studies have been made of the various contemporary youth and student organizations in Nigeria. What appears here is a meager effort to assess the role which some youth groups play in their criticism of the Government.

1930's when the Nigerian Youth Movement was the important vehicle for militant nationalism.[52] After World War II, youth wings began to appear with the new political parties which were formed. The most famous, undoubtedly, was the Zikist Movement, formed in 1946 by the militant members of the NCNC. It has the distinction of having been banned by the British Administration in 1950. Among the successors of the Zikist Movement, and treated as its heir, was the Zikist National Vanguard. In fact, the old name, Zikist Movement, was restored in November 1961, after the Government lifted the ban of 1950.

The Zikist Movement is still the militant and radical wing of the NCNC. It gets excellent newspaper notoriety, partly due to the fact that it does speak for an important element of the NCNC, and partly due, also, to the fact that the *West African Pilot* identifies itself with the Movement, and its President, Chief Adewale Fashanu, is director of the Nigerian National Press which publishes the Nigerian *Morning Post*. It was apparently this Movement which first exposed the fact that the Government was contemplating signing the Defense Pact. It was also in the lead of the agitation for the dismissal of the Prime Minister's expatriate secretary and his replacement by a Nigerian. Among other things, it has advocated: the appointment of ambassadors to all independent African states; a population census of Nigeria; the creation of a separate Ministry of Foreign Affairs and Commonwealth Relations; a republican form of government; the buying out of the partners in the Nigerian Shipping Line and the Nigerian Airways; negotiations among African leaders "with the sole aim of reducing tendencies of friction between African States"; the sending of an ambassador to Russia; and the lifting of the ban on Communist literature.[53] It has also called for the creation of a stronger central government, the creation of more states, and a "more vigorous and neutral foreign policy."[54]

At this writing it appears that the youth groups of the other parties do not represent programs essentially different from the parent body; certainly they do not appear to have a separate identity, as the Zikist Movement has. On the other hand, it appears that youth from all of the parties participate in the various students' unions, which have formed themselves into the National Union of Nigerian Students (NUNS), which in turn is affiliated with the International Union of Students.[55] The students' unions have passed

52 James S. Coleman, *Nigeria: Background to Nationalism* (Berkeley: University of California Press, 1958), pp. 224-229.
53 As outlined in an article by Chief Fashanu, *Morning Post*, January 13, 1962. The Zikist Movement has also condemned the radio network in the North owned by the Sudan Interior Mission, and has protested against the American Mercury Rocket Tracking Station in Kano. *Morning Post*, February 1, 1962.
54 *Daily Times*, November 6, 1961. It is instructive to note that Dr. Okpara, President of the NCNC, has categorically rejected the idea of the proposed COR (Calabar, Ogoja, and Rivers Provinces) state being carved out of the Eastern Region. See *West African Pilot*, November 4, 1961.
55 *Morning Post*, December 12, 1961. Because the IUS includes university students from the Soviet bloc, the NUNS is sometimes charged with being pro-Communist. *Ibid.* See also the *Daily Times*, December 12, 1961.

resolutions opposing the passport restrictions on travel to the Soviet bloc; asking the Government to call for volunteers to fight in Algeria; supporting a republican form of government; and defending the Lumumba Government in the Congo.[56] Students were in the lead in the riots over the Defense Pact; in the riots against the United States and Great Britain over the death of Lumumba;[57] and in charging, as a result of the Michelmore Post Card incident, that the Peace Corps was "a group of intelligent international secret service spies."[58]

The organization, however, which has received the greatest amount of attention since independence is the Nigerian Youth Congress. It was founded in 1960 by the leaders of the Zikist National Vanguard to provide a forum for all "progressive youths," irrespective of political party affiliation, to discuss the activities of the various Nigerian governments and to suggest reforms. "The Congress," Chief Fashanu said, "was to be a reform movement, not a political party."[59] However, at the first annual meeting of the Congress, radicals who were more radical than the Zikist Movement got control of the machinery and elected Dr. Tunji Otegbeye, a Lagos medical practitioner, as president. Aided by Mr. Olatunde Lawrence, until recently Principal of the Lagos City College, Dr. Otegbeye has veered the Congress into a virulent, and sometimes violent, antagonist of the Government and of the leading political parties. In fact, Otegbeye, Lawrence, and six students from the University College, Ibadan, were all convicted of leading the Lumumba riots of February 15, 1961.[60]

The most consistent theme of the Nigerian Youth Congress (NYC) is that Western Powers—meaning the Anglo-American bloc—are attempting to strangle Nigerian independence. In its vocabulary, the neo-colonial powers are Great Britain, the United States, Portugal, France, Spain, and oddly enough West Germany. The agents of neo-colonialism are the Peace Corps, Moral Re-Armament, and the International Confederation of Free Trade Unions (the similarities with the resolutions of the All-Nigeria Peoples' Conference cannot be missed here).[61]

Dr. Otegbeye, as spokesman for the NYC, has called for the nationalization of all oil companies and of all foreign firms; has referred to the 1970 date for the independence of all African states as "notorious"; has condemned the permission granted by the Government which allowed British soldiers shore leave for a few hours while en route by ship from Duala to London; has charged that expatriate employees of the Passport Office were often

56 *Ibid.* See also the *Morning Post,* November 1, 1961.
57 See *supra,* p. 47.
58 As described by Dapo Falashe, President of the Students' Union, University College, Ibadan, *Daily Express,* October 16, 1961.
59 *Morning Post,* December 3, 1961.
60 *Daily Express,* October 28, 1961.
61 *Morning Post,* December 15, 1961; *Daily Express,* December 15, 1961. Cf., also: *Nigeria, the Way Forward: Policy and Programme of Nigerian Youth Congress Adopted at the First Annual Convention, September 2-3, 1961* (Lagos: Ribway Printers, n. d.) , *passim.*

spies; and condemned the Government for having "sold" the sovereignty of the country by allowing the famous National Bank Case to be appealed to the Privy Council.[62] He has condemned the present boundaries of Africa (but made no suggestions how they might be altered), and demanded that Nigeria annex Fernando Po, the Spanish-owned island off the shore of Eastern Nigeria.[63] He has also, of course, condemned the Defense Pact, supported a republican constitution, and called for a strong central government.[64]

The character of Dr. Otegbeye himself may explain much about the NYC. He has, according to his wife, refused to buy land on the grounds that it is "unsocialistic." He regards all other organizations and parties in Nigeria as corrupt, but insists that the NYC cannot become corrupt because it is "based on strict socialist morality." He sees Nigeria as filled with spies and saboteurs: those who threw bombs in Ghana in 1961 before the Queen's visit were "British agents trained in Nigeria"; Britain and the United States have been "using Nigeria as a base to sabotage Ghana and other independent African States"; and the aim of NATO is to "enslave Africa forever."[65]

Dr. Otegbeye and his Nigerian Youth Congress were obviously beginning to embarrass a number of people in Nigeria, and it is not surprising that some measures were taken against him. When he made the mistake of referring to the Congress as a political party, Chief Fashanu seized the opportunity to order all members of the Zikist Movement, on threat of expulsion, to withdraw from the NYC.[66] This produced a mass resignation of NCNC stalwarts from Dr. Otegbeye's organization.[67] The Action Group followed suit in February 1962.[68] Meanwhile, the Government press has "found it difficult to comprehend what is their [NYC] loyalty";[69] and even the *West African Pilot* (December 5, 1961) charged it with being nihilistic. Furthermore, there are indications that the Government is investigating the organization.[70]

What all of these developments mean for the Nigerian Youth Congress is not clear. Until Chief Fashanu's expulsion threat, most of its membership, according to the *West African Pilot,* came from the NCNC and the Zikist Movement.[71] The NYC had never revealed its membership, either

62 *Morning Post,* December 15, 1961; *Daily Times,* December 4, 1961; *Daily Express,* October 6, 1961, and November 11, 1961; and *Sunday Express,* December 3, 1961.
63 *Daily Times,* December 14, 1961; *Daily Express,* December 3, 1961.
64 *Morning Post,* November 13, 1961, and December 15, 1961.
65 *Sunday Express,* December 3, 1961; *Daily Times,* December 5, 1961; *Morning Post,* November 13 and 28, 1961. Although Dr. Otegbeye has been accused of being a Communist, he denies this, and also denies that the NYC has ever received funds from Communist sources. *Morning Post,* December 15, 1961. See also: *West African Pilot,* February 17, 1962; and *Sunday Express,* December 3, 1961.
66 *Sunday Post,* December 3, 1961.
67 *West African Pilot,* December 7, 1961.
68 *Daily Express,* February 21, 1962.
69 *Morning Post,* November 28, 1961.
70 *H. R. Debates,* daily parts for November 27, 1961, p. 28.
71 *West African Pilot,* December 5, 1961.

before or after the mass resignations, so there are no indications of its size. At this writing, it is being alleged that its main support now comes from the Dynamic Party (a small militant party which urges a dictatorship for Nigeria)[72] and the Nigerian Trade Union Congress (NTUC—the radical, probably pro-Soviet, wing of the labor movement).[73] It may take months to reveal the full effects of the recent developments on Dr. Otegbeye's NYC.

In conclusion, it must be pointed out that the youth organizations, like others discussed above, seem to be applying pressures on the Government for a more dynamic and radical foreign policy, one which relies less on ties with the Anglo-American bloc, and either becomes strictly neutral or relies more on ties with the Soviet bloc. The reasons for the youth and student activities are undoubtedly varied and numerous, but Dr. Kalu Ezera seems to have used prescience to write the following *before* independence:

> There is, at the moment, a tremendous wave of frustration and disillusionment among the student groups at home and abroad as well as among the intelligentsia and the youths of the country in general. This frustration derives from a negative reaction to what these people rightly or wrongly consider to be a 'policy of drift' occasioned by the indecisive and confused political picture of the country where the parties shout hoarsely at each other with none in the ascendancy, and where corruption, like cankerworm, has eaten deep into the body politic. This type of frustration, unless arrested, would not augur well for the future of the country as it may bring in its train a tendency to revolution. Yet, in the absence of a single effective country-wide political party capturing power at the centre, it is difficult to see how the school of thought that advocates a sort of 'guided democracy' for the country could be prevented from growing faster after independence.[74]

Other opinions, less sympathetic, dismiss the youth movements as mere grumblers. An editor of the Government newspaper (*Sunday Post*, February 25, 1962) described the youth as "protestants . . . whose stock in trade consists not in putting forward alternative schemes to those of the governments but in denouncing what they regard as objectionable in existing ones. They are always protesting, seldom proposing." A similar view, oddly enough, was expressed by Dr. S. A. Aluko (himself only thirty-one at the time), Lecturer in Economics at the University of Ife and active participant in the All-Nigeria Peoples' Conference. Referring to "Nigeria's angry young men," he said (*Daily Times*, August 15, 1960): "The problems of this country are complex and they require a new antidote more realistic than making speeches at a parley of youths, many of whom are angry because

---

72 *Daily Times*, March 10, 1962. Dr. Chike Obi, leader of the Dynamic Party, has denied that there was any "official relation" between his party and the NYC. *Daily Express*, March 13, 1962.

73 *Sunday Express*, December 17, 1961; *Daily Times*, March 10, 1962. See also an advertisement in the *Morning Post*, December 14, 1961, announcing a mass meeting featuring NYC and NTUC speakers. Also the speakers at the mass rally which led to the Lumumba riots were Dr. Otegbeye and Mr. Imoudu (NTUC). *Daily Times*, February 17, 1961.

74 Kalu Ezera, *Constitutional Development in Nigeria* (Cambridge: the University Press, 1960), p. 260.

they are not yet permitted to enter into the club of those who share the good things of Nigeria."

It seems to this writer that those who dismiss the youth groups miss the intensity with which they hold their convictions. Certainly one must concede that their frustrations with the Government do not differ greatly from that of other articulate critics.

PRESSURE FROM THE TRADE UNIONS

As with the youth groups, much work remains to be done on the labor union movement in Nigeria. At the time of this writing, however, it can be stated that the labor movement appears to be hopelessly split, the ostensible reason being the question of international affiliation. Since the question obviously may affect foreign policy, some attention must be given to this subject.

The move which divided the labor movement occurred in early 1960 when the Trade Union Congress affiliated itself with the International Confederation of Free Trade Unions (ICFTU). A group within the union charged that there had been no agreement for such a move and immediately severed ties with the TUC. As a result, two national unions were formed—the Trade Union Congress of Nigeria (TUCN—affiliated with the ICFTU), and the Nigerian Trade Union Congress (NTUC—ostensibly unaffiliated, but aided by the World Federation of Trade Unions, WFTU).[75] The leaders of the TUCN are Alhaji H. P. Adebola, President-General and Mr. L. L. Borha, General Secretary; and of the NTUC, Mr. M. A. Imoudu, President and Mr. Ibrahim Nock, General Secretary; and in Nigeria the rival unions are often identified by the names of their leaders, rather than by the similar and therefore confusing names of the unions.

The TUCN sent Mr. Borha to the "Monrovia-minded" Pan-African Trade Union Conference in Dakar in January, 1962. There he called on the delegates not to be crippled by slogans of neutrality and unity. He said it was "folly to pretend Africans and Africa are outside the world, even if a slogan says this is so." He scorned those who claimed to be neutral by not openly affiliating with one of the international unions as follows:

Men who call themselves neutralists and condemn only one side are not neutralists. They are tools in the service of an ideological machine which feeds them not bread and butter, not social justice but empty slogans. . . . Let's acknowledge simple truth, there are no neutral men when the choice is between liberty and servitude.[76]

In elaborating on the stand taken by Borha, the TUCN has charged that the WFTU has been engaged in a plot to destroy "free" trade unions in

75 Increase Coker, "My Plan for a New United Labour Front," *Sunday Post*, March 11, 1962.
76 *Sunday Express*, January 14, 1962. One purpose of the Dakar conference was to explore ways of reconciling their differences with the Casablanca-backed All-African Trade Union Federation.

Africa "to give the communists an opportunity of taking over complete control of the trade union movement." In support of this claim, the TUCN has produced the photostat of an alleged letter on WFTU stationery, dated July 10, 1961, addressed to Charles Heyman, Director of African Affairs and the International Department of the Ghana Trade Union Congress, and signed by Ibrahim Zakaria, International Affairs Director of the WFTU, Prague.

The letter, if authentic, is significant. In it, Zakaria reminds Heyman that the main financial support for the All-African Trade Union Federation (AATUF) comes from the WFTU, but that such support may cease unless the AATUF can "guarantee that disaffiliation from the I.C.F.T.U. would be made obligatory for all affiliates of the A.A.T.U.F." Zakaria said that in order to "get the I.C.F.T.U. out of Africa" the WFTU might ask "our friends in Kamerun and Brazzaville to give up ties with us," although the "Chinese were reluctant to agree" with this move. He added that the Chinese "have been pushing Imoudu to affiliate with WFTU," but "that will have to change now." He reminded Heyman that he had given him WFTU funds to aid the NTUC through its former secretary, S.U. Bassey, but that he was not satisfied with the "progress so far."[77]

The TUCN, of course, charged that the letter gave final proof that the NTUC is "acting on orders from its bosses in the WFTU and in the Ghana TUC."[78] It also charges that the real issue which keeps the two national unions from effecting a merger is not the question of international affiliation; that could be resolved. The stumbling block, it maintains, has been the refusal of the NTUC to accept a clause in the proposed constitution for the merged unions to the effect that the central labor organization objects, as a basic principle, to the adoption of Communist ideologies.[79]

On the other hand, Mr. Imoudu of the rival NTUC, has argued that a central labor union for Nigeria must, like the nation, be neutral in world affairs. He charges that the rival TUCN has fallen under the sway of "working class enemies" from "far away Europe."[80] He has brought forth his own photostat of a letter allegedly written by a Mr. Irving Brown of the AFL-CIO to a Mr. George McCray of the United States embassy in Lagos, which he claims

clearly exposed the great harm already being done here in Nigeria by the battery of American spies in the guise of labour leaders in their efforts to sabotage the move of a most desired unity among [Nigerian] workers.[81]

As a result of the alleged letter, the NTUC officials claim to have written

77 Taken from the full text of the photostat as printed in the *Morning Post*, March 1, 1962.
78 *Ibid.*
79 *Sunday Times*, February 18, 1962.
80 *West African Pilot*, February 15, 1962.
81 *Daily Times*, January 31, 1962. Officials of the United States embassy claim, and a check of the Diplomatic List confirms, that there is no George McCray attached to the embassy. Nevertheless, Mr. Imoudu has asked the Nigerian Government to expel Mr. McCray and to declare Mr. Brown a prohibited immigrant. *Ibid.*

a letter to President Kennedy asking him "to put an immediate stop to the various American interventions in our affairs," and Mr. Nock later charged that the "State Department-run AFL-CIO" was trying to dictate the merger terms for Nigerian unions.[82]

NTUC's own international ties are somewhat inconsistent with its charges. It accuses the rival TUCN of receiving aid from the ICFTU, but that has never been kept a secret by either the TUCN or ICFTU.[83] On the other hand, Mr. Imoudu has denied receiving any aid or support from abroad,[84] although Mr. Wahab Goodluck, Assistant Secretary General of the NTUC in charge of external affairs, has openly declared just the opposite. Speaking at an annual labor conference at Jos in 1961, Mr. Goodluck said his union had received funds from Communist China, Ghana, and East Germany; had accepted scholarships for studies in Communist countries; and had been promised aid by the "Russian Labour Movement" which had not yet arrived. He also said his union encouraged Nigerians to go to Ghana and Guinea to get "identity cards" which would allow them to travel to Communist countries without a Nigerian passport. Finally, he said the NTUC had "delayed" affiliating with the WFTU in "the genuine interest of the unity of the Nigerian workers."[85]

The picture drawn here of the Nigerian labor movement is by no means as clear as it may appear. The Government, for example, selected Mr. Borha of the pro-ICFTU to attend the International Labor Organization Conference in 1961, which move, of course, was bitterly attacked by Mr. Imoudu.[86] On the other hand, a semi-Government conciliation body seems to have sided with Imoudu. The body was appointed, as a result of the All-Nigeria Peoples' Conference, to attempt to bring the rival unions together, and the Speaker of the House of Representatives, Mallam Ibrahim Jalo Waziri, consented to be its chairman. Yet, in what appears to be an unneutral statement for an impartial conciliator, Waziri has stated that the basis of merger must be one which prohibits international affiliation.[87]

Furthermore, the Government newspaper has taken the position that the source of the division between the rival unions is due entirely to the selfishness of the respective leaders. It says the Government has shown restraint

82 *West African Pilot,* February 12, 1962.
83 *West African Pilot,* January 14, 1962; *Sunday Post,* March 11, 1962.
84 *Sunday Times,* June 18, 1961; *Daily Express,* March 16, 1962.
85 *Sunday Times,* October 22, 1962.
   It may be significant to note that Mr. Imoudu, who has twice visited Communist countries, claims that he is a Marxian Socialist. When asked if he had also been invited to visit the United States, or had ever been offered aid by that country, he replied: "The very last thing America would do is to offer us aid or invite NTUC leaders to visit the United States. . . . America would wish to drag my Congress into its cold war ambitions and commitments, but as we are committed to working strenuously for world peace, there is fundamental difference of perspectives and as such the idea of the NTUC negotiating aid from America is out of the question." *Sunday Times,* June 18, 1961.
86 *Daily Express,* March 1, 1962.
87 *Sunday Express,* March 18, 1962.

in the matter because it is "resolved to make democracy work." It added, however, that for the Government "to allow this situation to continue is to abdicate its powers to garrulous and irresponsible trade union leadership." In a subsequent editorial, it said that both unions receive money from abroad, one (TUCN) openly, the other (NTUC) "by an underground route," and it called on workers to rise up and provide a remedy.[88]

Other newspapers have taken a similar position. The *West African Pilot*, although it has run a number of feature articles favoring the Imoudu faction (e.g., the issues of February 12, 15, and 19, 1962), has nevertheless said the dispute is a personal one among the union leaders and has called on the leaders to resign so that "a healthy, united trade union" could develop.[89] The *Daily Express* (February 1, 1962) has said that the merged union should join neither of the international unions. The *Daily Times* (March 10, 1962) says the "leaders, plagued with the lust for power, are to blame. The forces of confusion from outside backed by foreign money and international double-dealing have played their part." It suggests a plebiscite among workers to see which side has the greater support, the winner then being given government recognition. The Government should also insist, it adds, that no international affiliation should occur until the merged union is able to manage its own affairs.

The fascinating and inexplicable aspect of the whole matter is that neither the Government nor the press seems willing to discuss what the union leaders themselves regard as the issue—communism versus democracy. Disaffiliation with all international unions is hardly a solution when one side, while claiming non-affiliation, has been surreptitiously aided by an international union. In view of this fact, now apparently admitted by all, a law forbidding international affiliation, as suggested by many people, seems almost naive. Furthermore, apart from the unions of world wide scope (ICFTU and WFTU), African unionism is already divided between the "Monrovia-minded" Pan-African Trade Union Conference and the "Casablanca-minded" All-African Trade Union Federation. Yet no awareness of this fact seems to have been revealed so far in the public discussions. Truly, the pressures on the Government produced by the labor unions present a remarkably unclear picture at this writing.[90]

PRESSURES OF FEDERALISM

Theoretically, the Regions of Nigeria, as in any federation, have no voice

88 *Morning Post*, February 27, March 4, 1962.
89 February 28, 1962.
90 The picture is even hazier when it is noted that there are many local unions in Nigeria which are independent of both the TUCN and the NTUC, the largest being the Nigerian Union of Teachers, the Nigerian Civil Service Union, and the Plantation Workers Union of both the East and the West. Furthermore, out of a labor force of 700,000, only 140,000 workers belong to unions, and these are represented in 400 different unions. The exact number of these unions affiliated with either the TUCN or the NTUC is not known. See Increase Coker, "My Plan for a New United Labour Front," *Sunday Post*, March 11, 1962.

in foreign relations. The Constitution provides that external affairs is an exclusive domain of the Federal Government.[91] It was agreed at the Resumed Constitutional Conference in 1958 that:

there should be no Regional representative after independence in countries other than the United Kingdom, and that the title of a Regional representative in the United Kingdom should be changed from the present title of "Commissioner" to a title such as "Agent-General," in order to distinguish him from the High Commissioner of the Federation who would be appointed on independence.[92]

Federalism, however, by its very nature, is a system of strains and pressures, of compromise and balance. It is, as one eminent authority has pointed out, "the process by which adjustment is made between those forces making for disunity and those making for unity."[93] In foreign policy formation some of the pressures making for disunity stem from the Regions. There is, in fact, the feeling that "Nigeria speaks with too many voices," as Regional Premiers travel abroad seeking economic and cultural ties favorable to their Regions. It is inevitable that they "express their views about foreign and African affairs, views which do not always coincide either with the Federal Government's views or with each other."[94] This can be illustrated from a number of cases.

Premier Okpara of the Eastern Region wired President Nkrumah congratulations (on Ghana's becoming a republic) "on behalf of the Government and eight million people of Eastern Nigeria." He praised "Ghana's constitutional provision to surrender sovereignty to a United States of Africa" as a "bold and highly commendable step in the right direction and [which] is welcome by all who genuinely believe in the desirability of African unity." He added that he hoped "other African countries will soon follow this example."[95]

Later, however, Dr. Okpara became enraged at Nkrumah for "the dark forces of subversion and insult directed from Ghana through the so-called Dynamic Party against the citizens and most revered leaders of this blessed country."[96] He was referring specifically to charges that Ghana had contributed funds to the Dynamic Party in the latter's efforts to defeat the NCNC in the East, and to Nkrumah's criticism of Dr. Azikiwe's speech

91 The Exclusive Legislative List, Section 15.
92 *Report by the Resumed Nigeria Constitutional Conference, held in London in September and October, 1958* (Lagos: Federal Government Printer, 1958), p. 16.
93 Taylor Cole, "Emergent Federalism in Nigeria," *Constitutional Problems of Federalism in Nigeria,* edited by Lionel Brett (Lagos: Times Press, 1961), p. 10.
94 David Williams (editor of *West Africa*) in a contributed article to the *Daily Times,* October 4, 1961.
95 *Daily Times,* July 2, 1960.
    Another voice in Nigeria, though not a Regional one, was Chief Awolowo's congratulations to Nkrumah on behalf of the Action Group on the occasion of the fifth anniversary of Ghana's independence. He, too, commended Nkrumah's efforts toward African unity. *Daily Express,* March 8, 1962.
96 *Sunday Post,* February 18, 1962.

at the Lagos Conference of African States in January 1962.[97] It was at this time, however, that the Federal Government, through the Governor-General (Azikiwe), was sending Nkrumah congratulations on the fifth anniversary of Ghana's independence and commending him for his "fair share" of contributions "to the solution of world problems and the unity of Africa."[98]

Both of the Southern Regions have gone all-out to establish ties with Israel. Both Premiers Okpara and Akintola have visited Israel, and both of their Governments have maintained a policy of strict neutrality in the Arab-Israeli disputes.[99] This, of course, is in keeping with the Federal Government's policy which has been to establish close economic and cultural ties with Israel, and which succeeded in winning a loan from that country. When the loan was announced, the Northern Regional Government denounced the deal, saying that "it dissociates itself from the whole transaction and does not wish to accept any part of any such loan or export credit. The Northern Regional Government considers that acceptance of such a loan or export credit could be interpreted as involvement in the Middle Eastern controversies."[100] In fact, the Premier, Sir Ahmadu Bello, after declaring that the Northern Region would never ask Israel for help, added the rather ominous, and unclear, threat: "when we want help, we know where to go for it."[101]

The federal Prime Minister, obviously embarrassed—as a Moslem, as a Northerner, and as a deputy in the NPC to Sir Ahmadu—nevertheless reacted as the head of the federation. He said the introduction of religion into politics "will mean the end of happiness in Nigeria." He then asserted positively that the Federal Government would accept assistance from any country; would not involve itself in the Arab-Israeli dispute; would not force any Region to accept particular loans; but would not permit the objection of a Region to interfere with the Federal Government's constitutional authority to borrow money from abroad.[102]

The next, and perhaps most serious interference by a Regional Govern-

97 See *West African Pilot*, February 17, 1962; and *infra*, p. 95.

98 *Morning Post*, March 6, 1962.

99 See, for example, *Nigerian Outlook*, January 6, 1962; *Sunday Express*, December 24, 1961; and *Daily Express*, October 16, 1961. Cf., also: Arnold Rivkin, "Israel and the Afro-Asian World," *Foreign Affairs*, April 1959.

100 *Daily Times*, June 22, 1960.

101 *Ibid.*, June 15, 1961. The Northern Regional Government's newspaper spelled the matter out in the following antagonistic terms:

"The fact that Northern Nigeria will not receive aid from the Israeli Government in any shape or form is known to be a big headache to the Government of Israel.

"After all, the North Regional Government is entitled to choose its friends.

"The Israeli Government should know that it is an open secret that its Government is being run from the U.S.A. by the wealthy Jews there." *Daily Mail*, June 9, 1961.

It certainly is a novel argument, and one which portends trouble for a federal structure, for one of the units to assert the right to "choose its friends" independent of the central government's policy.

102 *Daily Times*, June 15, 1961.

ment in foreign affairs, came in the summer of 1961. Again the Premier of the Northern Region (who refused to accept a loan from Israel as an "involvement in Middle East controversies") was involved. In this case the Premier made a month-long tour of the Middle East (excluding Israel) and Pakistan. On arrival at the Karachi airport, he gave a press interview in which, to quote a non-Nigerian newspaper (*Times of India,* June 25, 1961), he said he was exploring "the possibility of promoting a pan-Islamic commonwealth or confederation." The southern Nigerian press immediately picked this up as a Regional incursion into the Constitutional prerogatives of the Federal Government and the Prime Minister.[103]

The seriousness of the alleged statement, and its implications for the Prime Minister, was emphasized in an editorial in the *West African Pilot* on June 27, 1961. The Sarduana, it said,

has taken the initiative to make statements on foreign policy, to the astonishment of all. He has invited the heads of moslem [sic] countries—Saudi Arabia, Sudan, and now Pakistan—to visit Nigeria. In doing so, the Sarduana has not only overreached himself but has also usurped the office of the Prime Minister, who is deputy head of the NPC.

. . . Sir Abubakar must now call him to order. If he does not, then, he would be adding strength to the lingering rumour that the Government of Lagos has its main artery in Kaduna—which we know is not true.

An editorial in the *Daily Express* (June 29, 1961) charged that the Sarduana had even said that his statement had "the full blessing" of Sir Abubakar, while still another (*Daily Times,* June 28, 1961) pointed out that the Northern Premier, as head of the NPC "which dominates the Government" of the federation, would have to be taken seriously.

The Federal Government, and especially the Prime Minister, was obviously embarrassed. Sir Abubakar said the Sarduana had discussed the tour with him fully before he left, and denied that the Northern Premier had ever spoken of a Moslem confederation, nor that he had a right to speak on such a subject.[104] The Northern Regional Government also issued an immediate denial of the press report saying that the Premier was merely

---

103 *Daily Express,* June 29, 1961 ("We think the Prime Minister owes the country an explanation."); *West African Pilot,* June 27, 1961 ("The South will never accept any suggestion that Nigeria is a moslem [sic] state."); and *Daily Times,* June 28, 1961 ("No, Sir Ahmadu.").

The depth of animosity and fear in the South against Nigerian ties with Moslem countries can be seen in statements from two parliamentarians. Mr. S. A. Ogedengbe (AG) asked the Government to appoint intelligent men as ambassadors, particularly, he implied, to Moslem countries. "If you are going to Mecca," he added, "on a Muslim pilgrimage it is all right [to send inferior men]. You can just get anybody, any fool can go there as long as he is literate." *H. R. Debates,* November session 1960, p. 166.

Dr. Kalu Ezera (NCNC) in a newspaper article on "Nigeria Middle East Politics," was less vitriolic but nevertheless blunt. Because of the NPC and the Northern Region, he said, "the notion that the enemy of our brother is also our own enemy must be drastically modified." *Daily Times,* July 29, 1960.

104 *The Truth* (a Nigerian Moslem newspaper), July 21, 1961.

concerned with "a unity of mind on cultural and spiritual matters" among Moslems.[105]

The serious nature of the accusations prompted the Northern Regional Government to issue a full report in its *News Letter* for July 1961. It denied that the Premier had ever made the alleged statement, and pointed out that when the Iranian Premier had suggested diplomatic relations with Nigeria, Sir Ahmadu said he "would bring this to the notice of the Prime Minister on my return to Nigeria." The *News Letter* went on to say that the Premier's trip had succeeded in its purpose, which it implied was to seek foreign aid. "The people," it said, "would soon see the practical demonstration of this in the money spent on development programmes." Finally, the *News Letter* asserted that:

The Prime Minister said that the Northern Premier had every right to try to bring about understanding between Muslims all over the world and that all Governments of Nigeria had the right to invite whom they liked to visit Nigeria, provided they inform the Federal Government.

Other incursions of Regional Governments in to the field of foreign affairs have also occurred, although the distinction between a Premier *qua* Premier, and the Premier *qua* private individual or party leader, is often confused at best. For example, Sir Ahmadu has asserted that he has lost confidence in the United Nations,[106] which has prompted the Prime Minister, who continues to call for full support of that international body, to note that everyone is entitled to his own opinion even when it is not shared by the Government.[107] Again, Sir Ahmadu condemned the United States for planning a resumption of atomic-bomb tests, while the Prime Minister has asserted that, in view of Soviet testing, "it would have been unwise of the American people to have decided otherwise."[108] On the other hand, to prove that Regions do not always have to make for disunity, each of the Regional Governments have made statements supporting the Federal Government's guarantees of protection of foreign investments in their respective Regions.[109]

The Eastern Regional Government, through the Eastern Nigeria Development Corporation has produced a rather anomalous situation by its partnership with some Israeli companies. This move prompted Jordan to ban all trade with the ENDC, although not, apparently, with any other Government of Nigeria, two of which also trade with Israel.[110]

Finally, the Western Region has come into criticism on at least three

105 *Daily Express,* June 29, 1961.
106 *Morning Post,* October 30, 1961.
107 *Africa,* November 1961, p. 40.
108 *Morning Post,* October 21, 1961, and March 6, 1962.
109 See, for example, *Daily Express,* October 28, November 9, 1961; and February 21, March 5 and March 15, 1962; *Daily Times,* December 14, 1961; February 26 and March 3, 1962; and *Morning Post,* March 5, 1962.
110 See *Daily Times,* January 6, 1962; and *West African Pilot,* January 5, 1962 (which editorialized that the ban was "something to laugh about") .

occasions for engaging in matters affecting foreign policy. The most serious charge was that it attempted to establish a Western Nigeria Information and Industrial Development Office in New York on August 9, 1961, without the approval of the Federal Government.[111] The news item to this effect prompted the Prime Minister to write a stern letter to Premier Akintola, pointing out the constitutional impropriety of such a thing. Said the Prime Minister:

> With only this information available at the time of writing, one naturally turns to the Constitution of Western Nigeria in order to discover, whether there is any provision under which your Government can open extra-territorial agency or organ for the avowed purpose of promoting any such object as you envisage.
>
> I consider it not open to argument that no agency other than the present Agent-General in the United Kingdom can constitutionally be established elsewhere by the Western Nigeria or indeed by any Regional Government. This seems to me to be the combined effect of Section 142 of the Federal Constitution and of Section 65 of the Western Nigeria Constitution. Besides, I need not remind you that ALL external affairs of the Federation or any part of it are the exclusive prerogative of the Federal Government.[112]

Premier Akintola answered that he too was surprised to read the news story, and that he could assure the Prime Minister it was false, for his Government had "never taken a decision to open such an office." He reiterated his own respect for the Constitution and added that: "It is by adhering strictly to its provisions that the unity of the Federation and the respect of the outside world for it can be assured."[113]

The two other occasions of criticism for the Western Region came from federal ministers. The Minister of Economic Development (Mallam Shehu Shagari) charged the West with seeking aid from France while "we were protesting about the French Atomic Bomb,"[114] and the Minister of Finance (Chief Festus Okotie-Eboh) charged the West with "unnecessary Ministerial tours abroad at the taxpayer's expense. They should know that this can only damage Nigeria's reputation in the eyes of the world."[115] Nothing further, however, has come of these charges.[116]

111 Reported in the *Daily Express,* August 11, 1961; the *West African Pilot,* August 11, 1961; and the *Western News,* August 16, 1961.
112 *Western News,* August 30, 1961.
113 *Ibid.*
114 *H. R. Debates,* March-May session 1960, p. 227.
115 *H. R. Debates,* August session 1960, p. 30.
   It might be pointed out, however, that the Action Group weekly probably reflects Regional frustrations when it laments that "in our Federation the Regions are left to fend for themselves, to go abroad to seek loans and foreign investments when in fact they should look up only to the Federal Government." *The Service,* November 11, 1961.
116 Although it might be noted that the Government newspaper has accused the Western Regional Government of pretending "to the outside world that their Government is the Federal Government." This charge stemmed from the fact that the Regional Government had invited Jomo Kenyatta to visit Nigeria. *Morning Post,* October 6, 1961.

CONCLUSIONS

From the beginning of independence, Nigeria has faced a bewildering array of internal pressures attempting to establish, alter, or repudiate the foreign policy of the country. The articulate challenges against the Government were by no means limited to Parliament. Non-governmental groups such as political parties, labor unions, university student unions, youth groups, newspapers, and others joined the radical politicians in condemning Government actions and policies. Although frequently hostile to each other, they often showed an unusual agreement on what was wrong with the country's foreign policy. Most of the groups, from inside as well as outside of the Government, called for a more positive non-alignment by lessening ties with the Anglo-American bloc and increasing them with the Soviet bloc. They pressed for more positive efforts toward some form of Pan-African union, and sought closer identification with the Casablanca bloc and less with the former French colonies. They demanded that the Government be more "dynamic" in condemning European colonialism in Africa; in pressing for early independence of all African colonies; in more vigorous condemnations of the South African government and apartheid; in supporting the dissolution of the Central African Federation; in supporting the Algerian rebels; and in strong condemnation of the Congolese Kasavubu, Mobutu, and Tshombe but not of Lumumba or Gizenga. Finally, they called for nationalization, particularly of foreign firms, even if it meant a reduction of foreign aid.

Overwhelmingly, therefore, the articulate pressures against the Government have been of a "leftist" tendency, to use an admittedly vague and indefinite term. The critics have shown an antipathy towards the Anglo-American bloc and little fear of the Soviet bloc; strong fear of Anglo-American colonialism but no recognition of Soviet colonialism; strong distaste for anything labeled capitalism and equally strong support for anything labeled socialism. They are obviously motivated by the belief that only a radical position on these and other matters would spell progress and demonstrate not only the true independence but the rightful power of Nigeria. It is clear that the pressures are for a *new* society, with an internally created image of itself in the world; with an exaggerated consciousness of race or Africanism; with a rejection of old tribal feudalistic values and the creation of a new economic society based on social consciousness or welfare rather than on capitalistic laissez faire; in short, a modern society of highly literate, mobile people enjoying all the fruits of modern science. The image of a modern Nigerian nation, of course, frequently clashes with the image of a modern Pan-African, or West African, nation, but both of these values nevertheless exist side by side. The pressures which the articulate liberals place on Government are largely in the form of criticizing the speed with which the Government is traveling toward these goals, and the fact that most or all of the old ties with colonialism (Britain) and neo-colonialism (Britain's ally, the United States) have not been broken.

It must be emphasized, however, that most of the articulate protest has been negative—the critics have been quite clear about what they oppose. On the other hand, they have not been able to give specific examples of what they favor. It is probably this factor which seemingly unites the disparate groups, but there is little doubt that the apparent unity would disappear if each stated its position in specific terms. In fact, the inability of the groups to unite demonstrates the extent of differences, tribal as well as philosophical, and reveals the pluralistic nature of Nigerian society. But pluralism still rests lightly in Nigeria as is revealed by constant pleas for parties to merge and form a National Government; for rival labor unions to unite into one single body; and for youth, student, and intellectual groups to coalesce into one national organization.[117]

The articulate pressures against the Government exist mainly in Southern Nigeria, Northerners maintaining an almost contemptuous silence on many of the issues. It is here that one form of federal strain enters the picture. Most of the articulate critics of Government must work through one of the Southern parties (as NEPU must work through the NCNC and the Bornu Youth Movement worked through the Action Group until that party was torn asunder in 1962) and/or such social groups as the Nigerian Youth Congress. Yet it is the conservative North, with its almost universally-supported NPC, which controls the Federal Government and in fact now has an absolute majority in the Parliament. The Government, therefore, faces no threat to its control from the articulate pressures as long as the present federal structure is maintained. On the other hand, there is no doubt that the federation itself does face the threat of dissolution from such pressures; that is, if the articulate Southern opposition groups are constantly frustrated in their demands, the temptation to win their way by non-democratic means will undoubtedly increase. It would probably be impossible, therefore, for the Government to ignore the pressures (and indeed it has not done so). It must be concluded, therefore, that one form of federal strain has resulted from the fact that the articulate radicals are overwhelmingly centered in the south, which can only pressure but cannot unseat the Government under existing institutions. These strains have existed from the creation of the federal structure; in fact, they were instrumental in creating that structure.

The other form of federal strain stems from the fact that Regional Governments are each controlled by a political party antagonistic to those which control the other Regions. It is this fact which explains the Prime Minister's stern rebuke of Premier Akintola for his alleged incursion into external affairs; and the same Prime Minister's efforts to explain away the alleged, and more serious, incursions of his party mentor, Premier Bello, into the same field. These "official" strains have come to the fore mainly since independence, and the seriousness of them will have to wait on a longer period of history to be evaluated.

117 The unreality, in the Nigerian context, of the opposition to pluralism was revealed by no less a man than Chief Dennis Osadebay, President of the Senate, who wrote an article entitled "Next? Nigeria Needs a One Party System." *Daily Times*, November 18, 1960.

V. Foreign Policy as Implemented since Independence

Pronouncement and implementation of foreign policy are intertwined. Pronouncement is the articulated generalizations of foreign policy in which government decision-makers declare national principles and goals in relation to events and forces outside of the state. As such, pronouncement attempts to say how the leaders will act when faced with future hypothetical events, and what action they will initiate to establish desired goals. Implementation of foreign policy is any concrete action taken as a result of a real or alleged situation outside of the state. As such, implementation may or may not conform to pronouncement. If it does not conform then implementation merely reveals that pronouncement did not mean what it appeared to mean. In any case, foreign policy is composed of both pronouncement and implementation.

On and shortly after independence, Nigerian decision-makers had reached agreement on a number of pronouncements. Furthermore, implementation of policy in certain areas (for example, Commonwealth and United Nations membership, and entry into the Defense Pact) came as no surprise to anyone. Pronouncement, however, except when related to a single, simple issue or event, is almost always abstract and as such can be given content only by implementation in time. Since implementation involves the power, real or imagined, of a state, it soon demonstrates the limits of its actions—which principles it will spend money, time, and arms on, and which it prefers to treat as vague goals. Nigeria, beginning independence with pronouncement, then faced the problem of implementation, which expanded and modified the pronouncement. Both were to be expected, of course. Expansion would almost certainly have had to come about as Nigerian leaders began more and more to interest themselves in world events—to initiate a position here, react to a crisis there, ignore a development elsewhere. Modifications of pronouncements, also, were to be expected, due in part to an increased awareness of issues, in part to following-up logically moves already made, and in part to vociferous internal pressures which the Government could not ignore. The following discussion, therefore, is devoted to implementation, and is treated topically rather than chronologically.

PAN-AFRICANISM

It would be impossible to overstress the emotional approbation in articulate Nigerian opinion for the terms "Pan-Africanism" and "African unity" today. The newspapers constantly feature articles on the subject; almost every prominent speaker has something to say on the matter; almost every public conference that could even remotely concern itself with the idea does so; the issue is raised almost daily in the deliberations of the Parliament; politicians, youth leaders, labor leaders, and students vie with each other, each claiming to "really" believe in some form of Pan-Africanism while the others are dragging their feet. One easily gets the impression in Nigeria that the idea of Pan-Africanism, as a positive virtue, originated in the country, and that the only thing which keeps it from materializing in fact are the evil machinations of false leaders, or the "divide and rule" policies of "imperialists," or the blindness of the leaders of other African states. Not a voice has been raised to condemn the idea as such. Pan-Africanism, like virtue, is lauded everywhere.

It is not difficult to understand the nature of the appeal for African unity. As an eminent "front bencher" of the NPC, Mallam Mohammed Muhtari, put it: "Whether we like it or not 'blackism' is our answer. We shall have to stand or fall together."[1] Coupled with the racial identity of Tropical Africans is the common history of almost all Africans as subjects of European colonialism. Before independence, all Africans seemed to speak with a common voice. The common political enemy was colonialism; the common internal enemies were undeveloped economies and the absence of national integration; the common psychological enemy was the debasement caused by the above; and the common goal was absolute independence. How natural that after independence many Africans, including Nigerians, should continue to think in terms of further common African development.

The question of African unity has been mentioned often in this study. In the election campaign of 1959, the Action Group had regarded the idea as an *"ignis fatuus";* the NPC regarded a West African Federation "as at present premature"; and the NCNC said the idea "should remain a long term one."[2] It has been noted that, in the months preceding independence, drastic shifts began to occur in the position of the Action Group, and many members of the coalition parties advocated positive action looking forward to African unity. It has been further noted that almost every form of parliamentary and extra-parliamentary pressure on the Government since independence has prodded it to seek some form of union. In interviews with Nigerians one gets the feeling of desperation: African unity must occur; Nigeria must lead in the development; yet the Government is not doing all it can to bring about the ideal.

The position of the Nigerian Government since independence, dominated as it has been by the Prime Minister, has been remarkably consistent with

1 *H. R. Debates,* March-May session 1960, p. 65.
2 See *supra,* pp. 16, 18, and 20.

both the NPC and NCNC policy statements of the 1959 election campaign. At no time have Sir Abubakar or Government spokesmen denied the efficacy of a union of African states, but they have consistently treated the matter as a long-term evolutionary process which may never actually result in political unification. The Prime Minister had stated his Government's position clearly in the foreign policy debate of November 24, 1960: he would contact African states in order to ascertain what their common interests were, but there was not to be talk of political union "before knowing exactly what our problems are."[3] He has constantly reiterated this position. In an interview in June 1961, he said (in the words of the interviewer): "Europe did not divide Africa—it united squabbling villages and made nations of them. These may join together now if their people wish it—but the pan-African state is not for this generation."[4] Nevertheless, in his 1962 New Year's message he was able to promise that Nigeria would continue to "foster the aim of African unity which is the common goal of all of us in Africa."[5] An even more incisive indication of his position came in February 1962, when he again renounced the idea that Nigeria should attempt to force itself on other African states as their leader, and then added the following revealing footnote: "Nigeria is big enough and does not need to join others. But if others wish to join Nigeria, their position would be made clear to them in such a union."[6]

That Sir Abubakar has not allowed his reservations to thwart all attempts at Pan-African cooperation is common knowledge. In fact, his role in the Monrovia, Lagos, and Addis Ababa Conferences deserves attention. The first was largely a reaction to a bloc of "radical" states—Ghana, Guinea, Mali, Morocco, and the United Arab Republic, later commonly referred to as the Casablanca Powers. Hardly had the Casablanca Conference ended, however, before it was suggested (apparently by Senegal) that "the uncommitted African countries—such as Togo, Nigeria, and Liberia—should organise a conference at which all African countries would try to reach and define a common policy toward the Congo."[7] The idea "caught on" and the focus of the proposed conference became larger than the Congo. Seven states agreed to be sponsors and to invite all independent African states (excluding South Africa and the unstable Congo) to participate. Guinea and Mali would invite the militant Casablanca Powers; Ivory Coast and Cameroun would invite the Brazzaville Powers; Nigeria and Togo would invite those "uncommitted" to either bloc; and Liberia would serve as host.[8] In all twenty states attended the resultant Monrovia Conference on May 8, 1961. In spite of the role of Guinea and Mali, neither they nor the

3 See *supra*, p. 50.,
4 *The Economist*, June 17, 1961, p. 1240.
5 *Morning Post*, January 2, 1962.
6 *Daily Times*, February 28, 1962. More recently, he even raised the following question: "Many small countries are living freely, why should African countries be joined together?" *Sunday Express*, April 15, 1962.
7 *The Economist*, April 29, 1961, p. 454.
8 *Ibid.*

other Casablanca Powers participated on the grounds that the conference was premature.[9]

It was probably this Conference, more than any previous event, which first brought Sir Abubakar to international attention. In fact, the Prime Minister is credited by observers with saving the Conference by offering compromises for some of the differences among the members.[10] Furthermore, the resolutions adopted by the Conference bear the unmistakable imprint of the Nigerian leader. The states present agreed to govern themselves on the principles of state equality regardless of size, non-interference in the internal affairs of other states, respect for the sovereignty of each state, condemnation of subversion directed from neighboring states, cooperation throughout Africa based on tolerance and the "non-acceptance of any leadership," and unity without political integration. They also resolved to set up a technical commission to work out details for cultural, scientific, and technical cooperation. They condemned colonialism, called on African states not to take sides on the Congo, condemned the further manufacture and stockpiling of nuclear weapons, condemned apartheid, approved the United Nations, and urged disarmament. They urged that African disputes be settled by peaceful means and that a commission should be created to promote such ends. Finally, they regretted the absence of some African states from the Conference and hoped they would attend the follow-up meeting to be held in Lagos.[11]

Prime Minister Balewa seems indisputably correct when, on his return to Lagos, he asserted: "As regards the principles which must underlie any realistic political co-operation between the countries of Africa, I am glad to tell you that the declared policies of the Federal Government received universal support."[12] Furthermore, as if to dispel any doubts about the real purpose of the Conference, he added:

Now the object of the conference in Liberia was not primarily to settle differences between the nations who attended but to try to create the right atmosphere for international co-operation in political, economic, cultural, and scientific matters.[13]

The Monrovia Conference had the appearance of creating in Africa a

9 Sudan also failed to attend because Mauritania was to attend, and Sudan, in deference to Morocco's claim to Mauritania, did not wish to appear to recognize the latter.
10 The editor of the *Daily Express,* under his pen-name of "Aiyekoto," said it was Balewa who kept the Conference from breaking up when Somalia (which claims some Ethiopian territory) insisted that border disputes be included in the agenda. Balewa suggested a brief adjournment "to clear the air," and after the break it was agreed that the dispute would not appear on the agenda but that machinery would be discussed for settling border disputes in Africa. On the other hand, "Aiyekoto" says that Balewa succeeeded in getting the question of French atomic-bomb tests in the Sahara added to the agenda in spite of the objections of some of the former French colonies. *Daily Exress,* May 11, 1961. Cf., also: *West Africa,* August 26, 1961, p. 930; *The Economist,* June 17, 1961, p. 1240; and *Africa Report,* June 1961, p. 5.
11 *Africa Report,* June 1961, p. 5.
12 *Sunday Times,* May 14, 1961.
13 *Ibid.*

conservative bloc to counteract the Casablanca one. Radical elements in Nigeria sensed this development and resented it. Chief Awolowo charged that the Monrovia Conference was "inspired and completely financed by the more important countries of the Western Bloc."[14] Also, he called on the Government to join Nigeria to the Ghana-Guinea-Mali Union, a move hardly calculated to strengthen the Monrovia bloc if Nigeria is in fact the dominant member of that group.[15] At the All-Nigeria Peoples' Conference, many delegates indicated a preference for Ghana over other African states, and the Conference even passed a resolution calling on the Government to make special contacts with the Casablanca Powers,[16] a move supported by radicals of the NCNC.[17] In the November 1961 session of the Parliament, some NCNC and NPC members were extremely critical of Nigeria's drift away from friendly relations with Ghana. The charges were serious enough to prompt a lengthy answer from the Foreign Minister who, rather than deny the rift, charged that Ghana had refused to cooperate with Nigeria.[18]

The effect of these criticisms may never be known, but it is instructive to note that, before calling the Lagos Conference, the Prime Minister made special efforts to meet mounting criticisms of his Government. Dramatically, he set out on December 10, 1961, to visit President Sékou Touré of Guinea, the obvious purpose being to woo this member of the Casablanca bloc to the Lagos Conference (by then firmly decided to begin on January 25, 1962). At the end of the visit, the two leaders issued a communiqué indicating that they "shared common views on external matters,"[19] but the Nigerian Prime Minister was only able to say that he "hoped" Mr. Touré would attend the Conference.[20] He had said a few days earlier that some of the Casablanca Powers had already indicated their intention to attend the "summit" meeting.[21] Whether they were relying on these tenuous statements or on more positive information is not known, but two Lagos newspapers, the *Daily Times* and the *Sunday Post*, announced that the Casablanca Powers were attending the Conference. The next five weeks witnessed a newspaper duel of the "he is, he is not" type. The Government newspaper and the *Daily Times* continued to assume that the Casablanca Powers would attend, while the *Daily Express* kept saying categorically that they would not. Foreign Minister Wachuku reminded everyone that the Casablanca Powers had *not* said that they would not attend, and on January 12, the *Morning Post* announced triumphantly that they were coming, at least to the pre-Conference meeting of foreign ministers.

On January 7, however, it was announced that President Nkrumah had

14 *Daily Express*, September 13, 1961.
15 *Africa Report*, July 1961, p. 11.
16 See *supra*, p. 60.
17 See *supra*, p. 68.
18 *H. R. Debates*, daily parts for November 20, 1961, pp. 27, 28, 38-39, 43, and 45.
19 *Daily Times*, December 18, 1961.
20 *Morning Post*, December 15, 1961.
21 *Sunday Times*, December 10, 1961.

proposed "terms" for the attendance of the Casablanca group: a pre-summit meeting of foreign ministers to harmonize the charters of the two groups, to be followed by another summit called jointly by the two blocs.[22] On January 20, two days before the scheduled pre-summit meeting of foreign ministers (the question of harmonizing the two charters was not on the agenda), Morocco and the United Arab Republic raised the question of inviting the Algerian Provisional Government.[23] Prospects were dimming for a conference attended by all independent African states (except South Africa, which was not invited) when Sir Abubakar pulled his trump card: he announced that the Anglo-Nigerian Defense Pact had been abrogated![24] Unfortunately, the Casablanca bloc had already met and decided against participation. An official statement issued from Accra gave the following two reasons: the Casablanca Powers had not been consulted as a group, and the Algerian Provisional Government had not been invited.[25]

The sore disappointment in Lagos was revealed in an extremely harsh statement by Dr. Azikiwe in the opening address to the representatives of the nineteen states who attended.[29] He reminded the leaders that just before the Monrovia Conference, the Casablanca states met and decided as a bloc not to attend. "Recently," he added, "we have witnessed the same tactics on the eve of the Lagos Conference." Claiming that there were many points of agreement between the two groups, he then added the following discriminating and significant observation:

But there is one basic difference of an ideological nature between the two groups, which should attract the serious attention of all who sincerely advocate African unity.

It is the conspicuous absence of specific declaration, on the part of the Casablanca States of their inflexible belief in the fundamental principles enunciated at Monrovia regarding the inalienable right of African States, as at presently constituted, to legal equality, irrespective of their area and population; the right of African States to self-determination; the right of African States to safety from interference in their internal affairs through subversive activities engineered by supposedly friendly States; the right of African States to be secure in the inviolability of their territories from external aggression.

Whilst the Charter of the United Nations provides for these safeguards, in general terms, it is very material to the subject of African unity that its votaries should declare publicly and recapitulate their faith and firm belief by adhering specifically to the principles made famous at the Monrovia Conference. Otherwise, it can be a matter for speculation whether these principles are capable of becoming spectres to haunt the conscience of those who would rather pay lip service to the Charter of the United Nations, whilst secretly they nurse expansionist ambitions against their smaller and perhaps weaker neighbours.[27]

22 *Sunday Express,* January 7, 1962.
23 *Morning Post,* January 20, 1962.
24 *Ibid.,* January 22, 1962.
25 *Daily Express,* January 22, 1962.
26 Absent were the Casablanca five, plus Tunisia, Libya, Sudan (over the Algerian issue), and Tanganyika (due to the resignation of Prime Minister Nyerere).
27 The full address was printed in the *Daily Times,* January 26, 1962.

Perhaps for the first time, a prominent Pan-Africanist had admitted that there are two blocs in Africa. The Nigerian Governor-General had clearly spelled out the difficulties between the two blocs—and in terms which seriously questioned the possibility of any union as long as each side held to its principles. For Dr. Azikiwe—Nigeria's foremost Pan-Africanist, and still probably the most powerful influence on the NCNC—to speak in such a fashion was indeed a harsh blow to those who believed a positive move for Pan-African union would result from the Lagos Conference. It was a tacit admission that the Lagos Conference was a continuation of the Monrovia Conference.

In spite of—perhaps because of—the absence of the Casablanca bloc, the Lagos Conference could hardly be called a failure. The most promising development was the initialing of a proposed Charter for the Inter-African and Malagasy Organization. It was a modest proposal in many ways in that it made no reference to political integration, emphasizing rather co-operation in economic, educational and cultural, health and nutritional, and political and diplomatic fields.[28] It agreed "to explore the possibility of building up the defence of the African and Malagasy States against external aggression and in safeguarding their territorial intergrity."[29] It reaffirmed the principles of Monrovia (which Dr. Azikiwe had described as the distinguishing factors between the two blocs). It proposed the establishment of three organs to give the organization permanence and administration: an Assembly of Heads of States and Governments (to meet at least once every two years); a Council of Foreign Ministers (to meet at least once every year); and a General Secretariat (to serve as "the central administrative organ").[30] Membership was open to any independent African state "under indigenous African rule."[31] It further proposed the creation of an Association of African and Malagasy Economic Cooperation and Development and a Permanent Conciliation Commission for the settlement of disputes, each to be effected by a separate treaty which should form an integral part of the charter.[32] The official languages were to be English and French, and the Charter would have come into force thirty days after two-thirds of the signatory states had deposited their ratifications.[33]

Certainly, if any charter could be said to have the imprint of Balewa's Government, this was it. It was the hesitant beginning of an African organization, although it is difficult to equate it with the Organization of American States (as some did) as long as a separate bloc existed on the continent which did not accept its principles. There was no pretense that sovereignty or nationalism were impaired in any way. The preamble made it clear that the Organization was made up of African states, not African

28 Article 2, parts a, b, c, and d, as printed in the *Morning Post,* February 5 and 6, 1962.
29 Article 2 (f).
30 Articles 8-25.
31 Article 4.
32 Articles 25 and 31.
33 Article 34.

peoples. The principles of absolute equality appeared weakened by the provision that decisions could be made by simple and two-thirds majorities, but the Charter carefully avoided obligating any member state to abide by a decision of the Organization. Caution permeated the Charter.

Reactions in Nigeria were mixed. The position of the radical wing of the NCNC was stated by Dr. Kalu Ezera who commended the Government "on the brilliant way and manner in which it very successfully handled the deliberations of the Summit Conference" but described the failure to invite the Algerian Provisional Government as "a blunder . . . Nigeria should not have adhered to" and he urged the Government to take the initiative in becoming the coordinator between the Casablanca and Monrovia blocs.[34] Mr. Imoudu of the Nigerian Trade Union Congress charged that the whole meaning of the Conference had been defeated because of the "distressing failure of the 'Monrovia' Group of States to recognise and provide for the representation of the Algerian Provisional Government in the Conference."[35] Similar views were expressed by the Students' Union of the University of Nigeria, Nsukka, as well as the pro-Action Group *Daily Express* (January 25, 27; February 12, 1962). An Action Group Member of Parliament said on the floor of the House that the Conference was a waste of £100,000.[36]

The Lagos Conference and its proposed Charter placed Nigeria permanently in the moderate or conservative camp of African states, and unless the Casablanca bloc yielded, established the fact that Africa was divided into at least two blocs. Also, the absence of Tunisia, Libya, and Sudan (along with the Casablanca states) made the new inter-African organization essentially a Tropical African affair. Furthermore, the gap between Nigeria and Ghana, already widened by Ghana's refusal to attend the Lagos Conference, was further widened by Ghana's reaction to Dr. Azikiwe's speech. A. K. Bardon, Chairman of Ghana's Convention Peoples' Party's Bureau of African Affairs, charged that Azikiwe's "speech was prepared in London and read in Lagos." Furthermore, he said, "not even a single country represented in Lagos has made any visible contribution to the anti-colonial fight in Africa." Reaction in Nigeria was unanimous. "Insolent" (*Daily Times,* February 14, 1962), "insulting as it is stupid" (*Daily Express,* February 17, 1962), "Dr. Nkrumah's megalomania," "the fuhrer of Accra" (*West African Pilot,* February 12, 1962), shouted the daily press while the Government filed a formal protest with Ghana.[37] The protests forced Nkrumah to dissociate himself from the article,[38] but the Government newspaper of Nigeria, the *Sunday Post,* was probably right when it commented on February 18, 1962: "It will . . . require time and a more sustained effort to clear the suspicion and resentment . . . formed over the past five years about the attitude of some of our friends and compatriots at Accra. . . ."

34 *H. R. Debates,* daily parts for April 3, 1962, pp. 15, 17, and 18.
35 *Daily Express,* January 27, 1962.
36 *H. R. Debates,* daily parts for April 3, 1962, p. 23.
37 *Daily Times,* February 14, 1962.
38 *Ibid.,* February 16, 1962.

The above references to the Charter of African and Malagasy Organization had to be written in the past tense simply because the Charter was never implemented. It did not go down to defeat, however, but became in essence the model of a new charter signed at the African Summit Conference at Addis Ababa on May 25, 1963.[39] Remarkably parallel to, and based on the principles of, the Lagos Charter, the new document represents a victory for the Nigerian position. In the first place, thirty-one African states were represented at the Conference, including the Casablanca Powers. That Casablanca was already declining was revealed in the sharp differences on objectives which occurred between Dr. Nkrumah of Ghana and Mr. Touré of Guinea. Nkrumah sent a plan to the pre-summit meeting of Foreign Ministers calling for close unity, with a common foreign policy for all of Africa, a common set of diplomatic representatives, a continental economic-industrial plan, a common currency, and a central bank. Touré opposed this plan on the grounds that it was an effort on the part of President Nkrumah to promote his own ambitions.[40] Later, he announced the demise of the Ghana-Guinea-Mali Union.[41]

In the second place, Prime Minister Balewa made a strong speech at the Conference condemning political unity and calling for the "practical approach" of economic, educational, scientific, and cultural cooperation "and by trying first to get the Africans to understand themselves before embarking on the more complicated and more difficult arrangement of political union." Among the principles essential for cooperation, he said, must be the concept of mutual respect, the concept of the equality of all states, and the recognition of existing boundaries. In what was apparently a correct evaluation, he concluded that "the practical approach is much preferred by the majority of the delegations. I am glad to say that the stand we have taken right from the beginning is the stand of nearly almost [sic] all the countries in this Conference."[42]

The moderate position of the Nigerian Prime Minister was also supported by Haile Selassie, Nyerere, Touré and Tubman, and even Nasser and Ben Bella.[43] These leaders persuaded the less moderate leaders to join them, and the Conference produced the new document called the Charter of the Organization of African Unity (modeled, as has been pointed out, on the Lagos Charter). Whether the new Charter "formally liquidated the Casablanca and Monrovia groups," as the weekly *West Africa* maintains,[44] remains to be seen. It does appear, however, that the Nigerian positions calling for caution and slowness in African unification movements, respect for boundaries, and anti-subversion, as well as its call for the elimination of "blocs," have now been accepted in principle by all of the African states (except South Africa). Nevertheless, the Addis Ababa Conference, like the

39 *Federal Nigeria*, June/July 1963, p. 1.
40 *New York Times*, May 20, 1963.
41 *Africa Report*, June 1963, p. 23.
42 *Federal Nigeria*, June/July 1963, p. 6.
43 *New York Times*, May 26, 1963.
44 *West Africa*, June 1, 1963, p. 597.

Lagos Conference, is merely a first step toward a very loose form of international cooperation. Since the motivations of the two "former blocs" appear to be different, there is no reason not to expect these differences to show up in the new organization if it ever becomes viable. In fact, a Ghana radio broadcast was quick to interpret the new Charter to suit Ghanaian meaning: for example, to interpret Article II (1-d), listing as one purpose of the Organization "to eradicate all forms of colonialism from Africa," as meaning "active and armed support for the struggle of dependent African territories against colonialism and apartheid."[45] Whether this is also the meaning for Nigeria may soon be known, since it (but not Ghana) is one of the nine states chosen to control a fund of £1,000,000 to aid various national liberation movements. At this writing, it appears that Pan-African movements are now under the control of the former Monrovia Powers and there is reason to believe that their pace will be slower and more moderate than that demanded by at least Ghana of the former Casablanca bloc.

What can be said about the concept of Pan-Africanism in Nigeria? There is no doubt that it has universal appeal, although it is also accompanied by a considerable degree of naïveté. The radicals tend to act as if the wishing will produce the fact. Since there appears to be little wishful thinking on the part of Government decision-makers, the radicals sense a lack of dynamism, or worse still of any real commitment, for Pan-Africanism. There is further naïveté in the refusal to consider what the end result of any sort of union would be like. In an interview with the writer, a prominent NCNC officer from the radical wing refused to admit that a West African federation must necessarily be dominated by Nigeria which has over half the population of the area. Obviously, there is little likelihood of Nigeria's joining such a federation if the other units, with less than half of the population, could outvote it. The NCNC officer dismissed this with the emotional insistence that Nigeria would join with a spirit of brotherhood and tolerance. This same officer was distressed, however, that Northern Nigeria, with over half the population of the Federation, should insist on dominating Nigeria merely because it represents most of the people. In the absence of universally accepted values in any part of Africa, it is obvious that any Pan-African state will have to be a bundle of compromises. Yet the fact that such a state will have to have machinery by which decisions are made is largely ignored.

Part of the refusal to face up to the political facts of any union of already existing states stems in part, it seems, from a general dislike of federalism. It seems ironic that many Nigerians were distressed over talk of a federal structure for both Congo and Kenya. In fact, many Nigerians are apologetic that Nigeria is itself a federal state. Pan-Africanism and distrust of pluralism make odd bedfellows, but they seem to coexist in the minds of many Nigerians.

Another problem which is often overlooked is that Pan-Africanism as a concept seems to contradict the effort in each African state, including

45 *Africa Report,* June 1963, p. 4.

Nigeria, to create a national consciousness (i.e., individual state nationalism) in the masses. While each state is attempting to create a national identification within its borders which supersedes local, tribal, or regional identification, it must also work for a West African, or Pan-African, identification. Two levels of nationalism must be encouraged at the same time—one loyal to Nigeria (or any other contemporary state) and one loyal to the grander scheme which has not yet even been identified.

It would be wrong, however, to imply that Nigeria's decision-makers have ignored these problems. The Governor-General certainly hinted at them in his address to the Lagos Conference. He was even more forthright in a series of articles in September 1961. At that time, Dr. Azikiwe pointed out that the deterrents to Pan-Africanism are "mainly anthropological, sociological, and ideological." Under these rubrics he listed the various disputes among and between African states; the language and racial barriers between North and Tropical Africa; the differences between French- and English-speaking Africans; the desire for an Islamic confederation among some African states; tariff and other economic barriers; and the differences over what kind of a political union to attempt. In spite of these barriers, he said he was still optimistic about Pan-Africanism: "but in spite of my optimism, I have never hidden my fears that the barriers to be overcome are many and variegated."[46]

It is not surprising that Nigerian leaders are beginning to think in terms of implementation. As noted earlier, the Action Group leader has now called for an attempt to unite regions first—North, West, Central, East, and South. In January 1962, Dr. Michael Okpara, in his presidential address to the NCNC, outlined a three-fold path to African unity: (1) a series of conferences should be held in each of the regions—North, West, Central, East, and South; (2) after a number of regional conferences based on cultural and technical cooperation, political federations should be created in each region; and (3) regional federations should be integrated into an all-African federation. He said that by this method African unity can be achieved "with the least amount of friction and tears." Drawing a lesson from Nigerian unity (where the South had to wait on the North) he warned that "African unity will be made at the pace of the slowest boat."[47]

Dr. K. O. Mbadiwe, at the time Personal Adviser to the Prime Minister on African Affairs, said the NCNC plan was the "Nigerian point of view,"[48] and Balewa himself recently corroborated this by advocating regional groupings as a first step towards African unity.[49] This would indicate that the Prime Minister's often repeated observation that Africans know little about each other has been accepted, and that efforts to Pan-African unity on any political level will have to be slow and cautious. In spite of what has been said, it must be pointed out that the Nigerian Government has

46 See the series on "Pan-Africanism" by Dr. Azikiwe in the *Daily Times*, September 4, 5, and 7, 1961.
47 From the full address as printed in the *Morning Post*, January 17, 1962.
48 *Daily Express*, January 25, 1962.
49 *Sunday Express*, April 15, 1962.

made no attempt to encourage regional political groupings. On the contrary, the Lagos Charter and its successor, the Charter of the Organization of African Unity, both envision an Africa-wide organization, although admittedly of the loosest sort, with no diminution of sovereignty.

Some conclusions can be reached about official Nigerian policy towards Pan-African political union. Such a union—at any level—is a long-term ideal which may never materialize. Nigeria is large enough so that it does not need to depend on unity with other states for viability. If other states wish to join Nigeria, that will be considered. Nevertheless, efforts toward continental cooperation among independent, sovereign states must be attempted. The former Casablanca states are too dictatorial, too intolerant of other states' opinions and rights, too narrow in outlook to embrace most African states. Therefore wider groupings, as at Monrovia, Lagos, and Addis Ababa must be attempted. The Casablanca Powers may join the Monrovia Powers (the reverse will never happen) but only by accepting the principles of the latter. Any attempt at political union—as opposed to cooperation—without a firm background of understanding is doomed to failure.[50] In effect, the Government's position has followed logically from the party manifestoes of 1959, radical criticism to the contrary notwithstanding.

The renunciation of the Defense Pact, timed as it was just before the Lagos Conference, revealed the extent to which the Government is willing to go now to try to bring about African cooperation. The obvious purposes of the abrogation at that auspicious moment were: (1) to disarm the Casablanca bloc whose spokesmen had continually charged that defense treaties with European Powers indicated a form of neo-colonialism; and (2) to placate critics at home. The Government appeared to realize, however, that the question of defense treaties, like that of Algerian invitation to Lagos, was a false issue.[51] The true issue had been in the nature of the

50 Some of these Nigerian principles were put to a test shortly after the Lagos Conference when President Olympio of Togo suggested that African union on a regional basis should begin with a union embracing Nigeria, Dahomey, and Togo and, if possible, Ghana. *Morning Post*, February 2, 1962. Dahomey has apparently endorsed the idea. Walter Schwartz, "Towards a Benin Union," *Daily Times*, February 27, 1962. Foreign Minister Wachuku has said that Nigeria fully supports the immediate formation of such a union. *Sunday Express*, February 4, 1962. However, the Prime Minister has been much more cautious. At a public meeting on February 20, 1962, attended by the writer, he said that all he knew of the proposed union was what had appeared in the press. He added categorically, however, that he would be opposed to a union like that of Ghana, Guinea, and Mali and added rather caustically that that union "exists only in Accra." For a press account, see *Daily Express*, February 22, 1962.
51 In fact, it must be admitted that the Government apparently abrogated the Defense Pact only in the formal sense, but plans to reap its benefits as before. This is clearly demonstrated in the official text of the abrogation as released to the press:
"The British and Nigerian Governments have been consulting together about the Anglo-Nigerian Defence Agreement. They have noted with concern that the scope and purposes of the Agreement have been widely misunderstood. In particular fears have arisen that in consequence of the Agreement, Nigeria's freedom of action might be impaired and that she might even be drawn into hostilities against her wishes. The text of the Agreement shows that these and other anxieties which have been expressed are wholly without foundation.

blocs themselves.[52] The Casablanca Powers had insisted on political union and were willing to use force and subversion to get it. They were largely motivated by an anti-European hatred and looked on African unification as a last dramatic expulsion of all European influence from the continent. The Monrovia Powers were much more national-minded and jealous of newly won independence. They seemed to harbor no hatred for Europe and in fact regarded their former rulers (and their ally, the United States) as friends who could help them. For them, Pan-African union was something grand which, in the course of time, might actually grow out of prolonged contacts among the various states. Nigeria was a leader in this school of thought. Its efforts to placate the Casablanca bloc at Lagos merely revealed the hope, justified at Addis Ababa, that the latter would calm down and join the majority of African states and at their pace.

"Nevertheless, in order to end misunderstanding, the two Governments have thought it wise to reconsider the need for a formal Agreement. As a result they have decided to abrogate the Agreement.

"Each Government will, however, endeavor to afford to the other at all times such assistance and facilities in defence matters as are appropriate between partners in the Commonwealth." *Morning Post,* January 22, 1962.

The Government newspaper editorial on the abrogation said that: "Nigeria is a democracy and the Nigerian people stepping out fresh from the unpleasant atmosphere of colonial rule, did not want any semblance of the vestiges of that rule; and they said so." It added however, that:

"For sometime it was difficult to distinguish this patriotic desire from the recklessness of an Opposition out to do damage and always preferring the doings of all others to the efforts of its own country; and Government could hardly do more than be cautious.

"The campaign against the Pact, however, continued, the subversive elements in the community as they are found everywhere, exploiting the less informed and the un-informed to stir up public anger, and lending a hand to those who could not bear Nigeria [to] go forward in their campaign of calumny."

In these circumstances, the editorial concluded, in order to end misunderstanding, the Government had to reconsider the Pact. It could not resist adding a parting shot (in its unusual effort to give the Opposition credit for forcing the abrogation):

"But this is certain, the loudspeakers of African nationalism, who batter the West against the East, with the only intention of getting the best of two worlds, must now find a new prop upon which to build their evil propaganda." *Morning Post,* January 24, 1962.

The new prop of the Opposition was soon made clear, for Chief Awolowo said the "military alliance with Britain is not yet completely broken." His evidence was the last paragraph of the formal text of renunciation, which, he said, cloaked "some secret understanding of an equally sinister nature as the original Pact itself."*Morning Post,* February 3, 1962.

Furthermore, the Government refused to accept a resolution in Parliament congratulating it on the abrogation of a pact "which was detrimental to its policy of non-alignment." Government spokesmen vigorously denied that the Pact was detrimental to Nigeria's policy on non-alignment, and accepted the resolution only after the offensive words had been eliminated. *H. R. Debates,* March-April session 1962, daily parts for April 3, pp. 7-15.

52 See the informative article by John Marcum, "How Wide is the Gap Between Casablanca and Monrovia?" *Africa Report,* January 1962, pp. 3 ff.

THE GREAT POWER BLOCS

In the first year and a half of Nigerian independence there is no doubt that its world focus was the Anglo-American camp (or what Nigerians refer to as the Western bloc). At the beginning of 1962, fourteen months after independence, Nigeria had opened foreign offices in ten African states;[53] one in Saudi Arabia; one in the United Nations; and three others—London, Washington, and Bonn. Even before independence the first economic contacts, apart from Britain, were with the United States, Israel, and the International Bank for Reconstruction and Development. Immediately before independence, the Minister of Finance had said that "No loan had been sought from or offered by the Government of Union of Socialist Soviet Republics [sic]."[54] One year after independence the list of countries which had given aid to Nigeria had grown to ten, all in the Western camp: Australia, Britain, Canada, West Germany, Japan, Israel, Netherlands, New Zealand, Pakistan, and the United States.[55] In keeping with the major party manifestoes of the 1959 federal elections, to the effect that closer ties would be sought with the United States, many Nigerian leaders have visited that country in the last two years, the most eminent being Sir Abubakar, Sir Ahmadu Bello, and Chief Akintola. Economic missions have made contacts primarily with the Western camp (including Israel and Japan), although Chief Okotie-Eboh has also headed an economic mission to the Soviet Union and Communist China. By and large, however, the first foreign contacts of an independent Nigeria have been overwhelmingly with the Anglo-American camp.

Besides those mentioned above, a number of events and policy statements have strengthened the hands of those who charge the Government with being pro-West.[56] The prime evidence has included the following: the Defense Pact; the sponsorship in the United Nations of the 1970 date for the

---

53 High Commissions existed in Ghana, Sierra Leone, and the Central African Federation; Embassies or "Offices" in Liberia, Ivory Coast, Cameroun, Sudan, Senegal, Congo (Léopoldville), and Fernando Po.

54 *H. R. Debates,* August session 1960, p. 347.

55 *H. R. Debates,* daily parts for November 20, 1961, p. 46 (Written Answers by the Parliamentary Secretary to the Minister of Economic Development).

56 Further evidence of the intensity of the belief that Nigeria is "pro-West" came as recently as April 18, 1962, when two Government Whips, vigorously supported by the Opposition, proposed the establishment of a Parliamentary Committee on Foreign Affairs to help the Government pursue a true course of non-alignment. The motion was moved by D. N. Abii (Whip) and seconded by Mallam Aminu Kano (Deputy Chief Whip), and was supported by other NCNC members, the most eminent of whom was Dr. Mbadiwe. The Foreign Minister vigorously condemned the move as an attempt to usurp both the powers of the Ministers and the House, and it was defeated by voice vote. *H. R. Debates,* daily parts for April 18, 1962, pp. 9-17.

One member of the Opposition even charged that the Nigerian Ambassador to the United States (J. M. Udochi) had become a staff member of the State Department, the proof being that he had named his son "John" after President Kennedy. *Ibid.,* daily parts for April 14, p. 22.

termination of all colonialism in Africa;[57] the Prime Minister's support of the American decision to resume atomic bomb testing;[58] the rejection of the Soviet "Troika" principle for United Nations administration;[59] the rebuff of Khrushchev's proposal for a summit meeting of heads of governments to discuss disarmament;[60] the ban of subversive (Communist) literature; the failure to establish embassies in any Communist countries; the refusal to attend the Yugoslav Conference of Non-Aligned States in September, 1961; the refusal to grant passports to students wishing to study in the Soviet Union or other Communist countries; the alleged rejection of Soviet scholarships; the alleged lack of enthusiasm in Government circles for the establishment of a Soviet embassy in Lagos;[61] the strong reliance on private enterprise in the mixed economy; the failure to establish embassies in certain neutral states, such as Guinea and Egypt, which allegedly have been disliked by the West; the Exchange of Notes, signed on October 1, 1960, by British High Commissioner Head and Prime Minister Balewa, whereby Nigeria accepted the rights and obligations of all British treaties that have application to Nigeria;[62] and other acts which seem to some people to support the West, particularly the United States, too freely.[63]

57 This had been regarded by radicals as a sell-out to Western colonialists bought at the price of the £80,000,000 loan from the United States. See the charge of I. A. Brown (AG), ibid., daily parts for April 14, p. 21.
58 Morning Post, March 6, 1962.
59 Daily Times, September 22, 1961. Balewa said: "I feel there should be only one [Secretary-General] and a first class man who is able, honest and sincere, who will have other assistants widely representative of the nations as much as possible."
60 Sunday Express, February 25, 1962. Nigeria was queried by Mr. Khrushchev because it is one of the eighteen members on the United Nations Disarmament Committee.
61 The Government Deputy Chief Whip (Aminu Kano) has charged, for example, that "there are thousands of Americans flooding into Nigeria, but that Russians have difficulty in getting in." West African Pilot, March 30, 1962.
62 See H. R. Debates, March-April session 1962, daily parts for April 3, p. 12; and Nigerian Tribune (Ibadan), November 28, 1960.
63 For example, the Minister of Economic Development (Waziri Ibrahim) defended United States aid in the following terms: ". . . I asked myself—what would America want in Nigeria, if they gave us a loan or some aid? Apart from getting a fair return from the investments of American businessmen, America would also want to see that democracy was retained in Nigeria. This is a democratic country and my feeling is that no hon. Member can quarrel with this if America's intention is not to interfere but to encourage us to prove that the private enterprise system and democracy are maintained." H. R. Debates, daily parts for April 4, 1962, p. 46.
   Again, when the Minister of Commerce and Industry announced that Nigeria had succeeded in recruiting distinguished economic advisers from the United States and West Germany, he refused to answer a question as to whether experts had also been sought in Russia. Ibid., daily parts for April 5, pp. 17-18.
   Still again, when Members of Parliament were pressing questions about racial discrimination against Nigerians in the United States, the Parliamentary Secretary to the Minister of Foreign Affairs gave the rather tolerant reply that "it is not always easy for any Government to check the excesses of certain elements of its nationals," but he added that Nigeria had "made it clear that unless all necessary steps are taken to prevent such acts, our people might be forced to retaliate." Ibid., daily parts for April 12, 1962, p. 30.

Attempts have been made to justify a "pro-West" position, even while denying that there has been a violation of the policy of non-alignment. Oddly enough, Chief Awolowo has offered the strongest defense by pointing out that Nigeria is a democracy and therefore holds basic values which are pro-Western and anti-Communist. Dr. F. U. Okeke (NCNC) recently took the same line in charging that it was unfair to accuse the Government of being pro-Western "after we have been under the democratic tutelage of democratic Britain for over fifty or sixty years." Continuing, he added:

We cannot in a day or two or even in a matter of years dispel the principles which we have imbibed from a democratic country like Britain and America. Certainly, we are a democracy. If you ask which camp we belong to, we have been under democratic principles and institutions for over one hundred years. Russia has not been here at all. We want them to come. We do not know the ideology of Communism or totalitarianism yet, or any other ideology. The one we have had is democratic principles which is pro-Western and there is no harm in our pro-Western attitude.[64]

Even Dr. Mbadiwe, while Adviser to the Prime Minister on African Affairs, said that the radicals do not realize that it takes years to win friends, and that while Nigeria is not "anti-East" it simply has to recognize that its ties now are with the West. As time goes on, he said, friendship and trade will be increased more and more with the "East" until some balance of relations between West and East occurs—"all on the basis of what is in Nigeria's interests."[65]

The Prime Minister himself expressed a similar sentiment in 1961 when he was charged with being too slow in establishing diplomatic relations with the Soviet bloc states: "I hope that [the] House will appreciate that some of these countries that are opening [embassies] are completely new to us but others we have been in association with for a very long time."[66]

The Government has modified some of the conditions which produced criticism, but it is not certain that pressures alone prompted the actions. Some modifications appear to be merely logical steps in an expanding role in international politics. On April 14, 1962, Foreign Minister Wachuku announced that the Russian Ambassador had finally found a home and office in Lagos.[67] He also announced that within a year Nigeria would open embassies in Moscow, Cairo, Conarky, Rome, and Addis Ababa; and

64 *Ibid.*, daily parts for April 14, 1962, p. 18.
65 Interview with the author, December 5, 1961.
66 *H. R. Debates*, March-April session 1961, p. 171. A similar response was made by Sir Ahmadu in 1960 when he was asked whether Nigeria should accept an alleged offer of a loan from Russia at 2½ per cent without strings. He responded: "That is not our policy. We have to work with those we are accustomed to." *Daily Times*, January 19, 1960. Perhaps one of the most "unneutral" statements was made by the Nigerian Ambassador to the United States who congratulated the latter on its orbital space flight in February 1962 and termed it a triumph for "all the Free World." *Daily Express*, February 22, 1962.
67 *H. R. Debates*, March-April session 1962, daily parts for April 14, 1962, p. 12.

High Commissions in Nyasaland, New Delhi, and Karachi.[68] On November 22, 1961, the Prime Minister announced that the ban on the importation of subversive literature (a colonial order dating from 1955) had been lifted. Sir Abubakar added a note of warning however:

The lifting of this ban is, therefore, an expression of faith by the Government in the common sense of the Nigerian people and their firm belief in democratic principles.

However, I wish to make one point perfectly clear. The Government is not oppossed [opposed?] to the imposition of a ban in principle. We shall retain and not hesitate to use our power under section 58 of the Criminal Code and re-impose the ban if we find that our faith has been misplaced and that this sort of literature directly threatens the security of the State or the sovereignty of our country.[69]

In March, 1962, the Passport Office was transferred from the Police to the Civil Service under the direct control of the Ministry of Foreign Affairs. As a result of the move, Mr. Wachuku announced that "it is now the policy of the Ministry . . . that all passports issued to adults should have an endorsement that will be valid for all parts of the world. Therefore the limitations which have been imposed before will be removed."[70] It must be noted, however, that when the Prime Minister announced the transfer of the Passport Office he added that some regulations were still necessary:

It is very common in this country for Nigerians who want to go to certain countries for perhaps certain evil intentions to run away from the Immigration Authorities and go to certain neighbouring countries to get passports to certain places.

He did not indicate the nature of the regulations, but he said that there "is a very large number of undesirables in and outside this country whom we should like to restrict their movements [sic]."[71]

As a result of radical pressures, Nigeria agreed not to press its motion for the independence of all African colonies by 1970, although it supported a resolution which set no date, thereby being milder than the Soviet proposal for "immediate" independence.[72] It has already been noted that Government response to pressures led it to abrogate formally, if not in spirit and practice, the Defense Pact which, radicals claimed, aligned Nigeria to NATO.[73]

On the other hand, the Government has refused to modify its policy in

---

68 *Ibid.*, p. 33. It is significant to note that only six months earlier Mr. Wachuku had said that Nigeria could not open an embassy in Moscow because there were no Nigerians who could speak Russian. *Ibid.*, daily parts for November 20, 1961, p. 38.

69 *Ibid.*, daily parts for November 22, 1961, p. 8.

70 *Ibid.*, daily parts for April 12, 1962, p. 10 and for April 14, p. 28.

71 *West African Pilot*, March 30, 1962.

72 *Ibid.*, November 29, 1961. Two months after withdrawing Nigeria's sponsorship of the 1970 date, Sir Abubakar still admitted with pride that it was a date which Nigeria had set, and he indicated that he still regarded it as the realistic one. *Daily Express*, January 29, 1962.

73 See *supra*, pp. 44-46.

some areas to meet the charge that it is pro-West. The Viscount Head-Balewa Exchange of Notes still stands. A mixed economic system has been frozen into the Six Year Plan, in spite of the strong criticisms that reliance on foreign private investors identifies Nigeria with Western capitalism. Although the Prime Minister has admitted that Russia has offered some scholarships, he said that when he queried the Soviet Government as to the fields involved—law, medicine, technology—no further response was forthcoming. He implied, but did not say specifically, that Soviet motives were *not* to train Nigerians in the fields which Nigeria needs.[74] It has already been noted earlier in this chapter that, even while abrogating the Defense Pact, Nigeria reasserted a special friendship with Britain, and when yielding to other pressures (as on subversive literature and passports) special qualifications were added, which leads one to question whether any basic changes of policy have resulted from radical pressures.

The question needs to be asked: What is Nigeria's position vis-à-vis the Big Power blocs? The Prime Minister himself has until recently consistently avoided using either the term "neutralism" or "non-alignment." Rather, he has said that Nigeria will not "associate itself as a matter of routine with any of the power blocs," and he explained that this meant that Nigeria "will not join either the Western or the Eastern, or any other bloc," but would "follow an independent line no matter from where the truth comes."[75]

On the other hand, Foreign Minister Wachuku has constantly rejected the term neutralism and asserted that Nigerian policy is one of non-alignment. This position he has explained as follows:

We have said it before on the Floor of this House, and elsewhere, that in matters pertaining to the African continent we cannot be neutral; in matters pertaining to common humanity we cannot be neutral. For instance, in the question of the atom bomb and the possibility of it wiping out the human race, we cannot be neutral because we happen to be members of the human race. But when it comes to a particular policy of a group of states or a group of powers, then we have to say 'No' when necessary and when we see it is 'Yes,' we shall say 'Yes,' but we shall be the final arbiters of our attitude.[76]

It is submitted that there is no difference in the two statements; that, in fact, the policy is pragmatic. The Defense Pact was entered because it was regarded as advantageous to Nigeria, but Britain's allies France and Portugal have not been spared criticisms for their policies in Africa. American aid has been welcomed, but Nigeria has voted against the United States' position a number of times in the United Nations.[77] The "Troika" was re-

---

74 The Prime Minister was answering questions at a public meeting at the University College, Ibadan, attended by the author, on February 20, 1962.

75 See *supra*, p. 49. However, in October 1962, the Prime Minister joined others in asserting that the policy "has never been one of neutrality, but rather non-alignment." Sir Abubakar Tafawa Balewa, "Nigeria Looks Ahead," *Foreign Affairs*, October 1962, p. 139.

76 *H. R. Debates*, daily parts for April 14, 1962, p. 29.

77 For examples, on many votes dealing with the Congo, the so-called United States "invasion" of Cuba, and on the Bizerta issue, see *United Nations General Assembly*, A/PV/985, pp. 322-24; A/PV/995; and A/PV/1006, p. 140.

jected because it would weaken the United Nations, an organization which Nigeria consistently supports. The 1970 date for independence of all African colonies was a compromise between those who advocated immediate independence and the intransigence of colonial powers to set any target date; and it can hardly be said that the spirit of compromise is totally contrary to the Prime Minister's practice. This spirit of compromise was most clearly demonstrated in the United Nations' vote on the seating of Communist China. The Prime Minister had stated categorically at independence that "Nigeria is going to see to it that Red China is admitted into the United Nations."[78] However, when the issue was worded in such a way that Nationalist China (with its 11,000,000 people on Formosa) would be left out entirely, Nigeria abstained.[79] In fact, Mr. Wachuku rejected the idea of expelling one member to get another in, and suggested that a compromise would be to seat both Chinas.[80]

Nigerian policy in relation to the power blocs is largely pragmatic, but it is probably too easy to leave it at this point. Historical, cultural, and opportunistic factors also enter the decision-making process. For example, the United States and its allies have offered many forms of aid to Nigeria, and without strings, while the Soviet bloc has offered none, except for technical personnel.[81] Furthermore, there is no doubt that the common English language between Nigeria and the United States has facilitated the great influx of Americans (particularly Peace Corps personnel) into Nigeria. This factor also helps explain the ease with which other Commonwealth citizens come to Nigeria. Also it can be added that in many ways Nigeria is to a large extent "Western" as opposed to Soviet or "Eastern." Its national history, its political institutions, its economic structure, its official language are "Western." Its educated elites were trained overwhelmingly in the "West"; its internal school system is British; and its money is tied to the sterling bloc. Many of these characteristics, however, also apply to Ghana; yet Ghana and Nigeria have created two distinct international images of themselves. The distinguishing feature probably lies in the fact that Nigeria is a federal state, and has projected into its decision-making

78 *H. R. Debates,* November session 1960, p. 251.
79 *Daily Express,* December 7, 1961.
80 *Morning Post,* January 19, 1962. *Time,* December 15, 1961, p. 32, said Wachuku even added that there was no indication from Red China that it wanted admission in the United Nations or that it was willing to abide by the Charter.

It is true that an Action Group front bencher (I. A. Brown) charged that Nigeria "willfully joined hands with America and Britain" on the issue in order to win United States aid. Mr. Wachuku said the allegation was "without an iota of truth." *H. R. Debates,* daily parts for April 14, 1962, p. 21. The Foreign Minister might have pointed out, furthermore, that the United States and Britain voted against each other on the issue.
81 Waziri Ibrahim, Minister of Economic Development, has said that Polish and Russian nationals, serving on United Nations' agencies, had given "the benefit of their professional and technical expertise," but when pressed as to why most experts had come from the Western bloc said that the "Eastern countries" had not offered them. *Ibid.,* daily parts for April 11, 1962, p. 5. For a table of foreign loans to Nigeria 1960-62, see *ibid.,* daily parts for April 2, 1962, p. 3.

in foreign policy the same caution and compromise it must use to harmonize the various internal forces on other matters.[82]

In the course of time there is no doubt that Nigeria's position vis-à-vis the power blocs will undergo alterations, and in African and colonial affairs and in some United Nations' affairs it will probably diverge from the Western position. On the other hand, during its formative months, since independence, it has made little effort to seek closer ties with the Soviet bloc. Rather than being anti-Soviet, however, its position appears to have been more one of simply ignoring that bloc as much as possible. Sympathy for Soviet-type dictatorship as a political ideal is indeed weak, while sympathy for Western concepts of democracy is a declared ideal of all important political leaders (undoubtedly supported by the knowledge of each faction that its chances for survival, as well as that of the federation, depends on democratic compromise). Similarly, Soviet economic concepts (monolithic state ownership and management of all means of production) receive practically no support, the overwhelming preference being for some form of mixed economy, a Western development. Disputes in this area are chiefly over degrees and balance, not all or nothing. It must be concluded, therefore, that Nigeria's policy of non-alignment is a pragmatic one, with no chance of an open blanket identification with either bloc, but with a strong tendency to give the Western bloc the benefit of any doubt except on questions of colonialism.

ECONOMICS AND FOREIGN POLICY

In forming an international economic policy Nigeria has been faced with two main problems: an internal and an external one. Internally the problem has been the creation of an economic climate conducive to attracting foreign investments and aid—governmental and private. Externally, the problem has been the European Common Market and Britain's application to join—raising the questions of Commonwealth preference and relations with the former French territories in Africa.

The Internal Problem. The problem of creating an economic climate conducive to attracting foreign investments and aid involves the question of guarantees against nationalization. In a more subtle sense, it also means an assurance to the Anglo-American bloc that no radical (i.e., "Communist") economic policies will be suddenly undertaken.

That a struggle exists in Nigeria over the question of nationalization at first appears to be a tempest in a teapot. Although the NCNC advocates Fabian socialism and the Action Group advocates democratic socialism, there appeared to be no real conflict over these terms and the question of nationalization in the election campaign of 1959. The prevailing atmosphere seemed to be that of 1957, when all of the Governments of the Federation (with the West then headed by Chief Awolowo) asserted that:

82 See *Infra.*, p. 136.

Our Governments have no plans for nationalising industry beyond the extent to which utilities are already nationalised, nor do they foresee any such proposals arising. Nevertheless they are anxious that there should be no doubt in the minds of overseas intrepreneurs that Nigeria will provide adequate safeguards for the interests of investors in the event of any industry being nationalised in the future. Should this occur, then fair compensation assessed by independent arbitration would be paid.[83]

The first indication of a shift in the policy of the Action Group came early in 1960 when Chief Awolowo urged that Nigeria, in seeking foreign investments, should say "in effect to foreign investors 'come to our aid in the meantime but in due course we will buy you out.' "[84]

Awolowo's comment prompted leaders to make statements attempting to clarify Nigeria's position. In New York the Sarduana said:

The scope for development is so vast, and the needs for new capital so great, that we should be acting to our own serious detriment were we foolishly to start nationalisation which would cut off at once the help we so much require.[85]

Dr. Okpara, President of the NCNC, said that his party was not planning any nationalization, and that talk of such "cannot aid in the wooing of outside capital in Nigeria."[86] The Western Nigeria Minister of Finance (and an Action Group leader), Chief J. A. O. Odebiyi, denounced what he called NCNC threats of nationalization and promised that foreign investments would be safe in the Western Region.[87] Sir James Robertson, outgoing Governor-General, and Dr. Azikiwe, his successor, both issued warnings against statements which would drive away foreign investors.[88]

Chief Awolowo answered these warnings by asserting that nationalization could not be totally ruled out, leading Chief Okotie-Eboh to warn against "wild statements" which damage Nigeria abroad,[89] and Okpara to charge that: "Those who are advocating nationalisation are communists and they should have the courage to say so." Okpara then added the following interesting comment: "We are not Marxists, we are not Communists. Socialism means fellowship, freedom and opportunity for all and my party believes in this principle."[90]

The disagreement appeared serious enough for Chief Okotie-Eboh (NCNC), the Federal Minister of Finance, to give some time to the question in his presentation of the Supplementary Appropriation Bill in the first Parliament after independence. He said he found it "most distressing" that, barely five weeks after independence, "people who should know better are propounding new and dangerous philosophies." These

83 Sam Epelle, *The Promise of Nigeria* (London: Pan Books, Ltd., 1960) , p. 244.
84 *H. R. Debates,* March-May session 1960, p. 31.
85 *Daily Times,* July 8, 1960.
86 *Ibid.,* October 20, 1960.
87 *Ibid.,* October 22, 1960. Cf., also Premier Akintola's assertion that his Government believes in "free enterprise and healthy competition." *Morning Post,* April 3, 1962.
88 *Daily Times,* October 27, 1960; *West African Pilot,* October 31, 1960.
89 *Daily Times,* November 1 and 2, 1960.
90 *Ibid.,* November 4, 1960.

philosophies include "loose talk of Nigeria being in the pocket of Britain economically, politically and otherwise," and "talk of nationalisation." He added that, "as far as I know, none of these philosophies was embodied in the election manifestos of the people who now propound these philosophies and theories."[91] He then asserted that:

Nothing . . . is more likely to deter potential investors than a threat that, once their investments have matured into a successful enterprise, they will be expropriated. No amount of talk of just and fair compensation can fully eradicate this fear.

The Minister said that some people cite Britain as an example of nationalization but he countered that Britain and Nigeria could not be compared.

In Britain, a highly developed economy had already emerged before certain basic industries were taken over by public corporations. A new nation like Nigeria cannot be built on the basis of nationalisation. I need, perhaps, only refer to the examples of America and Canada to illustrate how rapid and orderly development has been achieved by private enterprise effort, including a large measure of foreign capital, but without the over-hanging threat of nationalisation.[92]

He concluded his attack with the observation that:

Nationalisation, based on quasi-Communist ideas, is alien to our philosophy. It is in direct conflict with the far-sighted statement of foreign investments to which all the Governments of the Federation have fully and freely subscribed.[93]

Chief Awolowo answered by agreeing that underdeveloped states need the "requisite climate" to attract foreign capital, and he explained that is why the Nigerian Governments "have made provisions for aid to pioneer industries and also for granting new enterprises tax-free holidays when they are established in this country." These moves did not rule out the possibility of nationalization, he added, and suggested that Nigeria follow the example of other underdeveloped states—India, Burma, Ceylon, Siam, and Indonesia —who have nationalized industries and still "foreign investors . . . flock to" them.[94] In a fascinating bit of logic, he said the question of foreign aid does not even enter the picture, for donor countries really have no choice anyhow. In his words:

Furthermore, it must be clearly recognised, it must be borne in mind, that all the so-called civilised countries in the Western Democracies have now recognised that under-developed countries must of necessity be given aid by them. If they fail in these days of ideological conflict between the Western Democracies and the Eastern Democracies, or the Eastern Bloc, then they will lose whatever foothold they may have had in this place in the past. Consequently, the country has

91 *H. R. Debates,* November session 1960, p. 40.
92 *Ibid.,* p. 41.
93 *Ibid.,* p. 42.
94 *Ibid.,* pp. 81-83.

nothing to fear at all by discussing nationalisation and by saying or declaring that nationalisation cannot be ruled out of our national economy.[95]

His parting sally was to charge that:

the Government is mortally afraid of the growth and spread of Communism or Communist doctrine in this country. But you do not keep the bugbear of Communism out of your door by branding your critics Communists, by embarking on witch-hunting or red-hunting, or by bullying the hungry masses. Communism is a philosophy which grows automatically on the soil of much poverty and much discontent, to use the pregnant words of Bacon. At the moment, our country suffers terribly from the malady abject poverty and disease and rampant discontent.[96]

In view of the positive statement of the Minister of Finance, and the mildness of the opposition, one would have thought the issue was settled. It was not. Dr. Azikiwe, delivering his first Speech from the Throne as Governor-General, said: "My Government has no plans for the nationalisation of industry to any greater extent than the public utilities of this country are already nationalised."[97] When the traditional Motion of Thanks on the Speech from the Throne was proposed, Chief Awolowo moved that it be amended by adding the following: "but are of the opinion that the declaration regarding nationalisation contained in the Speech neither represents the true wishes nor accords with the best interests of the people of Nigeria."[98]

Apparently, Chief Awolowo was not stabbing in the dark. As the year 1961 wore on many of the articulate pressure groups discussed in the previous chapter began to make their voices heard in support of more nationalization. Suffice it to note that the pressures were sufficiently strong enough to compel the Government to call for a full-scale debate on this issue in the November 1961 session of the Parliament. The Minister of Finance threw the challenge to the Opposition by saying that if it would propose a motion on nationalization the Government would permit it to be debated.[99]

On November 29, Chief Awolowo moved: "That this House approves in principle the nationalisation of basic industries and commercial undertakings of vital importance to the economy of Nigeria."[100] His defense was

---

95 *Ibid.,* p. 83.
96 *Ibid.,* pp. 83-84.
97 *H. R. Debates,* March-April session 1961, p. 21.
98 *Ibid.,* p. 139.
99 It was on this occasion that Chief Okotie-Eboh made his now-famous remark about bearded revolutionaries in Nigeria. He said, among other things: "The fact that one bearded man in Lagos [apparently Dr. Otegbeye of the Nigerian Youth Congress] rises up and preaches nationalisation and communism does not mean that the people in the North, East or West are going to accept it. . . . It should be known that when people are trying to indoctrinate others to rise against a Government, they must be careful themselves because they cannot know where it will begin and where it will end." *H. R. Debates,* November session 1961, daily parts for November 17, 1961, p. 19. He said at this time that he would not say more on nationalization until the Opposition motion was proposed.
100 *Ibid.,* daily parts for November 29, p. 5.

based on the premise that "Nationalisation is the cornerstone, and an indispensable tool, of the politico-economic system called socialism." Nationalization was necessary, he said, to combat the three traditional evils of capitalism. First, capitalism, "of necessity, places a newly emergent and underdeveloped nation, such as ours, in a state of defenceless servitude" because foreigners own the major and minor extractive and secondary industries, the bulk of the shipping and commercial undertakings, and the distributive trade. Second, capitalism generates "excessive self-interest and utter disregard and disdain for the interests of others," as "our contact with the white race" bears out. In support of this charge he said: "It is said that only sixty families control and rule America's dollar empire," yet the United States has six million unemployed. "We do not know," he added, "how many white families dominate the economy of Nigeria." Third, capitalist agents of production—labor, land, capital, and organization— "are rewarded, not for what they actually do or produce, but in accordance with what the harsh, remorseless and impersonal and outdated mechanism of supply and demand dictates." In this context, he alleged that the laborer, "though indispensable to society, gets low wages" because what he supplied is "unusually plentiful in relation to demand."[101]

Finance Minister Okotie-Eboh personally defended the Government's position by moving to substitute for Awolowo's motion the following:

That this House
(i) Resolves that the nationalisation of industries and commercial undertakings beyond the extent to which public utilities, shipping, Airways, Railways, Power, Communications and Marketing Boards are already nationalised is not in the best overall interests of Nigeria;
(ii) welcomes the review of company and other legislation now being carried out by the Federal Government and other measures to ensure that such undertakings are conducted in the best interests of Nigeria;
(iii) welcomes the increasing participation by Nigerians in the ownership and direction of such undertakings; and
(iv) deplores irresponsible statements on nationalisation which have recently been made in Nigeria and overseas.[102]

As earlier, the Finance Minister's chief arsenal of defense was in the realm of foreign policy. He marshaled five arguments against nationalization. First, he said, it would be uneconomic to nationalize, because of the need "to recruit expatriate managers and technicians to manage the nationalised concerns," since Nigeria is desperately short of such talent. Second, what limited financial resources the Government has must be "deployed to build up the basic infra-structure," not to nationalize. Third, "we must remember that it adds nothing whatsoever to the growth of the economy, whether by increasing our productive capacity, making new opportunities for employment or in any other way, to take existing concerns into state ownership."

101 *Ibid.*, pp. 6-9. Chief Awolowo advocated the nationalization of all mining, the merchant marine, insurance, foreign-owned plantations, and "all pseudo-extractive and secondary industries like the timber and plywood industry. . . ." *Ibid.*, p. 6.
102 *Ibid.*, p. 10.

Fourth, past policies, directed "primarily towards foreign investment," but also encouraging investment by Nigerians, "have achieved a wide measure of success in creating a climate favourable to private investment in Nigeria." Fifth, "we all know that at least until such time as our own resources are adequate to sustain our further growth and development, there will be a continuing need for foreign investment in the private and productive sectors of our economy if economic growth is to be maintained and improved."[103]

Chief Okotie-Eboh elaborated on his fifth point. He said it would be difficult to attract aid or investment from financial institutions or "friendly governments" if they felt "that we were using our own limited resources to buy out undertakings rather than deploy them in ways which would contribute directly to the growth of our economy." In fact, he added, "Friendly Governments might well question the desirability of imposing additional burdens upon their own taxpayers to assist Nigeria in those circumstances."

He concluded with two rather crushing blows which went unchallenged. First, he said that of the statutory corporations already existing in Nigeria, "almost all of them pay exhorbitant salaries and they are invariably not properly managed. That is a statement of fact." Finally, he said that through taxation "we already enjoy a forty per cent share in the profits of all companies operating in Nigeria without risking a penny of our own limited financial resources in them."[104] In summary, he said that the Government was not arguing whether nationalization was good or bad in general but only that nationalization in Nigeria will not "secure an improvement in the lot of the mass of our people."[105]

Needless to say perhaps, the Government's position carried overwhelmingly in the voting on the motion and the proposed amendment. Certain conclusions seem warranted about Nigeria's economic policies. First, the articulate pressures for nationalization are sufficiently strong to compel the Government to counteract them repeatedly. Secondly, the Government, whatever may be the preference of the individual decision-makers, has consistently followed a policy based on the need to attract foreign investment—both private and governmental. Third, apart from the question of foreign aid, strictly economic arguments are used to discourage further nationalization, indicating that the individual decision-makers do in fact believe in the position they maintain. Fourth, in view of the *practice* of both Federal and Regional Governments, socialism appears to be a vague ideal prompting no doctrinaire solution, except for Chief Awolowo and some other articulate defenders. In fact, Chief Awolowo's main concern seems to be for national planning, and

103 *Ibid.*, p. 12.
104 *Ibid.*, p. 13.
105 *Ibid.* The Minister of Commerce and Industry (Dipcharima) argued also that he was "concerned with the practical rather than the doctrinaire approach to economic theory." From the practical approach, he said, "It follows that since we need capital and expert assistance to promote the development of our economy, and since we cannot provide these factors from within the country, we must get them from overseas." *Ibid.*, p. 16.

a greater interest in overall economic development from the central Government. Until the Six Year Plan was announced, he had consistently charged the Federal Government with lack of planning and with allowing economic matters to drift, a charge which many Nigerians support. These interests, rather than nationalization merely for the sake of nationalization, seemed to prompt Awolowo, who hoped that by pressing his position the Government would be forced to central planning on a broad and detailed basis. It is in this light that one must understand his constant plea for what he calls a "high powered" economic commission with strong powers of regulation.[106]

The significance of the Government's insistence that internal economic policy must be geared to the attraction of foreign aid and investment was revealed in March 1962, when the long-awaited Six Year Plan was released.[107] The Plan calls for an expenditure of £676.5 million, *one half of which (£338.8) must come from foreign loans and grants.*[108] Furthermore, for the total plan which involves all four Nigerian governments, the Minister of Finance has asserted the need for £200 million of private foreign investment during the six year period.[109] It was quite necessary, therefore, for the Government to make its internal economic policy unmistakably clear, for the success of the Plan stands or falls on the degree to which anticipated foreign aid and investment are forthcoming.

The External Problem. When Britain applied for membership in the European Economic Community, all members of the Commonwealth were disturbed. African members had reason to be the most disturbed of all, for sixteen African states (former French- and Italian-speaking colonies) were already associated with the EEC. While this meant a preferential market in Europe for the associated states, probably no insurmountable problems existed for the Commonwealth members as long as Britain remained aloof from the Common Market. However, when Britain sought membership the picture changed radically. Nigeria (and other Commonwealth states) immediately faced the problem of whether to seek associate status, thereby exploiting the vast new European market for their raw materials. Another attraction would be the possibility of participating in the Overseas Investment Fund set up by the Market to assist underdeveloped countries. A third advantage would be that Nigeria could compete in sales to the Market on a par with the other African primary producers which are already associate members.

106 He has maintained, for example, that while socialism means "public ownership of the means of production, distribution and exchange," democratic socialism is "socialism with a difference" for its advocates "a nationally planned economy, under which both the public and the private sectors will operate side by side." He admitted that part of the rift in the Action Group is due to the relative attention to be paid to each sector. "AG and Democratic Socialism," *Sunday Express,* January 21, 1962. See also the Action Group pamphlet, *Democratic Socialism* (Lagos: Amalgamated Press, 1960) , especially p. 11.
107 Federation of Nigeria, *Federal Government Development Programme, 1962-68,* Sessional Paper No. 1 of 1962 (Lagos: Federal Printing Division, 1962) .
108 *Ibid.,* p. 3, paragraphs 10 and 12.
109 *H. R. Debates,* daily parts for March 29, 1962, pp. 30, 33.

Conversely, the disadvantage of staying out is that Nigeria might not only lose its primary market—Britain—and thus have to seek markets elsewhere, but the "elsewhere" would probably exclude the vast new European Market.[110] Furthermore, the economic isolation which already exists between the former French and former British states in Africa would become frozen as each of these groups would tie its trade to different world markets.[111] This would greatly reduce the possibility of any strong Pan-African movement—economic or political—and thereby destroy the dreams of many Africans, including many Nigerians.[112]

On the other hand, if Nigeria were to become an associate member of the EEC, it would become more closely identified with Western Europe than it is now: its economic policy would be geared to, and it would participate in the decision-making of, the Market; it would be a partner in helping create a third economic bloc, competing with both the United States and Eastern Europe; it would have to forego membership in any other economic community; it would participate in common external tariffs against other markets; politically, the destiny of the Market would become to some extent Nigeria's destiny. As one Nigerian publication asked: "how does Nigeria ex-

---

110 Some statistics on Nigeria's foreign trade reveal the enormity of its reliance on Western Europe, and the nature of the challenge of the EEC. In 1959, Nigeria's exports and imports were as follows:*

EXPORTS		IMPORTS	
Country or Area	% of total Exports	Country or Area	% of total Imports
United Kingdom	51.1	United Kingdom	45.9
West Germany Netherlands Italy France Belgium Luxembourg } The Six	34.8	West Germany Netherlands Italy France Belgium Luxembourg } The Six	19.1
United States	7.3	United States	4.4
Japan	1.4	Japan	10.4
Others	5.4	Others	20.2
Total	100.00	Total	100.0

*Tables are adapted from *Handbook of Commerce and Industry in Nigeria* (Lagos: Federal Ministry of Commerce and Industry, 1960), pp. 120, 144.

111 Total Nigerian trade, both exports and imports, with other African states amounts to only 1 per cent. See the excellent article by H. M. A. Onitiri, "Nigeria's International Economic Relations: A Survey," *Nigerian Journal of Economics and Social Studies,* November 1961, pp. 13-38, especially the table on p. 38. Commented *The Economist,* January 20, 1962, p. 204: ". . . there is almost no inter-African trade and the whole area exhibits an extreme dependence upon the outside world, above all on the West. And this dependence is a factor making not for co-operation but for division between African states."

112 See "Eurafrica and Their Africa," *The Economist,* November 25, 1961, pp. 734-35.

pect to preserve her independence and remain true to her policy of non-alignment?"[113]

One of the earliest expressions of the Nigerian dilemma was made by Zanna Bukar Dipcharima (NPC), Minister of Commerce and Industry, on April 23, 1960. He pointed out that "the prices we get for our principal exports continue to decline." Part of the explanation, he said, was the "cheap American lard and soya beans being exported to Britain" which "terribly adversely affect our trade with the United Kingdom." While he had found both the United States and Britain sympathetic to Nigeria's problems, he added, all he could promise after independence was "to pursue this matter energetically through the appropriate international channels."[114]

Dipcharima found the threat of the European Common Market to be especially serious, as the following statement demonstrates:

The European Common Market remains a serious problem for the future of our exports. The latest information on the level of tariffs agreed by the Six in respect of commodities forming the substantial part of our exports is, to say the least, discouraging, particularly for our trade in cocoa and oil things. The ultimate effect of their development policy in the associated overseas territories must be to make the Community virtually independent of supplies from third countries.

Apologists of the Common Market point to the fact that the tariff reductions so far made by the Six have been extended to all members of GATT.

There is no disguising the fact however that the Common Market aims to develop the European Economic Committee [Community?] itself and its associated overseas territories at the expense of primary producers like ourselves. Not only will we ensure that the interests of such countries are kept in the fore-front in every discussion of the European Common Market but I intend to examine the possibility of joining other primary producing countries in forming a counter bloc.

The great industrial countries cannot do without our raw materials. We could, therefore, strike a better bargain if we the producers are to adopt a common front towards them. It is a pity and sad reflection of the state of affairs in the world today that while the industrial countries are progressing by leaps and bounds, we the primary producing countries of the world suffer humiliation in financial matters.[115]

The only alternative for Nigeria, he concluded, was "to find new markets for our produce," and in

expanding Nigeria's share of the world's trade our policy will then be to promote multilateral trade over as wide an area as possible thereby enabling us to sell our goods in the most favourable market and to buy our imports from the cheapest source available.

He added, however, that Nigeria would continue to honor its "existing international trade obligations" and after independence would seek to "join

113 *The Service,* October 21, 1961, p. 7.
114 *H. R. Debates,* March-May session 1960, p. 627.
115 *Ibid.*

the GATT since its principles offer the best chance for a steady and orderly expansion of world trade."[116]

In keeping with the Minister's intention of finding new markets, negotiations for such were begun immediately after independence. These have now resulted in trade agreements (the only ones signed to date) with Poland and Czechoslovakia.[117]

Britain's decision in 1961 to apply for membership in the European Economic Community threw the Nigerian economic policy into confusion. The first reaction was hostile. The Minister of Finance said at the Commonwealth Finance Ministers' Conference in Accra: "Nigeria cannot join the European Common Market. Nigeria is at present actively trying to promote an African Common Market."[118] His position appeared to be fully supported in Nigeria.[119] It was only a short time thereafter, however, before the Minister of Commerce and Industry was reported as saying that if the EEC pursued an "open and liberal trade policy, Nigeria will try to become an associated member of the Common Market."[120] He later branded the report as mischievous and false and added that "if the European Common Market would make Europe prosperous and therefore make it a better buyer of African products, then good luck to them."[121]

There is no doubt, however, that Dipcharima's comments, whether accurate or not, revealed a state of indecision in the Government. This was most clearly revealed in Chief Okotie-Eboh's budget speech the following March (1962), given at the time of the announcement of the Six Year Plan. He said that Nigeria's relations with the EEC and with "our fellow African states" are "intimately related to each other." As to relations with African states, he said:

As must be clear from the results of the recent Conference held here in Lagos, Nigeria attaches the greatest importance to the closest possible economic co-operation with other African states and particularly, initially, with the other West African states. This will doubtless in time lead to the establishment of at least a West African Common Market comparable in concept to the present European Common Market. It would be idle to underestimate the magnitude of the difficulties which must be resolved before this can come to pass.

116 *Ibid.* In this same session the Minister of Finance was distressed that loans from the United States Development Loan Fund "could only be made on the basis of their being tied to United States exports." This means, he said, that Nigeria "cannot obtain the goods she needs in the cheapest available market" and is "a complete negation of a declared multilateral policy." *Ibid.*, p. 82.

117 *Daily Times,* September 20, 1961 and November 14, 1961.

118 *The Service,* October 21, 1961.

119 The NCNC paper supported Okotie-Eboh "with pride." *The Cock,* October 7, 1961. The Government newspaper of the Northern Region condemned the Market as a plan "to make Africans 'drawers of water and hewers of wood.' " *Daily Mail,* July 4, 1961. The Action Group weekly charged that associate membership in the Market would violate Nigeria's policy of non-alignment. *The Service,* October 21, 1961, p. 7.

120 *Sunday Times,* October 15, 1961.

121 *Daily Express,* October 27, 1961.

First is the complexity of the manifold problems involved in reconciling the interests of the nations which formerly belonged respectively to the British and French spheres of influence in Africa. Secondly, is the fact that, unlike the countries which go to make up the European Common Market, whose economies are broadly complementary to each other in that by far the greater volume of trade takes place between the member countries themselves almost all the trade of the African countries is with the outside world, frequently in competition with each other.[122]

He expressed the hope that "Nigeria will become the industrial heart of an African Common Market," but admitted that, before such could become a reality, "there must be far greater industrialisation." He felt that progress had already been made in some fields, "notably the co-ordination of customs administration and plans for international highways" which would facilitate "trade and commerce between all the West African States." He concluded by expressing confidence that, "given patience and mutual understanding, all the present difficulties will be speedily resolved."

On the question of relations with Europe itself, he said:

Two major points are relevant to the consideration of Nigeria's relationship with the European Common Market. First, our trade with the present member countries is large and increasing—over sixty-eight million pounds in the first nine months of 1960 and over seventy-eight million pounds in the corresponding period of 1961. The six countries together constitute the most rapidly growing market in the world today. Clearly, we must seek to maintain and increase our trade with them.

The second point concerns the position of Great Britain. Even before Great Britain applied for membership of the Community, Nigeria was faced with the grave problem of discrimination against her and in favour of the former French and Belgian territories associated with the Community. That this problem has not yet become acute has been due partly to the representations we have consistently and firmly made to the Common Market countries and partly to the fact that the Common Market itself has not yet got fully under way and no quantitative restrictions have therefore been placed on our exports. This problem will remain whether Britain joins the Community or not. If she does join, our problems will be immeasurably more complex and their solution vital to our continued development.[123]

He added that he wished to make it clear that Nigeria "cannot, and will not, contemplate any form of agreement or association with the Community which in any way savours a colonial or neo-colonial relationship," and that Nigeria would insist that "our vital interests be fully protected and in a manner commensurate with our national sovereignty." With these reservations, he concluded:

. . . we approach the whole complex question with a completely open mind. The pattern of events is changing almost daily with suggestions and counter-suggestions from all sides. Many detailed studies are being made, both in

122 *H. R. Debates,* daily parts for March 29, 1962, p. 29.
123 *Ibid.*

Nigeria and elsewhere, but until a very much clearer picture emerges, Nigeria cannot fully determine where her true interests lie.[124]

In spite of the open-mindedness which had replaced the first antagonistic reaction to the Common Market, as Britain continued to negotiate for membership the Nigerian leaders established a policy. In October 1962, Prime Minister Balewa announced that "Nigeria will, in no circumstances, seek association" with the EEC, but would attempt to obtain "a guarantee of access to its market and to a reasonable share in the expansion of that market for those commodities that would be particularly affected by import tariffs and quotas."[125] The Governor-General, in his Speech from the Throne in April 1963, indicated Nigeria's new approach. "In view of Nigeria's rejection of associate status with the European Economic Community," he said, "a vigorous policy of export promotion will be pursued on a global scale in order to secure new markets for our produce."[126]

The following month, in a radio report on the Addis Ababa Conference, the Prime Minister pointed out that one of the themes which he dwelt on was the need for "an African Common Market based on certain groupings— a North African Grouping, which will include the Sudan; a West African Grouping which will extend to the River Congo; an East African Grouping, which will include almost all the Central African countries." He said that coordination among such groups would create "a successful African Common Market which should increase the inter-State trade on this Continent." While his plan was not adopted, he added that the Conference did welcome a plan to establish an African Development Bank and agreed to appoint a preparatory economic committee "to study in collaboration with governments and in consultation with the Economic Commission for Africa the various economic African problems and to submit their findings to Member States."[127]

It would appear, therefore, that Nigerian economic policy has now shifted from Europe to Africa, and that moves will be made to attempt to improve inter-African trade, although the difficulty of such a move for primary producers seems formidable indeed. In the meantime, of course, trade with non-African states must be continued. Its massive Six Year Plan depends on foreign aid and investment and its trade patterns, therefore, will be tied for some time to come to non-African states.[128]

SPECIAL AFRICAN PROBLEMS

1. *Relations with the Republic of South Africa.* It would probably be impossible to exaggerate the antagonism which all African Negroes feel

124 *Ibid.*, pp. 29-30.
125 *Commonwealth Survey*, November 9, 1962, p. 902.
126 *West Africa*, April 6, 1963, p. 371.
127 *Federal Nigeria*, June-July 1963, p. 3.
128 Cf., *West Africa*, April 13, 1963, p. 397. See also Wolfgang F. Stolper, "The Development of Nigeria," *Scientific American*, September 1963, p. 168.

toward the apartheid policy of South Africa. Nigerians are no exception to this feeling, and indications of Government policy had been revealed even before independence. On April 5, 1960, a private member's bill had been passed which urged "the Government to take appropriate steps to ban the importation of South African goods in this country."[129] This motion was the immediate result of the Sharpeville killings, but did not rest on that one incident alone; rather it reflected the opposition to everything connected with the South African Government. The Minister of Commerce, Zanna Bukar Dipcharima, promised that from that day onward, "no white South African will be employed by this Government."[130] Others encouraged the expulsion of South Africa from the Commonwealth, and some even talked about war with that friendless country.[131] The Prime Minister had indicated a hardening of his attitude toward South Africa in the August session of 1960.[132] In his inaugural address as Governor-General, Dr. Azikiwe summed up the Nigerian attitude well when he said that Nigeria would regard it as "a mark of disrespect and an unfriendly act" if any country with whom she has friendly relations indulged in race prejudice in any shape or form, "no matter how it may be legally cloked."[133]

It was not surprising, therefore, that the Nigerian leader went to the Commonwealth Prime Ministers' Conference in March 1961 determined to challenge South Africa's race policy. In fact, many people credit South Africa's withdrawal from the Commonwealth almost exclusively to Sir Abubakar's opposition. The South African Prime Minister, Dr. Verwoerd, spoke of the " 'unbridled attacks' made by the Prime Ministers of India, Nigeria and Ghana."[134] The pro-Action Group *Daily Express* had its full front page (March 19, 1961) devoted to Balewa's return from the Conference. Bold headlines of "WELCOME SIR" headed the editorial which followed:

Your role at the Commonwealth Prime Ministers' Conference has been described as laudable.

We think it is more. It was heroic. It was great. It was a masterpiece of statesmanship.

129 *H. R. Debates,* March-May session 1960, p. 152.
130 *H. R. Debates,* March-May session 1960, p. 139.
131 Cf., for example, *ibid.,* pp. 134-152.
132 *H. R. Debates,* August session 1960, p. 190. As early as January 1960 the Prime Minister had questioned whether South Africa and Nigeria could both remain in the Commonwealth, *H. R. Debates,* January session 1960, p. 90. In May he said, in relation to South Africa as a member of the Commonwealth: "If a member gives trouble to other members why not kick him out?" *Daily Times,* May 3, 1960.

In October 1960, Sir Ahmadu Bello, leader of the NPC and Premier of the Northern Region, said South Africa should not be readmitted to the Commonwealth. *Daily Times,* October 14, 1960.

In November 1960, Chief Awolowo said: "if the worst comes to worst, it would be the duty of Nigeria in partnership with the Prime Minister of Malaya, and with any other Prime Minister, to see that South Africa is not readmitted into the Commonwealth." *H. R. Debates,* November session 1960, p. 200.
133 *Federal Nigeria,* November/December 1960, p. 1.
134 *African World,* April 1961, p. 3.

Your role was all these and more because you were truly Nigerian in tone and temper.

That's what this bubbling, bumptious, big nation wants you to do—to step ahead with courage, confidence and concrete proposals—and to reflect the true greatness of great Nigeria.

Cheers Sir! Many many cheers.

Sir Abubakar himself left the impression that he may have played the leading role. At a press conference, he said that at one stage of the Conference he had threatened to withdraw Nigeria from the Commonwealth if South Africa was not willing to modify its racial policy because "I could not imagine how I would look at my countrymen when I came back home." Continuing, he said: "I gave it hot to South Africa, and they gave it back to me during the sharp exchanges across the conference table. But I am particularly pleased about the outcome of the conference."[135]

Whether Balewa played the leading role, or merely shared it with Nehru and Nkrumah, is not known. India and Ghana had, of course, met with South Africa numerous times before without seeing that country withdraw; but the 1961 Conference was also different since South Africa was re-applying for membership as a republic. The evidence is that the Nigerian Prime Minister played an important role in this Commonwealth development.[136]

Further evidence of Nigerian intentions toward South Africa came at the International Labor Organization meeting in June 1961. There the Nigerian Minister of Labor, Mr. J. M. Johnson, moved a resolution to the effect that South Africa should be asked to quit the organization. The motion carried 163 to 0, with 89 abstentions.[137]

These moves, apparently, were merely the beginning of Nigerian attacks on the South African Republic. "Kicking South Africa out of the Commonwealth does not solve the problem [of apartheid]," the Prime Minister said.[138] It is not surprising, therefore, to find the Nigerian Foreign Minister at the front of the United Nations censure of South Africa in the fall of 1961. In fact, Mr. Wachuku told the Nigerian House of Representatives that it was the result of a "snap move between Liberia and Nigeria that

135 *Sunday Times,* March 19, 1961.
136 See *The Economist,* June 17, 1961, p. 1240. David Williams, editor of the influential journal *West Africa,* in a contributed article to a Nigerian newspaper, said the departure of South Africa from the Commonwealth "can be attributed to him [Balewa] personally." *Daily Times,* October 4, 1961. However, see the excellent and informative article by J. D. B. Miller, "South Africa's Departure," *Journal of Commonwealth Political Studies,* November 1961, pp. 56ff., who points out that there was no foregone conclusion about the outcome of the Conference when it first began, but that positions gradually hardened among the Afro-Asian and Canadian Prime Ministers leading finally to South Africa's withdrawal of its application.
137 *Daily Express,* July 1, 1961. Among the abstainers were the government and employer delegates from the United States, Western Europe, Australia, Canada, and New Zealand. *Africa Report,* July 1961, p. 11.
138 *Sunday Express,* March 19, 1961.

we succeeded in getting South Africa censured."[139] Furthermore, the Minister added, "we are determined that South Africa will either change her policy of *apartheid* or pull out of the continent."[140] To press these points further, he concluded,

it was at our suggestion at the United Nations that the Security Council was asked to consider applying the provisions of Article 6 of the United Nations Charter, which says that when a member continues to disobey or infringe the Charter of the Organisation, then the possibility of such member's expulsion must be considered under Article 6 of the Charter. We, in conjunction with other African states, brought this Resolution to the Political Committee and it was passed. Now, we want the Security Council to consider the possibility of expelling South Africa from the United Nations under Article 6.[141]

Second thoughts apparently appeared on the expulsion bid, however, for Nigeria did not press the issue further.[142]

Another move against the Republic of South Africa occurred in November 1961, when the Federal Minister of Internal Affairs, Alhaji Usman Sarki (NPC), decided to expel the South African Dutch Reformed Church from the Federation. Apparently, this Church had only twelve members in Nigeria, operating exclusively in the Northern Region, but the Church's identification with apartheid was enough to justify the extreme action taken by the Minister.[143]

The coup de grâce of Nigerian relations with South Africa came in the November 1961 session of the Parliament. At that session the Attorney-General and Minister of Justice (Dr. T. O. Elias) introduced a bill, the effect of which was:

to make sure that the privileges of membership of the Commonwealth which nations from that country [South Africa] have enjoyed so far, come to an end, and all South African nationals will henceforth be treated as foreigners.[144]

The only opposition to the bill was from a member who feared that it might imply recognition of the Republic. Mr. Wachuku allayed his fears by asserting that "our attitude is that South Africa is a colony" controlled by a minority. "Therefore," he concluded, "our attitude towards South Africa is one of Liberating the Africans."[145] The motion, of course, carried unanimously in a roll-call vote.[146]

139 *H. R. Debates,* daily parts for November 23, 1961, p. 14.
140 *Ibid.*
141 *Ibid.*
142 The Minister, in speaking to the House, did not tell that body that he had had second thoughts on expelling South Africa. In fact, a few days earlier, on a United States television program, he had been asked about the expulsion move and said: "She may expel herself but as far as I am concerned censure is enough for the time being if that will make them think." *Daily Express,* October 17, 1961. Cf., *Newsweek* (International), October 23, 1961, p. 29.
143 *West African Pilot,* November 27, 1961.
144 *H. R. Debates,* daily parts for November 23, 1961, p. 11.
145 *Ibid.,* p. 14.
146 *Ibid.,* p. 16.

Finally, it might be noted that Sir Abubakar has now freed himself from Dr. Ezera's charge that Dr. Verwoerd regarded him as a moderate. In fact, it was Dr. Verwoerd who came, unknowingly, to the Prime Minister's defense. Balewa had told the House of Representatives that, in the interests of peace, he would visit any part of Africa including South Africa, if invited. This move prompted the South African Prime Minister to charge that Balewa was "not a moderate on the question of White and non-White relations but a fanatic in his cause." It must be admitted that Nigerian newspapers seemed to headline this statement with a great deal of satisfaction.[147]

Moves to date indicate that Nigeria's general moderation on international issues cannot be expected to apply to South Africa, and vigorous moves in relation to that unhappy country may well occur again from time to time.[148]

2. *The Congo.* The official Government position on the Congo has been based on four premises: (1) uncertainty as to whether the Congo Government under Lumumba represented the people; (2) belief that the peoples of the Congo are themselves divided; (3) belief in the need for Congo unity; and (4) determination to give full co-operation to the United Nations on Congo matters.

The first official statement on the Congo came in the Prime Minister's address to the United Nations on the occasion of Nigeria's becoming the ninety-ninth member of that organization. He said that there was much about the Congo that remained obscure to him, especially about the actual machinery of transfer of power, whether the Congolese were consulted or not, and whether the Constitution was imposed by Belgium rather than agreed upon by both. Nevertheless, he added, certain factors had to be kept in mind. First, "Africa must not be allowed to become a battleground in the ideological struggle"; second, in creating a "real political life in the country itself, it will be necessary to start at the bottom by seeing that local and provincial authorities are established while maintaining the essential unity of the country"; third, the "Congolese people were right to appeal to the United Nations Organisation for help and advice in rebuilding their country rather than to turn to any individual power." He then commended the United Nations' action to date, recommended a fact-finding commission with no representation of the big powers, and called for the holding of new elections "to find a government capable of governing."[149]

147 See, for example, *Daily Times,* April 13, 1962: "P. M. Blacklisted"; *Morning Post,* April 13, 1962: "Premier who was kicked out of the Commonwealth: I Fear This Man Balewa"; and *Daily Express,* April 13, 1962: "Verwoerd Spurns It All."

148 In fact, Mr. Wachuku boasted that: "If hon. Members examine our record [towards South Africa] within the past twelve months in the light of those who have been there [in the United Nations] for 15 years, 12 years or even 4 years, I think Nigeria will be given credit, and hon. Members will, no doubt, be proud of our achievements and our records." *H. R. Debates,* daily parts for November 23, 1961, p. 14.

149 *Federal Nigeria,* September/October 1960, p. 13.

Subsequently, Mr. Jaja Wachuku, at that time Federal Minister for Economic Development and Nigerian Representative to the United Nations, was appointed chairman of the United Nations Conciliation Committee to the Congo. He said that the Commission should work for the peace, unity, and stability of the Congo, and that, therefore, dismemberment should be discouraged.[150]

In the November 1960 debates on foreign policy in the House of Representatives, the Government was strongly challenged by the Opposition Leader, Chief Awolowo. He said that the Congo situation may appear "complicated and mystifying to some people but if we have correct orientation, an ideological orientation, it will not be difficult to know what the answer is to the Congo situation."[151] He said elections had been held which resulted in Mr. Kasavubu becoming President and Mr. Lumumba becoming Prime Minister, but that unfortunately Mr. Lumumba had confused the issue by inviting the United Nations in to deal with "some dissident elements." United Nations intervention, he said, has made the "confusion more confounding" for that organization "has allowed itself to be the instrument of Belgian imperialism." The "correct attitude" for the United Nations, he added, "should have been to go there and support and uphold the Government of Mr Lumumba and Mr Kasavubu."[152] He concluded by criticizing Sir Abubakar for suggesting the fact-finding commission and the holding of the new elections.[153]

Prime Minister Balewa felt compelled to answer these criticisms, and in doing so revealed again his unwillingness to take extreme positions. He said he would not have suggested new elections

had there emerged from their elections even one single Party with a quarter of the seats in the House. But this did not happen. All the Parties came with very small numbers and none of them was even in a position to command one quarter of the Assembly. I heard also that there was a vote of confidence on the Prime Minister of Congo but the vote of confidence was given to him by an Assembly which did not have a quorum.[154]

Sir Abubakar said that Nigeria was doing all it could to assist the United Nations in the Congo, and that he had, in fact, instructed the Nigerian troops sent there as follows:

You are going to the Congo as soldiers; nothing less, nothing more. You will go there as soldiers. You are to listen and to obey the United Nations command.

150 *Ibid.,* November/December 1960, p. 10.
151 *H. R. Debates,* November session 1960, p. 200.
152 *Ibid.,* p. 201.
153 *Ibid.* Chief Enahoro, foreign policy spokesman for the Action Group, had criticized the Prime Minister's stand at the United Nations as follows: "On the Congo he was original but he was largely wrong, and on matters where he was not original or wrong he was silent." *Ibid.,* p. 125.
154 *Ibid.,* p. 251.

And whatever you are told just do it as soldiers. You should have no interest whatsoever in the affairs of the Congo.[155]

The Government has scrupulously followed the advice of the Prime Minister. Mr. Wachuku, Chairman of the United Nations Conciliation Commission to the Congo, said, shortly after his appointment, that any solution in the Congo must provide for the unity and stability of that country, and that especially dismemberment must be avoided.[156] In March 1961, Mr. Wachuku roundly criticized Mr. Nkrumah of Ghana for assuming the role of spokesman for all Africa, and charged that the Casablanca Powers, led by Ghana, would only make the situation worse.[157] In May 1961, Mr. Wachuku welcomed the arrest of Mr. Tshombe who, he said, was not working in the interest of the Congo,[158] and in November 1961, as the situation began to stabilize itself, he credited the United Nations with saving the Congo, despite the failure of many states to support that Organization.[159]

Without going into details on the Congo crisis, it seems clear that the Nigerian Government quite early took a moderate position, worked for a solution which reflected political compromise among the Congolese themselves, envisaged a single Congo out of the former colony, and gave full support to actions and decisions agreed upon in the United Nations.[160]

3. *Atom Bomb Tests in the Sahara.* Nigerian resentment of French atomic-bomb tests in the Sahara have already been mentioned.[161] On April 5, 1960, the Prime Minister had promised the House of Representatives that if France persisted in the tests "we will definitely take positive steps when we have the power, to see how we can deal with countries who treat us in this way."[162] On November 17, after independence, the Parliamentary Secretary to the Prime Minister reported that there was no truth to the rumors that France was surreptitiously testing bombs in the desert. "On the contrary," he said, "I have every reason to believe that the French Government is reconsidering any plans it might have had for these tests in the interests of friendly relations among African countries."[163]

155 *Ibid.* By November 18, 1960, the Minister of Defense, Muhammadu Ribadu, was able to announce that one Nigerian battalion, the 5th, had already left for the Congo (Kivu Province), and that the Prime Minister had agreed to send another battalion and a Brigade Headquarters at the United Nations' request, to be stationed in Katanga. *Ibid.,* p. 36.

156 *Federal Nigeria,* November/December 1960, p. 10.

157 *Daily Times,* March 19, 1961.

158 *Daily Express,* May 8, 1961. At a later date, Mr. Wachuku, as Foreign Minister, said: ". . . any country that dares to suggest that Katanga will by any means be taken out of the Congo is an enemy of Africa so far as we are concerned." *United Nations Review,* November 1961, p. 19.

159 *H. R. Debates,* daily parts for November 20, 1961, p. 37.

160 For an excellent account of the position of the "moderates" (including Nigeria), see Robert C. Good, "Four African Views on the Congo Crisis," *Africa Report,* June 1961, pp. 3 ff.

161 See *supra,* p. 33.

162 *H. R. Debates,* March-May session 1960, p. 131.

163 *Ibid.,* November session 1960, p. 21.

The Parliamentary Secretary was proven wrong in December 1960, when France conducted its third bomb tests in the Sahara. Nigeria immediately broke off diplomatic relations with France, ordered the French Ambassador, M. Raymond Offroy, and his entire staff out of the country within forty-eight hours, and placed an embargo on French aircraft and shipping. The Prime Minister had called Mr. Offroy to his office at 7:30 P.M. on January 5 and personally handed him the ultimatum, effective from 8:00 P.M. The entire French staff was caught up in a hectic period of confusion and frustrations as they vacated their homes, sold their cars, and prepared to leave. On the morning of January 6 telephone service was cut off in the French embassy, further frustrating staff members attempting to make last-minute preparations to settle their affairs. The telephone authorities denied knowing anything about it, and also denied that the cut-off was due to a Government order. The French staff had to leave by car since the air and shipping embargoes were effective immediately. The French Ambassador was not even given the courtesy of an escort to the Dahomey border. Radical reaction in Nigeria was immediate and unanimously commendatory of the Government action.[164]

Within a week, Dahomey and Niger had sent delegations to Nigeria begging that the embargoes be lifted on goods moving to and from their territories. All equipment to build the new harbor at Contonou was imported on French ships through the Lagos port; and 90,000 tons of Niger groundnuts (its chief export) were stranded on Lagos docks waiting to be loaded into French ships. The Dahomey delegate said "The future is bleak and repellent, Monsieur," and the Niger delegate said "We should not be punished for the sins of France." Special concessions were soon granted to these countries.[165] At the Monrovia Conference in May 1961, Nigeria formally lifted the ban on all aircraft and shipping effective from May 18. The official announcement given to the press said that France had given assurance that no further nuclear tests would be carried out in the Sahara. The announcement further said that Nigeria had been importuned by the Governments of Dahomey, Niger, and Chad to lift the embargoes because their development plans were "being retarded by the denial of Nigerian port facilities to French shipping on which these countries largely depend for their imports of capital goods."[166]

Balewa, however, although he ordered the French out originally, said he would not invite them back in. "It is a matter of national prestige," he said, and if it wanted to re-open its embassy, France would have to apply to Nigeria to do so.[167] France did resume its air traffic into Nigeria in 1961,[168] but at the time of this writing had not re-opened an embassy.

164 See *Daily Times* and *Daily Express* for January 6 and 7, 1961.
165 *Daily Times*, January 16, 19, and 20, 1961.
166 *Daily Express*, May 18, 1961.
167 *Morning Post*, October 31, 1961. He added, however: "We want them to come so that we can open one in France too." *Africa*, November 1961, p. 40. See also *H. R. Debates*, daily parts for November 23, 1961, pp. 8-9.
168 *Daily Express*, November 2, 1961.

In retrospect, the Nigerian move appears to have been precipitate. No other African state felt constrained to take such harsh action. The only major effect of Nigerian action was to injure the economies of former French colonies near Nigeria and dependent upon her ports. Furthermore, the Algerian Provisional Government, in its cease-fire agreement with France, has made the Nigerian move ironic by agreeing that France would continue to have atomic testing rights in the Sahara for a number of years. Finally, Nigeria has been embarrassed because President de Gaulle has been in no hurry to reestablish diplomatic relations. That the Nigerian Government would like to rectify the mistake is now clear. Mr. Wachuku has said that if the French are willing to come back, "we shall certainly receive them," and Mr. T. O. S. Benson (NCNC), Federal Minister of Information, has made what appears to be a special plea for French return. In Paris, as a guest of Air France, he pointed out that he and other Nigerians did not hesitate to travel in France at all. "All this is clear evidence of the goodwill between our two countries," he said; and a newspaper item added that Benson's remarks indicated "the satisfaction the Nigerian Government would derive from any French move to resume diplomatic relations."[169]

It would appear that in at least one case where Nigeria became "militant" and "dynamic" its action later was only to be regretted. Nevertheless, Nigeria, as a member of the United Nations Disarmament Committee, has consistently followed its stand by recommending that Africa be declared a nuclear-free zone.[170]

4. *Other Issues.* Nigeria's deep interests in African affairs have already been demonstrated: its attempts to foster inter-African cooperation, its disagreement with Ghana and other Casablanca states, its strong rejection of any form of cooperation with South Africa, its resentment of any kind of atomic bomb testing on the continent, its conciliatory role in the Congo, and its interest in the gradual but complete demise of colonialism on the continent. One can hardly say that Nigeria is neutral about Africa.

It can be said, however, that Nigeria's African policy, except for South Africa and the Sahara bomb tests, tends to be cautious, conciliatory, and conservative. In spite of its congratulations to the Algerian Provisional Government for the cease-fire agreement which presaged the impending independence of Algeria, it refused to recognize the Provisional Government. On the other hand, it exchanged High Commissioners with the Central African Federation, which was not only not independent but the possibility of its ever becoming independent was growing dimmer with each passing day. To confuse matters more, the Government expressed sympathy and encouragement for Kenneth Kaunda, nationalist leader of Northern

169 *Morning Post,* March 17, 1962. Cf., also, *H. R. Debates,* daily parts for April 5, 1962, p. 4, where Mr. Wachuku said that "preliminary discussions" have been held between Nigeria and France on "the presumption that the testing of nuclear devices and weapons on African soil by France has been discontinued."

170 *Morning Post,* March 24, 1962; *United Nations Review,* December 1961, p. 12.

Rhodesia, while at the same time Joshua Nkomo, nationalist leader of Southern Rhodesia, was quoted as charging Nigeria with "aggression against the African people" by its diplomatic recognition of the Central African Federation; and Foreign Minister Wachuku had announced the intention of Nigeria to open a "High Commission Office in Nyasaland"![171]

Other illustrations of caution and conservatism, even on African affairs, exist. An interesting, almost humorous, case involves Angola, recently torn by bitter strife with Portugal. In April 1962, a Mr. Holden Roberto, who claims to be the Prime Minister of the Angolan Government-in-Exile, visited Lagos seeking support for his cause. Sir Abubakar told Mr. Roberto that Nigeria can help in training the administrative and medical staff of the Provisional Government. "But," added the Prime Minister, refusing to be trapped into a commitment, "we cannot assure you of training your armed forces of the Police and the Army because it will mean that we are training you to fight your African brothers in the South."[172] His caution paid off in only three days, when Mr. Bervardo Domingo arrived in Lagos to denounce Roberto and to declare his party leader, Mr. Mario de Andrade, the true leader of Angola. He came to seek Nigerian assistance "for the genuine cause of the Angolan people."[173] It is not known whether the Prime Minister made the same offer to Domingo as to Roberto.

A more serious problem, and one which threatens to cause bitterness among Nigerians, involves Fernando Po. This Spanish-owned island off the coast of Eastern Nigeria (in reality it is closer to what is now Western Cameroons), is a source of employment for Nigerians, chiefly Eastern Ibos. Recruitment of Nigerians began in the 1920's and was unregulated until a labor agreement was negotiated with the Spanish authorities in 1942. Today, for each Nigerian recruited, the Federal Government is paid £3 and the Eastern Region £2 by the Spanish Government. There are about 30,000 contract laborers on the island.

Early in 1962, Peter Enahoro, respected editor of the *Sunday Times,* under his pen-name of "Peter Pan," wrote a series of articles entitled "The Brutal Island." He charged that, besides the 30,000 contract laborers, there are 70,000 Nigerians working on Fernando Po without benefit of contract; that Nigerians constitute 70 per cent of the total population; that laborers are treated as slaves; and that the Nigerian Government has not sufficiently protected the Nigerians there.[174]

At this same time, Lola Martins began a series of articles in the *Daily Express* (February 22, 23, 1962) making similar charges. However, he claimed that Nigerians number 47,000 out of a total population of 100,000. The Government newspaper (the *Sunday Post,* April 1, 1962) joined in with a lengthy article by Eze Ogueri II entitled "The Island of Horror."

171 Cf., *Sunday Post,* September 17, 1961 and *Sunday Times,* April 8, 1962; and *H. R. Debates,* March-April session 1962, daily parts for April 14, p. 33.

172 From the official communiqué of the conference between Sir Abubakar and Roberto as printed in the *Morning Post,* April 26, 1962.

173 *Sunday Times,* April 29, 1962; and *Sunday Express,* April 29, 1962.

174 *Sunday Times,* February 18 and 25, and April 1, 1962; *Daily Times,* March 23, 1962.

These articles helped stimulate a popular demand for territorial expansionism in Nigeria, which buttressed the demands already made by the Nigerian Youth Congress that Nigeria annex the island.[175] A spate of letters to the editors (the *Sunday Times* said it received "hundreds of letters from readers") demanded action. Samples of the comments were as follows: "Any map of Nigeria without Fernando Po is, from this day, incomplete"; "I suggest that we use any kind of force, constitutional or belligerent, to terminate Spanish rule on the Island"; "The challenge of Fernando Po is one of national prestige"; "The only language that impresses the Spaniards is force"; "How many delegations did the Indians lead to the Portuguese about Goa!"; "I have been sick, sick, sick"; "We should annex the island";[176] "Fernando Po is part of the Federation of Nigeria"; "Fernando Po is Nigeria."[177] A national newspaper editorial said that "What Goa was to India . . . Fernando Po is to Nigeria," but later said that "No responsible, intelligent Nigerian ever expected the Prime Minister to lead invasion forces to the Island."[178] A Government newspaper editorial said that if Nigeria

finds for a fact that Fernando Po is being used as a base to carry out illegal activities against Nigeria, she will naturally be justified to act, strengthening her case with the fact that the territory, in any case, cannot rightly belong to far away Spain.[179]

Finally, Dr. Ezera announced that he had filed a resolution in the House calling on the Government to devise a way of acquiring the island,[180] but later in the House he refused to move the resolution on the grounds that "quiet diplomacy is more effective than noisy diplomacy" and besides the motion might embarrass the Government.[181]

The expansionist fever was exacerbated when the Government newspaper quoted the Prime Minister as saying in a press interview that Nigeria "might be compelled to apply certain measures, even if it meant annexation of the Island, if peaceful negotiation failed to solve the situation."[182] Immediately an official statement was issued denouncing the quotation as "far from the truth," and adding:

175 *Daily Times,* December 14, 1961; *Daily Express,* December 3, 1961.

176 Each of the above quotations was taken from a different letter, which with others of a similar nature, appeared in the *Sunday Times,* March 18, 1962.

177 *Daily Express,* March 30 and January 31, 1962.

178 *Ibid.,* February 2, 1962, and March 12, 1962.

179 *Morning Post,* March 12, 1962. This Government newspaper also featured an article which spoke of the "rage and fury which now tends to be developing in the minds of our people over the attitude of the governments of the Federation on the issue." *Ibid.,* March 15, 1962.

180 *Daily Times,* March 20, 1962.

181 *H. R. Debates,* daily parts for April 3, 1962, p. 30. This did not prevent an NPC member, S. D. Lar, from declaring on the floor of the House that Nigeria should annex the island. *Ibid.,* daily parts for April 14, p. 26.

182 *Sunday Post,* March 11, 1962.

In fact, Sir Abubakar has always declared at home and abroad that Nigeria has no aggressive intentions.

Nigeria's attitude, according to Sir Abubakar, is that of peaceful negotiation and not of any territorial ambitions or forceful annexations of any neighbouring state.[183]

In an attempt to allay further the mounting chauvinism, the Minister of Labor, J. M. Johnson (NCNC), made a statement to the House of Representatives. He said that no Nigerian was forced to work on Fernando Po, that 97 per cent of the laborers renewed their contracts when they expired, and that in 1961 alone 1,694 Nigerians were granted permission to settle there by the Spanish authorities. Furthermore, he said:

Those who shout so much about the annexation of Fernando Po seem to forget that the future of the Island depends completely on the indigenous people of the Island, and it is the avowed wish of this Government to see that all colonial peoples in Africa are granted independence.

Finally he asserted that "Our Government has no intention now, or at any other time, of playing the role of an aggressor nation."[184]

Nigeria was clearly faced with a popular demand for expansion. This element has entered the thinking of many new states since 1945; consider, for example, Goa, Kashmir, West New Guinea, Morocco's claim to Mauritania, Ghana's claim to Togo, and Somalia's claim to part of Ethiopia. Nigeria was similarly threatened with being caught up in a ground swell of popular demand for aggression. The main elements were forming: first, an alleged insult to the state; then demands for positive actions to rectify the wrong; and finally a refusal to accept any solution other than absorption of the territory of contention.

It seems unlikely that the issue is dead, but the positive statements by the Prime Minister and the Minister of Labor calmed the troubled waters at the time. There is no evidence that the Government ever gave any thought to using violence on the island. In fact, the Government even refused to send a delegation of pressmen, as "Peter Pan" had suggested, to report on conditions in Fernando Po on the grounds that "the present state of mind of our pressmen" would cause them to look "for the distasteful instead of the pleasant."[185] On the other hand, the Government has agreed to discuss the charges with the Spanish authorities "in the very near future."[186] The refusal of the Government to be stampeded into hasty action demonstrates again the conciliatory and conservative nature of Nigerian foreign policy.

A new facet of Nigeria's African policy was revealed in January 1963 as

183 *Morning Post,* March 13, 1962. In fairness to the Prime Minister, there is no doubt that he had been misquoted, for no other news account of the interview included the alleged statement.
184 *H. R. Debates,* daily parts for March 31, 1962, pp. 3-4. Note that it was after this ministerial statement that Dr. Ezera decided not to press his motion.
185 From the statement of the Minister of Labor, *ibid.*
186 *Sunday Times,* March 18, 1962.

the result of the assassination of President Sylvanus Olympio of Togo. From the beginning, Nigeria (joined by Guinea and Liberia) refused to treat the event as an internal matter (as did Ghana, Senegal, and Dahomey). Supporting Sékou Touré's charge that the assassins were supported by non-Togolese, Mr. Wachuku hinted that the plot had been engineered in Ghana, and even went so far as to warn that "For the purpose of security, Nigeria considers her boundary extends to the Ghana-Togo border."[187] Sixteen of the Monrovia Powers met in Lagos on January 24 to discuss the situation and help prevent a power vacuum in Togo. However, after the first bursts of outrage, further investigation seemed to support the Ghana contention that the revolt was indeed an internal matter, almost embarrassingly devoid of international intrigue. Nevertheless, Balewa and Touré adamantly refused to recognize the provisional regime of Grunitzky, even after it was given legitimacy by overwhelming voter approval in a May 7, 1963, election. Furthermore, the Nigerian and Guinean leaders were able to persuade the summit conference at Addis Ababa later in May not to invite the new Togo leaders (thus leaving only Togo and South Africa unrepresented among independent African states). In fact, as of the first week in June, 1963, only ten African states had granted *de jure* recognition to the new government, and they made as strange a collection as those which withheld recognition. The recognizing states were Cameroun, Central African Republic, Chad, Congo (B), Dahomey, Gabon, Ghana, Malagasy Republic, Senegal, and Somali Republic.[188] The only explanation for the adamant position of Nigeria and Guinea is that they believe the revolt *did* have foreign help and that recognition might, therefore, encourage further subversive activities. However, only Ghana of the former Casablanca bloc had recognized the new Togo Government by mid-1963, and since Nigerian leaders clearly distrust that country and suspect it might benefit from unrest in Togo, they have apparently decided not to give the new regime the benefit of the doubt. In conclusion, it appears that in many ways the Togo case is *sui generis*, and that other cases of non-recognition by Nigeria must occur before a clear-cut pattern of policy is discernable.

RELATIONS WITH MOSLEM STATES

Nigerian relations with Moslem states, even those in Africa, are indeed quite restricted. We have noted in the last chapter the nature of some of the pressures on the Government produced by the fact that the dominant religion of the North is Islam. Yet the pattern of relations with Moslem states is only incidentally based on religion. Among the first embassies established abroad by Nigeria were those in Saudi Arabia and Sudan, the first because of Mecca, the objective of the Moslem pilgrimage, the second because the Sudan lies directly on the land route of pilgrims from Nigeria to Mecca. The pilgrimage presents a potential for strained relations. It is claimed

187 Helen Kitchen, "Filling the Togo Vacuum," *Africa Report,* February, 1963, p. 9.
188 *Africa Report,* June 1963, p. 25; and *West Africa,* May 25, 1963, p. 567.

that fifteen thousand Nigerians go on pilgrimage each year. Over the years many impecunious travelers have been stranded somewhere en route. Rumors exist to the effect that "thousands of Nigerians are in the slave camps of oil rich sheiks in Saudi Arabia."[189] Chad has said that the problem of impoverished Nigerians in that country has compelled it to place restrictions on Nigerian pilgrims: they may enter only at Lake Chad and have one month, after reporting at the Fort Lamy control post, to pass on through to Sudan.[190] However, the most shocking news to Nigerians was the allegation by the Nigerian Ambassador to Sudan, Alhaji Ahmadu Waziri, that there are two million Nigerians in that country, most of them stranded destitutes.[191] He claimed that the Nigerians could not earn enough money to return home because of Sudan's law which debars aliens from participating in trade and business and permits naturalization only after seventy-five years of residence! To this explosive situation has been added the Saudi Arabian requirement that pilgrims must now deposit £100 before entering the country in order to pay for their repatriation if necessary. In response to these pressures, Nigeria now requires each pilgrim to obtain a passport (previously travel permits had been used) and to prove that he has £286 to cover his expenses, including the £100 demanded by Saudi Arabia.[192] Furthermore, the Northern Regional Government recently agreed to repatriate six thousand stranded pilgrims in Saudi Arabia at £3 per pilgrim.[193] Only time will reveal what further agreements can be reached to smooth the situation, but there is no doubt that the problem of pilgrims will have the attention of the Nigerian governments for some time.[194]

It seems safe to conclude that the problems of Moslem pilgrims alone decided the question of opening embassies along the land route to Saudi Arabia. This is buttressed by the fact that Nigeria has not opened embassies in other, and certainly more important, Moslem countries. Furthermore, if proof is needed that Islam itself has not been the determining factor, diplomatic relations with Israel were established from the beginning of independence. Relations with Middle East states, therefore, have not been based on religion. This seems remarkable indeed, when one considers the religious evangelism of the Sarduana; the fact that the dominant NPC is overwhelmingly Moslem in membership; and the fact that the Prime Minister is regarded by all as a devoutly religious Moslem. The key undoubtedly lies in the conciliatory nature of the Prime Minister (who feels that he must speak for all of Nigeria); the fact that he has abhorred the mixing of religion and politics; and the nature of the coalition which prompts the NPC to be ever mindful of the reaction of its southern partner.

189 *West African Pilot,* February 7, 1962.
190 *Daily Times,* March 5, 1962.
191 *West African Pilot,* January 5, 1962.
192 *Daily Times,* December 14, 1961.
193 *Sunday Times,* April 15, 1962.
194 The Western Region, for example, set up a Pilgrim Welfare Board in 1958, and now supplies a physician in Saudi Arabia to care for the pilgrims from that Region. "Welfare of Pilgrims to Mecca," *Daily Times,* March 19, 1962.

CONCLUSIONS

A number of issues since independence have been noted to which Nigeria has responded in such a way as to indicate a foreign policy. On many issues and for many countries there simply has been no policy. Latin America has received practically no attention. Asia has been largely ignored except for India and Pakistan and the focus of relationship with these countries has been the Commonwealth. No official interest has been shown in the Kashmir dispute, the China-India border disputes,[195] the troubles in Southeast Asia, or Indonesia's claims to West New Guinea. Relations with Japan, while friendly, have been slightly strained by the fact that Japan buys almost nothing from Nigeria but sells Nigeria 10 per cent of its imports. Relations with other so-called non-aligned states *as such* have been limited indeed, colored by the one instance in which Nigeria refused to attend the Yugoslavia Conference of Non-Aligned States in September 1961 because it was insulted by the hesitation of some powers to invite it. The Foreign Minister has said the Big Powers must solve the Berlin dispute, although he once suggested that Berlin should be surrendered to the United Nations.[196] On disarmament, he has urged the Big Powers to reach agreement, but has been willing to sit on the Disarmament Committee as a representative of a non-aligned state to help facilitate agreement.

The Government newspaper has said (*Sunday Post,* September 10, 1961) that there are three concentric fields of activities in Nigeria's foreign policy: "the immediate circle of activity is Africa, then the Commonwealth and then the world community." In many ways, of course, this is too simple. That there is a concern for Africa goes without saying, and as recently as October 1962, Prime Minister Balewa reasserted this principle: "We belong to Africa and Africa must claim first attention in our external affairs."[197] But on some issues the Commonwealth and the world community have colored reactions to African situations; for example, the diplomatic relations with the Central African Federation is apparently based on its Commonwealth membership, and sponsorship of the 1970 date for African colonial independence was a compromise between African reluctance for any delay and general reluctance (outside the Soviet bloc) to risk another Congo by undue haste. Although the Commonwealth may be the second circle of interest, Nigeria's deep interest in and friendship for the United States cannot be denied, and certainly its economic focus on Western Europe is stronger than that on the rest of the world.

Some of Nigeria's reactions to African problems (South Africa, French atomic-bomb tests) have been highly charged emotionally and colored

---

195 Since the above was written, Prime Minister Balewa has condemned China's attack on India. *New York Times,* November 11, 1962.

196 See *H. R. Debates,* daily parts for November 20, 1961, p. 39, and the *New York Times,* October 11, 1961.

197 Sir Abubakar Tafawa Balewa, "Nigeria Looks Ahead," *Foreign Affairs,* October 1962, p. 136.

with a considerable quantity of antagonism. Others (Congo, Fernando Po, the question of Moslem pilgrims) have been marked by a spirit of conciliation. On the question of African unity, while a spirit of conciliation has generally prevailed, the Lagos Conference revealed that Nigeria was reaching a limit of tolerance toward the Casablanca bloc.

The thread of consistency in Nigeria's foreign policy has many strands. The chief principles on which it has been guided appear to be the following:

1) *Pragmatism.* Nigerian leaders have been strongly concerned with what works both in the international field and produces harmony at home. Even pragmatism, however, requires a concept, a "picture in the mind," of what a thing is like that is working. The Nigerian conception of African cooperation does not see any form of political unification as working, hence the pragmatic approach has been to move cautiously to see what would work. This pragmatic approach has also been conditioned by the other principles discussed here.[198]

2) *Non-intervention.* This principle has generally been interpreted so strictly by Government leaders that, although they believe they ought to lead Africa, they refuse to take any initiative in this matter until asked.

3) *Peaceful negotiation.* Even on highly emotional issues, Nigeria has tended to encourage negotiation. It has refused to take a doctrinaire and dogmatic stand from which compromise is impossible. The only two exceptions probably are its reactions to apartheid and the use of African soil for atomic-bomb experiments. In the first case, it is impossible for this writer to see how any Negro state could possibly accept the thesis that human activities should be restricted on racial grounds. Furthermore, science has so thoroughly exploded the myth that human ability has racial variables that it can be defended only by superstition. In relation to the second issue, Nigerian leaders feel that atomic-bomb testing in the Sahara is an affront to all Africans. In both cases the Nigerian reaction demonstrates the importance of Africa in its foreign policy.

4) *Work from the known to the unknown.* An independent Nigeria has first fostered contacts with Great Britain, the United States, and Israel in receiving foreign aid and technical assistance. It has been careful to preserve its trade relations with Western Europe. It has not, however, failed to criticize certain allies of the Anglo-American bloc, particularly France, Belgium, and Portugal.[199] On the other hand, it has cautiously entered trade treaties with Poland and Czechoslovakia, but criticized Russia for not paying its United Nations obligations for the Congo operation.[200]

5) *Non-involvement in non-African disputes.* So carefully have Nigerian leaders observed this principle that they have found it necessary to repeat a number of times that Nigeria will not take sides in the Arab-Israeli dispute, in spite of its Moslem population. It has avoided other non-African disputes

198 Since the above was written Sir Abubakar himself has asserted that Nigeria's policy "has been a pragmatic one." *Ibid.*
199 For strong criticisms of Portuguese and Belgian policies in Africa by the Foreign Minister, see *H. R. Debates,* daily parts for November 20, 1961, pp. 37-38.
200 *Ibid.*

equally well. Even in the Red China-Formosa dispute it has refused to approve the seating of Red China in the United Nations (which it favors on the grounds of universality) at the expense of the expulsion of Formosa.

6) *Support of the United Nations.* It is obvious that Nigeria has supported the United Nations fully in its first eighteen months of independence. It has even agreed to purchase $1,000,000 worth of United Nations bonds.[201] It has not, however, disagreed sharply with the United Nations on any issue and perhaps the real test of this principle will not come until it does.

Undoubtedly the list will lengthen with time and in response to new issues. By and large, however, it must be concluded that Nigeria's foreign policy, in its first three years, has been pragmatic, conciliatory, conservative, African-centered, friendly to certain powers in the Anglo-American camp, largely indifferent to the Soviet bloc, and strongly pro-United Nations.

201 *Morning Post,* March 22, 1962.

VI. Evaluation[1]

This study is in many ways provisional. Foreign policy in any state is a continually growing development, but in a new state one can only show beginnings. A new state, however, provides a laboratory for the study of those first efforts. One can spotlight a relatively brief period of time in which the state moved from having no foreign policy to the establishment, whether consciously or unconsciously, of a definable foreign policy, no matter how many gaps and contradictions may appear. It probably takes at least a generation and a succession of Governments (Administrations) before a country's foreign policy has sufficiently fixed goals and patterns to give it a strong degree of predictability. The best one can do therefore, when viewing one government in operation only three years, is to consider party policies, Government rationalizations, internal and external pressures, and actual responses. The virtue in studying Nigeria lies in the fact that one is able to focus on the formative stages of its policies toward the outside world.

Many elements converge to shape a state's foreign policy: size and geographical location; industrial and military might; governmental structure; the extent of agreement in the society on national goals; the power of interest groups; and the alternatives open to decision-makers. Following is a brief evaluation of these elements as they relate to Nigeria.

Size and Geographical Location. These elements have already been discussed at length and it need only be pointed out here that Nigeria's size and location have already contributed to certain patterns. Its location could hardly have made its interest in Africa less intense. In fact, its role in African affairs can only increase. Whatever happens in Africa, particularly in West Africa, cannot fail to be important to Nigeria. This much, however, is true of all African states. Nigeria adds the element of size and therefore the power, or illusion of power, which goes with it. It rapidly became a leader of one of the African blocs (indeed it was instrumental in creating one of the blocs) and just as rapidly moved to prominence in the United Nations, from having its representative chosen as Chairman of the Concilia-

1 Since conclusions have been given at the end of sections and chapters, no effort shall be made to repeat them here but instead a general evaluation shall be attempted.

tion Committee on the Congo, to membership on the Disarmament Committee, to an almost-successful attempt to obtain a seat on the Security Council. It is already quite clear that in all African affairs and many international affairs, Nigeria will more and more be a power for other nations of the world to deal with.

Industrial and Military Might. Industrial and military might are yet so inadequate that a policy dependent on them has hardly been mentioned in Nigeria. As their potential is expanded, however, as they certainly will be, Nigerian reliance on them for foreign policy decisions can be expected to increase. Already a considerable pride is noticeable in connection with the Nigerian troops used in the United Nations' operations in the Congo; and Nigeria's superior road and port facilities have had to be relied upon by its less fortunate neighbors.

Nigeria is fortunate in that it has no traditional enemies. Nevertheless, it may itself soon be regarded as an enemy by certain African leaders (such as Dr. Nkrumah) who seek to dominate and coerce other African states to pursue their goals of unification. This factor, as well as the national pressure in any country to have a deterrent force, helps explain why Nigeria already is devoting over 17 per cent of its budget for its army.[2]

Governmental Structure. There is much about Nigeria which distinguishes it from other African states. It is pluralistic, multipartite, and as yet, tolerant of opposition, all rare features in Africa. This is not to say that Nigerians prefer these "disruptive" features. In fact there is now a trend toward one-party rule in each of the Regions, accompanied by the usual Governmental neglect of dissident groups inside each Region and frequently by clear-cut persecution of those who fail to support the dominant Regional party.[3] The irony in this situation is that precisely because each party is entrenched in its Region, the Central Government is forced to be democratic. The NPC, which now has a majority at the center, realizes that since its majority comes overwhelmingly from the North it must coalesce with at least one of the Southern parties. This will always leave the other Southern party to form the Opposition, which has been officially recognized. To recognize an Opposition and accept its constant goading and criticism, which many regard as a luxury, is to concede a basic tenet of democracy—majority rule in a system which guarantees minority rights.[4] Put another way, it means that

2 See Vernon McKay, *Africa in World Politics* (New York: Harper & Row, 1963), pp. 400-01.

3 See the excellent study by John P. Mackintosh, "Electoral Trends and the Tendency to a One Party System in Nigeria," serialized in *The Service*, April 7, 14, and 21, 1962. Cf., also K. W. J. Post, *The Nigerian Federal Election of 1959* (London: published for the Nigerian Institute of Social and Economic Research by Oxford University Press, 1963), Chapter 8.

4 This is not to suggest that all democratic forms have disappeared from the Regions. Although the Northern Region does not now officially recognize an Opposition, the Western and Eastern Regions still do. However, the dominant party in each Region does represent and speak for the dominant interests there. The point is that Regional Governments are not faced with the destruction of their Region by mistreating opposition forces there. The Central Government, on the other hand, has

neither the Central Government nor Parliament is absolute. Furthermore, the Central Government has accepted this fact by acceding the principle of the supremacy of the Constitution, as was revealed in the National Bank Case.[5]

The evidences of democracy on the federal level explain much about the formation of foreign policy in Nigeria. They explain why Nigeria, unlike so many African states, has been unable to have one-party domination, and has had therefore to shape a policy which was at least a verbal compromise between Northern conservatism and Southern radicalism.[6] They also explain why Nigeria has not created a charismatic leader who could unite the country behind a single monolithic set of values. After all, independence came easily after Nigerians accepted the fact that few common values (apart from independence) exist among their disparate groups. No Nigerian leader of today was imprisoned by the British or was otherwise treated so as to become a common symbol around which to rally all the people. The most likely candidate for charismatic leadership, Dr. Azikiwe, has been shunted to the political hinterland of the Governor-Generalship (since October 1, 1963, the Presidency). Sir Abubakar lacks the fire and venom to be such a leader. On the contrary, his spirit of compromise makes him the leader necessary to harmonize the various interests. There simply is no leader and no issue around which charismatic characteristics can develop.

Tolerance of constant criticism has revealed another aspect of the democratic process: The Government has been forced to a fuller and more frequent defense of its policies than a government without such criticism is likely to give. To the extent that citizens wish to know the bases of policy, the leaders have supplied it rather fully. Also, unlike many leaders of other African states, Nigerian decision-makers have had to rely on rational defenses to counter the cogent arguments of a capable Opposition. As a

---

to accommodate a federal structure in which each Region is firmly controlled by a different party, each of which could possibly wreck the federation if pushed too far.

5 The National Bank was established by the Western Regional Government, and to embarrass that Government, pressures were placed on the Central Government to investigate the whole operation of the Bank. In the Commissions and Tribunals Act, 1961, Parliament empowered the Prime Minister to appoint a commission of investigation whose functions would not be subject to judicial proceedings. The Federal Supreme Court declared portions of the Act null and void on the grounds that: (1) the provision of the Act which excluded the Courts from entertaining any matter regarding a commission appointed by the Prime Minister transgresses the human rights clauses of the Constitution; (2) the provisions empowering the Commissioners with judicial authority violates that part of the Constitution dealing with Courts; and (3) those parts of the Act which are still valid apply only to the Federal Territory, not to the Regions. *Doherty* v. *Balewa,* Federal Supreme Court 326/1961.

6 The Government was unable or unwilling, however, to tolerate without a reprimand what it regarded as an improper criticism of Nigeria's foreign policy by Chief Awolowo outside the country. In a strict party vote, he was censured for the speech he made in London in September 1961. *H. R. Debates,* daily parts for November 30, 1961, p. 30. Cf. *supra,* p. 64.

result, they have made a minimum use of largely-undefined emotional terms such as neo-colonialism, Big Power immorality, economic imperialism, or African personality.

The Central Government, it would seem, is bound to be democratic. Even if the Opposition could be stifled, any coalition of Northerners and Southerners would have conservative and radical elements. Only if the majority NPC decided to govern alone, thus excluding the South, could dictatorship occur, but it seems unlikely that the South would accept such a move without a civil war.

The Nigerian experiment with federalism is promising. All of the important leaders in the country have accepted it as the best under the circumstances. In view of the entrenched positions of the various parties in their Regions, the only alternative to federalism would be the creation of three separate states, which all leaders now reject as a calamity. The creation of the new Mid-West Region in late 1963 does not seem to alter this picture materially. Foreign policy, therefore, as it continues to evolve, will also continue to be a compromise between the conservative and radical elements. As such it will also probably continue to appear "out of step" with other African states as it agrees with one group at one time and another group at another time.

Extent of Agreement on National Goals. A significant aspect of the articulate criticism of the Government lies in the fact that it is all one-sided. The critics are all radical in the sense that they demand rapid changes made with enthusiasm and verve. They are generally equalitarian, with visions of a society in which wealth is rather evenly distributed, but no blueprint is proffered. Many of them (but not the Action Group) deplore the divisiveness of federalism and advocate unitary government, but do not suggest how it can be created in Nigeria. In external affairs the radicals have an "enemy"—colonialism. This enemy is all bad and the cause of all that is wrong in Africa. Where colonialism itself has given way, neo-colonialism has replaced it whereby the former metropole continues to exercise sinister control through expatriate office holders, expatriate business firms, defense pacts, and unequal economic agreements. Where the metropole has been eased out, its ally the United States has insinuated itself in to continue the work. The radicals see economics in nineteenth-century terms as a struggle between laissez faire capitalism and true social equality, and cannot concede that laissez faire has long ceased to exist in so-called capitalistic states and that social inequality is entrenched in so-called socialistic states. Because of all these factors, the enemy for the radical is Western Europe, and states identified with Western Europe. On the other hand, the external "friend" is hardly identifiable. The radicals, with probably very few exceptions, do not see Soviet communism as the alternative. The Soviet bloc states would be welcomed only to balance the influence of the Anglo-American bloc states. The Action Group and most of the NCNC radicals have clearly repudiated the dictatorship of the Soviet system, and other radicals seem to give little attention to the Soviet experiment as a model for Nigeria. The radicals do, however, make much use of terminology usually identified with communism, such as "correct social orientation," "true socialist morality," "proper concern for proletarian values," "monopolistic capitalism," "exploitation of the masses," etc. Nevertheless, these are also terms of European Social Democracy and it appears to be in that sense that most of the radicals use the terms. Thus while the radicals appear to have a fairly clear image of the external enemy they do not have a clear concept of the external friend.

The tensions in Nigeria over foreign policy are sharp indeed. The articulate radicals represent a large precentage of the university educated and professional people. They are deeply conscious of race and "Africa"; and these prompt them to call for dynamism in creating the Nigerian image. Dynamism means taking a strong stand in expressing the true soul of the nation against all the wrongs of the past. It means the adamant rejection by a Negro state of every insult by white men. The radicals cry for national expression and see in the conservative Balewa Government too great a tendency to think things through. They speak of the rumor (not substantiated by this author), for example, that Balewa did not think to condemn the Sharpeville killings in South Africa until an expatriate (white) friend suggested to him that he do so. The radicals are uneasy and distrustful. To many of them, Northerners are "Uncle Toms," binding the nation more and more to alien values. They are frustrated also, for none of them look to a recrudescence of Nigerian values and institutions—after all, as one backs up a few years, "Nigeria" as a common description disappears. Negative though they may be, the radicals are displeased with Nigeria's image and friends abroad. They would, furthermore, reverse Nigeria's friends and enemies in Africa. Conservatism, they believe, belies the demands for change, for equality, for free expression in Nigeria; it covers up corruption at all levels; it ignores the need for Nigeria to find new, truly indigenous answers to problems; it refuses to recognize that Nigeria's greatness over the years can only be guaranteed in the Great African State, not in the present conglomeration of petty nationalistic states. These are the thoughts that motivate radical responses and help explain the intensity of radical antagonism to the Government. The tension is great, and the real challenge of the Government over the next few years is to accommodate it, placate it, and where possible erase it by agreeing or pretending to agree with radical sentiments. Whether a truly conservative Government can do this is not known, but some moves in this direction have been made in the latter months of this study.

The effort to accommodate in one state strong blocs of conservatives and radicals puts Nigeria to the challenge. The almost total absence of a clearly definable middle position merely exaggerates the situation. Almost all articulate expression supports either the conservatives or the radicals, and society appears to be bifurcated. Some exceptions exist, of course. The radicals of the NCNC, while frustrated over Government conservatism, still support the coalition in voting. Chief Awolowo, though generally critical of the Government, has also supported it from time to time. Sir Abubakar has made it a point to commend the Action Group leaders occasionally. While the illustrations do not reveal any great tolerance, they at least reveal that differences are not yet frozen into uncompromisable rigidity. Nevertheless, dangerous situations are developing. Less and less tolerance seems to emanate from the Government towards the radicals of the Nigerian Youth Congress, the Imoudu faction of the labor movement, and the Dynamic Party. Even more disquieting was the precipitate action by which the Federal Government stepped into the Action Group crisis in May 1962. The crisis itself was between radical and conservative positions in the party, and the Federal Government's position clearly favored the conservative Akintola faction. Furthermore, the conservative national leaders once seriously considered a preventive detention law, directed against "subversive elements from any quarters."[7] That radicals are now beginning to fear for their freedom is revealed by the fact that Mr. Samuel Ikoku (militant General Secretary of the Action Group and Opposition Leader in the Eastern House of Assembly) fled from Nigeria to Ghana in the midst of the Action Group crisis. He did so to escape a restriction order which was placed on all leaders of the Action Group.[8] The conservative-radical cleavages in Nigeria are not restricted to issues of foreign policy, but foreign policy has provided the sharpest focus of the differences.[9]

It has been alleged that the greatest weakness in the formation of national goals is the absence of ideology. None of the political party leaders seem to have a "picture in their mind" of what Nigeria or Africa ought to be like in even one or two decades. With Nigeria's potential for becoming the greatest power in Africa (on the basis of the traditional elements of national power), none seem to see the ramifications of this in terms of the opportunities and obligations such power calls forth, whether in diplomacy, use or threat of force, arbitration of disputes, African international cooperation or organization, or even of Pan-Africanism, however defined.

The NPC, and therefore the Government, appears to have no concrete image of Nigeria as an African leader, although there is also certainly no image of any other African state as leader. The admitted ignorance about the rest of the continent produces only vagueness in much of its policy. Radicals at times appear to be developing an ideology, but this always dissipates when party loyalty is called for. While the NCNC has a more pronounced ideology than the other two parties, its role must now be subordinated to that of the NPC. Much of the frustration in the NCNC is due to the inability of many members to accept that subordination, even with the compensation which comes from participating in decision-making

7 *Daily Express,* June 11, 1962. Significantly, the preventive detention act failed of passage in the Parliament.
8 *Morning Post,* June 13, 1962.
9 Mr. Ikoku said the Action Group crisis was produced by reactionaries both inside and outside of the Action Group. In fact, all who differed with his wing of the party were listed as lackeys of neo-colonialism. It was primarily Action Group foreign policy, he said, which angered "the right-wing leadership" of Nigeria and prompted the punitive action. In his words, the Action Group "demanded a foreign policy truly independent of London and Washington. It advocated neutralism as between the Western and Eastern power blocs." *Ibid.*

and the prestige and power of having some members in the cabinet. The Action Group struggle between the Awolowo and Akintola factions may delay indefinitely the formation of ideology there.

Ideology, as used here, refers to a body of principles and goals, rigidly defined and uncompromisingly adhered to. Few states or political parties within states advocate or practice such an ideology, but it is clear that some states come closer to it than others. In Africa, it is submitted, the Casablanca states tried to establish a radical ideology, with rigid ideas about Pan-Africanism, non-alignment, and neo-colonialism, which was countered by the refusal of the Monrovia bloc states to use these terms in a rigid sense. Nigeria was, of course, a leader in the latter group.

While Nigeria does not have an ideology in the sense used here, one cannot conclude that it has no conceptualization of ends sought, nor that it will compromise any and all positions. Nigerian decision-makers have established national goals, some more rigid, some less rigid, than others. For example, there is no doubt that one goal is rapid and massive internal economic growth. Foreign policy has been adapted to that end, but with flexibility, not rigidity. Thus when leaders saw no advantage for Nigeria as an associate member of the European Economic Community, they rejected the idea but did not then repudiate all its ties with Europe as rigid ideology might have demanded. Other illustrations are discussed elsewhere in this book, especially Chapter V.

With all states, national goals can usually be divided into at least three categories: those involving its vital interests and for which it will risk all; those it will make all-out effort short of war or the threat of force to achieve; and those it declares as goals but rarely initiates action stronger than resolutions to achieve. A policy of pragmatism or realism is one which assesses each goal on the willingness and ability of the state to defend it; that is, it categorizes goals on the basis of its means to achieve them with the power at its disposal. Nigeria has been quite realistic in its foreign policy. Unlike Ghana's goal of a politically united Africa, or Somalia's goal of obtaining part of what Ethiopia possesses (both unrealistic in the face of absence of power to bring them about), Nigeria has advocated goals resolvable by negotiations and discussions, or goals which demand no more than support of resolutions.

Nigeria has been careful, for example, not to question the boundaries it has inherited, and it freely accepted, without bitterness, the results of a plebiscite in Southern Cameroons which attached that territory to the Cameroun Republic rather than to Nigeria. When a popular mood for expansionism arose in relation to Fernando Po, the leaders were careful to reject any thought of aggression and to insist on negotiation, not to take over the island, but to protect Nigerians there. While understandably incensed at apartheid, its leaders have not threatened the use of force in South Africa. Although opposed to the continuation of colonialism in Africa, Nigeria has been cautious in its demands for immediate de-colonialization. While international affairs have been especially dramatic at times, Nigeria has tended to focus its attention on domestic affairs, serving to urge moderation and conciliation in external disputes and relying on the United Nations, where possible.

Power of Interest Groups. At this time the power of interest groups which would alter Nigeria's foreign policy does not seem formidable, but their potential is an unknown quantity. Their very existence calls for research and study, and some investigations are now under way on at least marketing women's organizations and unemployed school leavers. Much more needs to be undertaken. There is no doubt that a new generation of technicians, businessmen, professionals, and political leaders is in the making. They will naturally seek their place in the Nigerian sun. There is also no doubt, as Henry Bretton points out, that "continued frustration of groups dissatisfied with the social and economic order of things results in violent eruptions sooner or later."[10] Bretton also apparently believes that such frustrations now exist in Nigeria, that they will be continued, and that they will produce those "eruptions." Taylor Cole also recognizes these forces but concludes that "unifying [rather than divisive] pressures in Nigeria are increasing in their impact."[11] In any case L. Gray Cowan offers counsel in the following statement:

There are pressures building up inside and outside Nigeria which may bring about a radical change in the Nigerian position. . . . The rising generation of younger Nigerian leaders may well be prepared to sacrifice a continuing relationship to the West if this relationship appears likely to threaten Nigeria's potential position of leadership in African politics.[12]

The above remarks remind us that the Nigerian political scene is not static; on the contrary, more than so-called developed states and many underdeveloped ones, Nigerian society is in dynamic flux. This can only produce new groups, and change or disappearance of old ones. One social consensus in rapid succession may yield to another. In such a society, the "fixed" of one moment becomes a mere stage of on-going change, and predictability even less certain than usual. In the Nigerian context we can only say that interest groups are as yet poorly organized and even more poorly understood by the present level of scholarship. To date, they do not seem to have had much impact on foreign policy formation.

Alternatives Available. Alternatives have to be assessed on the possible courses the present decision-makers might have taken, and on what another Government (say a more radical one) might have made. The question of alternatives rests not on whether any have been proffered but whether the political setting would permit them. The North would certainly prefer closer relations with Moslem countries, but the South would never accept this. Furthermore, economic relations with Israel have assisted both of the

10 Henry L. Bretton, *Power and Stability in Nigeria* (New York: Praeger, 1962), p. 27.
11 Taylor Cole, "Emergent Federalism in Nigeria," in Robert O. Tilman and Taylor Cole (eds.), *The Nigerian Political Scene* (Durham: Duke University Press, 1962), p. 62. See also Cole, "The Independence Constitution of Federal Nigeria," *ibid.*, p. 86.
12 L. Gray Cowan, "Nigerian Foreign Policy," *ibid.*, p. 143.

Southern Regions as well as the Federal Government. Closer ties with the former Casablanca states would (supposedly) please radicals, yet widespread distrust of both Nasser and Nkrumah (even in radical ranks) exists, and a move in this direction would certainly alienate part of the NCNC. Even if radicals were to win power in Nigeria, it seems unlikely that they would be any more willing than Balewa to subordinate Nigeria to a non-Nigerian leader, and even more unlikely that Nkrumah would join a union with a Nigerian leader.

The only alternative to close identification with the West would be a stricter neutralism (since a converse closeness with the Soviets does not appear to this writer to be a policy of any group which could possibly win office). Neutralism, apparently, would mean a refusal to support any position in a dispute in which one of the power blocs is involved. Since the Big Powers are involved, or can involve themselves, in almost any dispute, a policy of neutralism would rather effectively silence the voice of a nation on the most important world problems. However, neither the Balewa Government nor those who seek to replace it have advocated this kind of muted role for Nigeria. All factions see a role for Nigeria which clearly involves taking stands on important issues. This form of neutralism, therefore, does not appear to be an alternative. The real conflict over this question appears not to be one of neutralism, but of self-respect: that is, alternative proposals for the most part do not reject any real benefits to Nigeria which come from the West but do suggest that the receipt of benefits be accompanied by criticism of some part of the West. The radical's alternative to Balewa's ties with the West would be to maintain the ties (or most of them) but demonstrate the independence of the country by repeated denunciation of certain policies identified with the West.

This is not to say that the Balewa Government may not itself come to be more critical of the West, but at this writing such a move would be a matter of degree only. It is difficult to see how any moves which jeopardize the success of its Six Year Plan would be to Nigeria's benefit. Since its success depends so heavily upon support from certain Western powers it seems quite unlikely that a strong anti-Western position will develop.

Given the political power of the North and the continued conservatism of the NPC, it would seem that alternatives to present foreign policy would come slowly and in response to issues (domestic or international) not now apparent.

CONCLUSIONS

From the above, it is clear that the elements of foreign policy in a new state can be assessed much as in old states. In Nigeria the difference is that the relative position of various elements is still fluid. It is perhaps too early to talk in terms of predictability, yet trends are already evident, and the patterns of any one moment surely help shape the future. It is in this sense that "Foreign policy itself is a continuum beginning with the birth of the nation and ending only with its death."[13]

It is obvious, of course, that this study did not focus on the birth of a nation. On independence Nigeria could not be likened to a baby with no values or patterns of operation, but rather to a son trained to function in a certain way, to use an analogy of the Prime Minister himself.[14] This contrasts it with the Congo, which was still seeking to find workable institutions three years after independence. Furthermore, Nigeria's independence came with a minimum of bitterness and ill-feeling, in contrast to some of the Casablanca states, but comparable to the Brazzaville states. Nigeria, therefore, like the Brazzaville states, does not see the outside world as hostile and avaricious. Offers of aid and assistance from a state it already knows, and its friends, are not automatically suspect as long as care is taken to see that unacceptable conditions (strings) are not attached. New friends are to be created slowly, and not with a haste that repudiates the old and then discovers that the new cannot be relied upon.

As a new state which is underdeveloped, Nigeria will need to rely for some time on external assistance. This means that it cannot be isolated completely from the wealthier states of the world. Nigeria approaches these states without apologies. Its Government leaders have not engaged in repeated attacks on either of the two world giants, and can therefore approach each with clean hands.

Its conservatism, however, seems to identify Nigerian interests more with the Anglo-American position than with the Soviet one, just as radicalism in Ghana or Guinea tends to produce the opposite identification, though in neither case is it possible to say that they "belong" to one bloc or the other. Furthermore, a state can hardly be a colony or a "neo-colony" if its leaders seek to expand the power of the state; if an army answerable to its leaders defends it; if foreigners are present only on the sufferance of the state; if entrenched foreign interests know that their present and future position rests on the will of the Government; and if treaties are negotiated (not imposed). Nigeria is as independent as any other African state. To charge that it is not independent when the decision-makers are making the decisions they want to make (even though conservative) is to imply that there is only one true way for an ex-colony to act. In spite of the tendency, therefore, of some Nigerians and other Africans to question the "true" independence of Nigeria, the evidence certainly supports the observation of Taylor Cole: "Since achieving independence on October 1, 1960, Nigeria has had full responsibility, in name as well as in fact, for the maintenance of national defense and for the conduct of foreign relations."[15]

Leaders of many new states appear to believe that independence means a

---

13 Hans J. Morgenthau, "The American Tradition in Foreign Policy," in Roy C. Macridis (ed.), *Foreign Policy in World Politics* (Englewood Cliffs: Prentice-Hall, 1962), p. 202.

14 See *supra*, p. 27.

15 Cole, "Emergent Federalism in Nigeria," *op. cit.*, p. 60.

release from any international obligations. They frequently act as if their role is merely to make demands which older states are duty-bound to grant. It is a mark of a state's maturity when its leaders realize that international (like domestic) politics creates inequality of power, and that states (like individuals) freely make grants, loans, or concessions only when there is hope of gaining a greater value. The Nigerian Government has revealed a considerable maturity in a number of ways, the most recent being the following observation by the Prime Minister:

We know that there is no assistance without some strings attached, and that those who invest in our country have a right to expect that their investment is secure, or that grants made to us are used in the over-all interest of the people rather than for the benefit of a few privileged persons. This, in fact, accords with our own national policy, and we cannot see a conflict of views or interests in this. We seek assistance, not only because we need it, but also because we think we deserve it. This is a challenge to those advanced nations which really desire to see the new African states stand on their own feet and make their own particular contribution to the peace of the world and the happiness of mankind.[16]

James Coleman concluded in his great work that "Nationalism in Nigeria . . . is a manifestation of long-dormant peoples groping their way to nationhood in order that they may enter the life of the world community as equal participants."[17] It is apparent that Nigeria has now arrived, that the federal nature of the "nation" has survived the first strains of independence, and that Nigeria has begun to enter the life of the world community, not merely as another new state but as probably the most important state in Africa and as such destined to play an ever-increasing role in world decisions.

16 Sir Abubakar Tafawa Balewa, "Nigeria Looks Ahead," *Foreign Affairs,* October 1962, p. 134.
17 James S. Coleman, *Nigeria: Background to Nationalism* (Berkeley: University of California Press, 1958), p. 414.

Appendix

Draft Defence Agreement between the Government of the United Kingdom of Great Britain and Northern Ireland and the Government of the Federation of Nigeria*

Sessional Paper No. 4 of 1960

Whereas the Federation of Nigeria is fully self-governing and independent within the Commonwealth;

And whereas the Government of the Federation of Nigeria and the Government of the United Kingdom of Great Britain and Northern Ireland recognise that it is in their common interest to preserve peace and to provide for their mutual defence;

And whereas the Government of the Federation of Nigeria has now assumed responsibility for the external defence of its territory;

Now therefore the Government of the Federation of Nigeria and the Government of the United Kingdom of Great Britain and Northern Ireland have agreed as follows:—

ARTICLE I

The Government of the Federation and the United Kingdom Government each undertake to afford to the other such assistance as may be necessary for mutual defence, and to consult together on the measures to be taken jointly or separately to ensure the fullest co-operation between them for this purpose.

ARTICLE II

1. The two Governments will foster the closest co-operation between the armed forces of the two countries. In particular, the United Kingdom Government will, on request, furnish the Government of the Federation to such extent and on such terms as may be agreed between the two Governments with assistance for the training and development of the armed forces of the Federation and other assistance as set out in this Article.

*Exclusive of Annex.

2. The United Kingdom Government will, if so requested by the Government of the Federation, provide personnel to assist in the staffing, administration and training of the armed forces of the Federation.

3. The United Kingdom Government will make available facilities for the training of members of the armed forces of the Federation. In particular places will be made available for officers cadets and other ranks at training establishments in the United Kingdom, such as the Royal Military College, Sandhurst, the Royal Naval College, Dartmouth, the Mons Officer Cadet School, Aldershot, the Staff College, Camberley, Arms Schools, Arm and Service Schools and other training establishments and on such instructional and specialist training courses as may be necessary. If at some future date the Federation creates an Air Force, the United Kingdom Government will likewise provide training on a similar basis for Federation officers and personnel.

4. The United Kingdom Government will, in consultation with the Government of the Federation, make every effort to ensure for the armed forces of the Federation an adequate supply of such modern weapons (including new types of weapons which may be developed) as may be considered necessary and suitable for the armed forces of the Federation.

5. The United Kingdom Government will, if so requested by the Government of the Federation, consult with the Government of the Federation with a view to making available to that Government any warships which may be required by the Royal Nigerian Navy.

6. The United Kingdom Government will, at the request of the Government of the Federation, make available any expert advice and assistance in operational and technical matters which may be necessary to the armed forces of the Federation. The United Kingdom Government will also provide, if requested by the Government of the Federation, professional and technical advice in the planning of the base installations which are to be constructed for the Royal Nigerian Navy.

7. The United Kingdom Government will pay landing fees for the use of civil airfields in the Federation by the aircraft referred to in Article III of this Agreement (not being aircraft of or under the control of the armed forces of the Federation) at the rate applicable to civil aircraft of comparable size and will reimburse the Government of the Federation any extra expenditure incurred in this connection by the Government of the Federation at the request of the United Kingdom Government for the provisions of any supplies, services and facilities additional to those required by the Government of the Federation for its own purposes.

ARTICLE III

The Government of the Federation and the United Kingdom Government each undertake to accord to military aircraft of and aircraft under the control of the armed forces of the other unrestricted overflying and air staging facilities in the Federation and in the United Kingdom and dependent territories respectively.

ARTICLE IV

On request by the United Kingdom Government, the Government of the Federation agrees to make available facilities at Kano and Lagos airfields for the holding of tropicalisation trials of aircraft. Should the Government of the Federation so request, the United Kingdom Government will make available to the Government of the Federation the general results of such trials.

ARTICLE V

The Government of the Federation and the United Kingdom Government will afford each other an adequate opportunity for comment upon any major administrative or legislative proposals which may affect the operation of this Agreement.

ARTICLE VI

The arrangements relating to Status of Forces shall be those contained in the Annex to this Agreement.

ARTICLE VII

In this Agreement:—

"the Government of the Federation" means the Government of the Federation of Nigeria;

"the United Kingdom Government" means the Government of the United Kingdom of Great Britain and Northern Ireland;

"the two Governments" means the two Governments abovementioned;

"dependent territories" means United Kingdom colonies, protectorates and trust territories, but excludes the Federation of Rhodesia and Nyasaland;

"the Federation" means the Federation of Nigeria;

"military aircraft" includes aircraft operating under charter for the purposes of the armed forces of the United Kingdom or the Federation.

ARTICLE VIII

This Agreement shall come into force on the date of

In witness whereof the undersigned, being duly authorised thereto by their respective Governments, have signed this Agreement.

DONE at .... in duplicate, this ....
day of 196

For the Government of the United Kingdom
of Great Britain and Northern Ireland
....

For the Government of the Federation of
Nigeria
....

Index

Abii, D. B., 46, 48, 101n
Abubakar, Sir; *see* Balewa
Action Group (AG), 10n, 15, 17, 18, 29n, 30, 33, 34, 38, 51, 53, 62-67, 71, 75, 81n, 87, 89, 108, 140; Jos Congress of 1962, 65-67; policy shift, 26, 35, 51; rift, 66; vote in 1959 election, 23; *see also* Akintola; Awolowo
Adebola, Alhaji H. P., 77
Aderemi, Sir Adesoji, 66
Adjei, Ako, 48n
AFL-CIO, 78-79
Africa, primacy of in Nigerian policy, 6, 34, 41, 42, 55-62, 64, 69, 75, 86, 122, 126-30, 132, 134, 135, 139, 140
African Common Market, 41, 59, 116-18
African Military High Command, 60n
"African personality," 33, 34, 39n, 51, 138
Afro-Asian states, 12
AG; *see* Action Group
Agunbiade-Bamishe, O., 65n
Ahmadu, Sir; *see* Bello
"Aiyekoto," 65n, 91n
Akintola, Chief S. L., 38, 65-67, 82-85, 87, 101, 108n, 140, 141; *see also* Action Group; United People's Party
Akpan, P. O., 30n
Akwiwu, E. C., 31, 39n
Algeria, 50, 59, 74, 93, 95, 126
Alignment, 16, 17, 34, 35, 39, 42
All-African Trade Union Federation (AATUF), 77n, 78
All-Nigeria Peoples' Conference, 54-62, 65, 70, 74, 76, 79, 92

Aluko, Dr. S. A., 76
Amechi, Mbazulike, 60n
American Mercury Rocket Tracking Station (Kano), 73n
Angola, 63, 127
Apartheid, 7, 30, 32, 36, 64, 86, 91, 97, 120, 121, 133, 141
Arab-Israeli conflict, 61, 64, 82, 133
Atomic bomb tests in the Sahara, 15, 30, 33, 36, 85, 91n, 124-126, 132, 133
Australia, 101, 120n
Awolowo, Chief Obafemi, 9, 15, 16-17, 23, 29, 33, 37, 39, 44-46, 47, 48, 50, 51, 62-67, 100n, 107-9, 119n, 123, 137n, 139, 141; on Communist bloc, 16-17, 63, 109-10; on democracy, 16-17, 63; on Pan-Africanism, 16, 63-64; on Western bloc, 16-17, 63; *see also* Action Group; Leader of the Opposition
Azikiwe, Dr. Nnamdi, 8, 11-13, 15, 17, 21, 23, 24, 37, 38, 44, 45n, 55, 59, 68n, 69, 81, 82, 93, 95, 98, 108, 110, 119, 137; *see also* Governor-General

Balewa, Sir Abubakar Tafawa, 9, 10n, 15, 27, 38, 39n, 44, 47, 51, 52, 55, 58n, 62, 64, 69, 70n, 83, 90, 91, 93, 96, 98, 99n, 101, 102, 104n, 105n, 118-20, 122, 123, 125, 129, 130, 132, 137, 139, 143, 145n; *see also* Prime Minister
Balogun, Chief Kolawole, 59
Bardon, A. K., 95
Bassey, S. U., 78
Belgium, 17, 63, 114n, 117, 122, 123, 133